Enduring violence

Manchester University Press

New
Ethnographies

Series editor
Alexander Thomas T. Smith

Already published

The British in rural France: Lifestyle migration and the ongoing quest for a better way of life Michaela Benson

Ageing selves and everyday life in the North of England: Years in the making Catherine Degnen

Chagos islanders in Mauritius and the UK: Forced displacement and onward migration Laura Jeffery

Integration, locality and everyday life: After asylum
Mark Maguire and Fiona Murphy

An ethnography of English football fans: Cans, cops and carnivals
Geoff Pearson

Literature and agency in English fiction reading: A study of the Henry Williamson Society ...
Adam Reed

International seafarers and the possibilities for transnationalism in the twenty-first century
Helen Sampson

Devolution and the Scottish Conservatives: Banal activism, electioneering and the politics of irrelevance Alexander Smith

Enduring violence

Everyday life and conflict in eastern Sri Lanka

Rebecca Walker

Manchester University Press

Copyright © Rebecca Walker 2013

The right of Rebecca Walker to be identified as the author of this work has been asserted by her in accordance with the Copyright, Designs and Patents Act 1988.

Published by Manchester University Press
Altrincham Street, Manchester M1 7JA, UK
www.manchesteruniversitypress.co.uk

British Library Cataloguing-in-Publication Data is available

Library of Congress Cataloging-in-Publication Data is available

ISBN 978 1 5261 0863 0 *paperback*

First published by Manchester University Press in hardback 2013

This edition first published 2016

The publisher has no responsibility for the persistence or accuracy of URLs for any external or third-party internet websites referred to in this book, and does not guarantee that any content on such websites is, or will remain, accurate or appropriate.

Printed by Lightning Source

For A.H. and the *ammas* of eastern Sri Lanka
and
for Craig, thank you for all the happiness

Contents

List of plates	*page* ix
Preface	xi
Acknowledgements	xv
List of abbreviations	xvii
Series editor's foreword	xix
Map 1: Map of Sri Lanka provinces and districts	xx
Map 2: Map of administrative boundaries, Batticaloa	xxi
Map 3: Map of areas in Sri Lanka controlled by the government and the LTTE	xxii
1 The beginning of the end	1
2 Mapping spaces and lives: Batticaloa and the east	29
3 Living and learning in Batticaloa	60
4 Between violence and the everyday: questions of the ordinary	83
5 Meena's story	98
6 '*Kutti annar maram*' (my older brother's tree)	130
7 In light of new beginnings	148
Bibliography	168
Index	187

List of plates

1.1 A woman sitting outside her tsunami-destroyed house, Kallady (Batticaloa) (2005). Image: Rebecca Walker   *page* 10
2.1 Mother's meeting, Batticaloa (2006). Image: Rebecca Walker   53
6.1 Returning to the sea, Kallady (Batticaloa) (2005). Image: Rebecca Walker   146
7.1 Children playing in the sea, Batticaloa (2005). Image: Rebecca Walker   166

Preface

Conversations in the dark

Sitting in the shadowy darkness of another evening of power-cuts in Batticaloa, eastern Sri Lanka, my friend Rajini (not her real name) turned to me and commented, 'Batticaloa is like a cemetery. Everything is dead and broken.'[1] It was March 2007, and I was back in Sri Lanka after a seven-month break in the UK for my final month of research into the effects of violence on the everyday lives of people in eastern Sri Lanka. My host family, of whom Rajini was a member, had warned me that the situation had worsened since my last visit. My return coincided with a dramatic escalation of conflict, as the government forces stepped up the pace of attacks on the Liberation Tigers of Tamil Eelam (LTTE), through an intense campaign of shelling to 'clear' the LTTE out of the east of the island, parts of which had been under LTTE control since the late 1980s. What others and I did not know was that this period of fighting marked the beginning of the end of the war between the Tigers and the Sri Lankan government. The offensive saw the LTTE, already weakened by a fractional split in the movement in March 2004, routed from the east by mid-2007. The government then shifted its focus to the north of the island and between 2008 and 2009 advanced towards the LTTE's *de facto* administrative capital of Kilinochchi (Map 3: xxii), which it captured in January 2009. Finally, on 19 May 2009, after trapping the LTTE on a small strip of land along the north coast along with thousands of civilians, the government forces declared victory after killing almost the entire leadership of the LTTE. The brutal and bloody final battle brought the end to a conflict that had ravaged the island of Sri Lanka for almost three decades.

Batticaloa, or in Tamil *Mattakkalappu* (meaning 'muddy lagoon'), a district situated halfway down the east coast of Sri Lanka, has been one of the most disrupted and devastated areas of the island since the conflict started.[2] Framed on either side by the sea and the lagoon, the district formed a part of the northern and eastern regions of Sri Lanka that the LTTE sought to secure and establish as Tamil Eelam (see maps 2 and 3: xx–xxii). At the time of my arrival in January 2005, Sri Lanka was just coming to terms with the enormity of the tragedy of the 2004 South Asian tsunami, which on the east coast alone had taken more than

3,000 lives, devastated homes and livelihoods, and left thousands more displaced (World Health Organisation [WHO] 2005: 1).

Against the backdrop of an unravelling ceasefire, failed peace talks, and a chaotic tsunami response, the political situation, which had experienced a temporary reprieve after the tsunami, was once again worsening day by day. The power-cuts that we were experiencing were a part of this – a consequence of the shelling by the Sri Lankan army from their main camp situated in the centre of Batticaloa town. Starting in the early hours of the morning after a short lull, the shelling would continue intermittently until around midnight. Lying side by side on our mats in the front room of the house, the family and I would wake to the entire house shaking and the fan swinging precariously above us. In the darkness, we would reach out to one another – listening, whispering, and waiting until sunrise would cast the noise in a less hostile light.

Although our evening rituals were often disrupted by the lack of power, there was also something inviting about the intimacy and stillness that the darkness created. As the sun disappeared behind the lagoon and people locked themselves away inside their homes, the family and I would sit, sticky and uncomfortable in the stilted March heat, chatting to one another. Forced together, in those shared moments we would talk, laugh, reflect, lament, and debate in ways we had not done before. Despite (or perhaps because of) the fact that circumstances were so tense and frightening, the hushed conversations that emerged in the darkness felt intimate and honest. Deep-seated feelings, fears, memories, and speculations that had until now been folded away behind the crevices of everyday busyness would be stirred and shared. For all of us, it seemed to be easier to be honest and vulnerable in this particular space, the darkness providing a blanket of protection and allowing the normal boundaries of conversations to be transgressed. Perhaps our increased awareness of our own mortality, our fragility in the wider setting of physical destruction, meant that we needed to feel somehow connected in the moment.

In that present moment for us in that household in Batticaloa, the past realities of similar times of violence told us that danger was close, but also that people survive. Those realities also told us that we were relatively safe compared to those in the more exposed areas of the villages. We knew that what were hopeful futures could turn into violent presents and eventually slip back to form memories of violent pasts once again. Yet, at the same time, the future remained open and shaped by possibility, for we knew the reality was that people did keep going and did strive for something different. It was not only violent memories that created the self and the future but the constant *endurance* of the everyday that opened up to alternative meanings and imaginings of other everydays.

It is these evening conversations in March 2007 reflecting on how people endure violence and the sharing of thoughts and feelings regarding life in Batticaloa that have provided the impetus for this book. What unfolded in those dark evenings reflected what has become my main focus – the significance of connections, intimacy, and space – for revealing how people in Batticaloa deal with violence in their everyday lives. Widening the discussion from one household by the lagoon to many diverse and different stories about how people shape their lives through, around, and outside of violence, this book provides an exploration of the lives of Tamil-speaking people in the eastern district of Batticaloa. Questioning what is understood by 'everyday violence', it asks what it is to live with violence on a daily basis and, in turn, what particular spaces of non-violence or relative safety might look like. At the centre of this book are the experiences of a small, local, human rights group that formed amongst mainly Tamil-speaking people in Batticaloa, with whom I lived and worked, alongside during my fieldwork in Sri Lanka. Although many of the group members had worked together on human rights issues, and particularly women's rights for many years, the group was officially formed in the wake of the 2004 tsunami and at a time when violence was again escalating. Known as the *Valkai* group, the group aimed to provide forms of assistance and create networks of support for families affected by the violence across the eastern region of Sri Lanka. The kinds of activities the group were involved in included visiting families whose loved ones had been killed, 'disappeared', or taken by the government forces or one of the Tamil militant groups, organising meetings for mothers whose children had been forcibly abducted by the LTTE or breakaway group, the TMVP (*Tamil Makhal Viduthalai Pulikal* – Tamil People's Liberation Tigers), and bringing families together for tree-planting ceremonies.³ Sometimes the family visits involved helping to locate and reclaim the body of a loved one, or obtaining a death certificate, and, at other times, providing small amounts of financial support to a family during a particularly difficult time. Overall, the work of the *Valkai* group sought to create safer spaces for families to be supported at a time when violence and fear shaped most daily interactions, and even the simple acts like sending your child to school or attending the funeral of a friend were marked with threat and widespread, pervasive fear.

Notes

1 In order to protect the identity of the family, all names listed here and in the rest of the book are pseudonyms.
2 Incorporating 'Mattakkalappu' and other place names into the vocabulary of this book, I will no longer italicize these words.
3 Under international law, a state commits an enforced disappearance when it takes a person into custody and denies holding them or disclosing their whereabouts. 'Disappeared' persons hereafter referred to as disappeared are commonly subjected to torture or extrajudicial execution and cause family members continued suffering. An enforced disappearance is a continuing rights violation – it is ongoing until the fate or whereabouts of the person becomes known (Human Rights Watch [HRW] 2008a: 4).

Acknowledgements

Over the two years that I spent in eastern Sri Lanka, I was extremely privileged to find myself a part of a very special group of people engaged in courageous work amidst a climate of violence and fear. During my time in the household by the lagoon, I was able to share many small and wonderful moments as well as many tragic and painful ones. I was given far more in terms of love, support, and experiences than I could ever give back. More than anything, my years of fieldwork were a learning experience, ones in which I learnt much about grief and hope, taught by those who lived through both, every day. Therefore, I first have to thank my Batticaloa family without whom this book and the research behind it would never have come into existence. To AH, S, P, JT, VK, and SR – my time in eastern Sri Lanka would have never been the same without the rich experiences of life that you showed me. You welcomed me in before you barely knew me and invested your time, spirit, and, most of all, courage in showing me where trust and hope can be found even in the darkest of experiences. Being a part of your family has left an indelible mark on me, and the sustenance of my experience has propelled me to move on and grow. Much of what I learnt from you is now embedded in the way that I see things and approach life. AH – as a mother, friend, and teacher you taught me more about patience, awareness, and strength than anyone else I know. You seemed to always have the energy to fight the battles others couldn't and had the courage to look critically at what was closest to you. As I grew in awareness of my own vulnerabilities, I also learnt about the unwavering commitment of people like you who seem to live so that others could too. Thank you to JT for keeping me laughing through horrible times, to SR for being a great sister, and to P for doing a great job as a little brother. I also extend my thanks to all the *Valkai* people and those connected to the group who included me in their networks and friendships, particularly Daniel, S and Y. To all the mothers, and to the girls at the orphanage, especially Sinthu, thank you for investing time and trust in me, sharing your stories and looking after me as if your own.

To all of you mentioned so far I have to admit that there will be times in this book where I will invariably have made mistakes and unintentionally misrepresented people and situations. For this, I can only apologise, and emphasise the fact that I have always sought to present as accurate account as possible. However, the process of writing and rewriting, and the passing of time inevitably wear at experiences and stories. Furthermore, I never presumed that what I have written in this book could not be told better by those of you who have lived every narrative, and experienced the everyday fear, risk, and endurance. Yet, I also recognise that the task of writing often falls at the feet of those who are somewhat removed from the context and who are afforded the luxury of stepping away from daily violence. I have, therefore, written this book with the hope that one day you will write something that will be far more powerful than any anthropologist could ever produce. In writing this book, providing that I do not increase the risk you already face, and that no one is hurt by my work, then I hope you will think it worth the effort and risk.

There are, of course, many more people that I want to thank – more than I am able to name here, people who have encouraged me throughout, cheered from the sidelines, and actively shoved me over the hurdles in order to reach the finish. I am extremely grateful for the support and encouragement of my Ph.D. supervisors Prof. Jonathan Spencer and Prof. Tony Good, who pushed and pulled me through the Ph.D. process and helped me believe in my own abilities. Thank you to Prof. Dilip Menon at the Centre for Indian Studies in Africa (University of the Witwatersrand, Johannesburg) for the encouragement, support, and opportunity to continue my work on Sri Lanka during the post-doctoral fellowship. Thank you also to Sharika, KB, Kath, Dhana, and Timmo (and many others); you have all provided me with much support and extended your friendship across countries and continents as I moved from Edinburgh to Sri Lanka, back to Edinburgh, and now to Johannesburg. I would have been lost without you all. Glynis, thank you for the Friday writing sessions and for reading every chapter I have sent you. Mum, dad, and all my siblings – thank you for being so patient with me and for always being there.

To Craig, thank you for putting up with all the stress, tears, frustration, and serious caffeine addiction. You have kept me laughing, loved, and running throughout this writing process. I have never been happier than with you and you helped me find calm and balance at the most crazy of times. Thanks must also be extended to Gill Morton, without whose support, insight, and wisdom I could not have got to where I am now. Thank you for carrying my hope until I felt able to realise it, and for helping turn what felt impossible into an achievable process.

Finally, there are many who have been a part of my life yet not managed to complete their journeys. Their memories have been with me throughout this and will always be so. To G. W (1956–2007), your energy and enthusiasm were infectious and kept me laughing all the way to Trincomalee. To Y. H (1958–2006), your memory, like your sons' lives in the leaves and branches of *Kutti annar maram*; I hope that you now have the peace you were denied in the last years of your life. Finally, to my friends Meeto (1978–2006) and Sasi (1979–2005), if only you could have danced a while in someone else's shoes, then you would have seen yourselves for the beautiful, young women you were.

Abbreviations

ADB	Asian Development Bank
AFP	Agence France-Presse
AGA	Additional Government Agent
AI	Amnesty International
BRC	British Red Cross
CFA	Ceasefire Agreement
CFR	Council on Foreign Relations
CIRM	Centre for Information and Resources Management
CPO	Child Protection Officer
DS	Divisional Secretariat
EPDP	Eelam People's Democratic Party
EPRLF	Eelam People's Revolutionary Liberation Front
EROS	Eelam Revolutionary Organisation of Students
FCE	Foundation for Co-Existence
FCO	Fisherman's Cooperative Society
FP	Federal Party
GA	Government Agent
GAM	*Geraka Acch Medeka* (Free Aceh Movement)
GN/GS	Grama Niladhari/ Grama Sevaka
GoSL	Government of Sri Lanka
HRW	Human Rights Watch
HSZ	High Security Zone
IASC	Inter-Agency Standing Committee
ICES	International Centre for Ethnic Studies
ICG	International Crisis Group
ICRC	International Committee of the Red Cross
IDMC	International Displacement Monitoring Centre
IDP	Internally Displaced People
ILO	International Labour Organisation
INFORM	Information Monitor (Human Rights Organization)
INGO	International Non-Governmental Organisation
IPKF	Indian Peace Keeping Force

IRIN	Integrated Regional Information Networks
ISGA	Interim Self-Government Authority
JBIC	Japan Bank for International Cooperation
JHU	*Jathika Hela Urumaya* (National Heritage Party)
JVP	*Janatha Vimukthi Peramuna* (People's Liberation Front)
LTTE	Liberation Tigers of Tamil Eelam
MBRL	Multi-barrel Rocket Launchers
MOU	Memorandum of Understanding
NVA	National Unity Alliance
OCHA	United Nations Office for the Coordination of Humanitarian Affairs
PA	People's Alliance
PLOTE	People's Liberation Organization of Tamil Eelam
PTA	Prevention of Terrorism Act
P-TOMS	PostTsunami Operational Management Structure
PTSD	Post-Traumatic Stress Disorder
RAW	Research and Analysis Wing (India)
SLA	Sri Lankan Army
SLFP	Sri Lanka Freedom Party
SLMC	Sri Lanka Muslim Congress
SLMM	Sri Lanka Monitoring Mission
SLRC	Sri Lankan Red Cross
STF	Special Task Force
SU	Sihala Urumaya
TEA	Tamil Eelam Association
TEC	Tsunami Evaluation Coalition
TELO	Tamil Eelam Liberation Organization
TMVP	*Tamil Makhal Viduthalai Pulikal* (Tamil People's Liberation Tigers)
TNA	Tamil National Alliance
TRO	Tamil Rehabilitation Organization
TULF	Tamil United Liberation Front
UNHCR	United Nations High Commissioner for Refugees
UNICEF	United Nations International Childcare Fund
UNP	United National Party
UPFA	United People's Freedom Alliance
UTHR(J)	University Teachers of Human Rights (Jaffna)
WB	World Bank
WHO	World Health Organisation

Series editor's foreword

At its best, ethnography has provided a valuable tool for apprehending a world in flux. A couple of years after the Second World War, Max Gluckman founded the Department of Social Anthropology at the University of Manchester. In the years that followed, he and his colleagues built a programme of ethnographic research that drew eclectically on the work of leading anthropologists, economists and sociologists to explore issues of conflict, reconciliation and social justice 'at home' and abroad. Often placing emphasis on detailed analysis of case studies drawn from small-scale societies and organisations, the famous 'Manchester School' in social anthropology built an enviable reputation for methodological innovation in its attempts to explore the pressing political questions of the second half of the twentieth century. Looking back, that era is often thought to constitute a 'gold standard' for how ethnographers might grapple with new challenges and issues in the contemporary world.

The *New Ethnographies* series aims to build on that ethnographic legacy at Manchester. It will publish the best new ethnographic monographs that promote interdisciplinary debate and methodological innovation in the qualitative social sciences. This includes the growing number of books that seek to apprehend the 'new' ethnographic objects of a seemingly brave new world, some recent examples of which have included auditing, democracy and elections, documents, financial markets, human rights, assisted reproductive technologies and political activism. Analysing such objects has often demanded new skills and techniques from the ethnographer. As a result, this series will give voice to those using ethnographic methods across disciplines to innovate, such as through the application of multi-sited fieldwork and the extended comparative case study method. Such innovations have often challenged more traditional ethnographic approaches. *New Ethnographies* therefore seeks to provide a platform for emerging scholars and their more established counterparts engaging with ethnographic methods in new and imaginative ways.

Dr Alexander Thomas T. Smith

Map 1 Map of Sri Lanka provinces and districts.
Source: Government Survey Department of Sri Lanka (2005a)

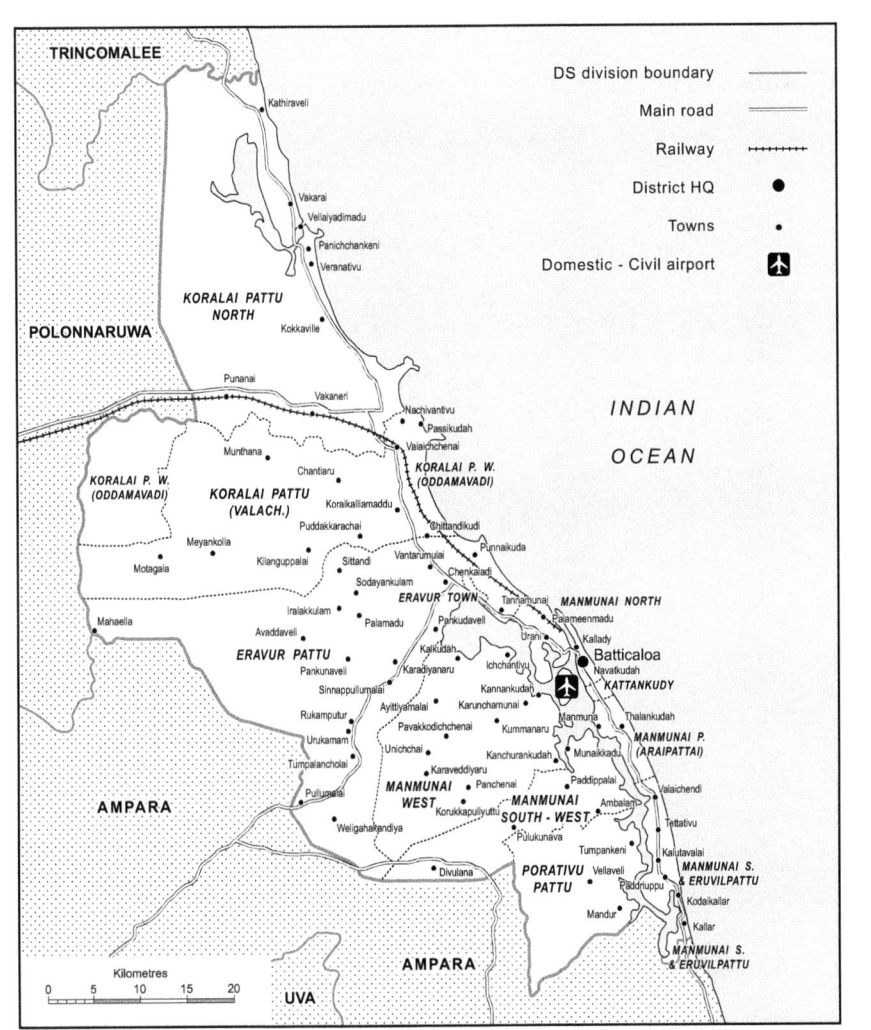

Map 2 Map of administrative boundaries, Batticaloa.
Source: Government Survey Department of Sri Lanka (2005b)

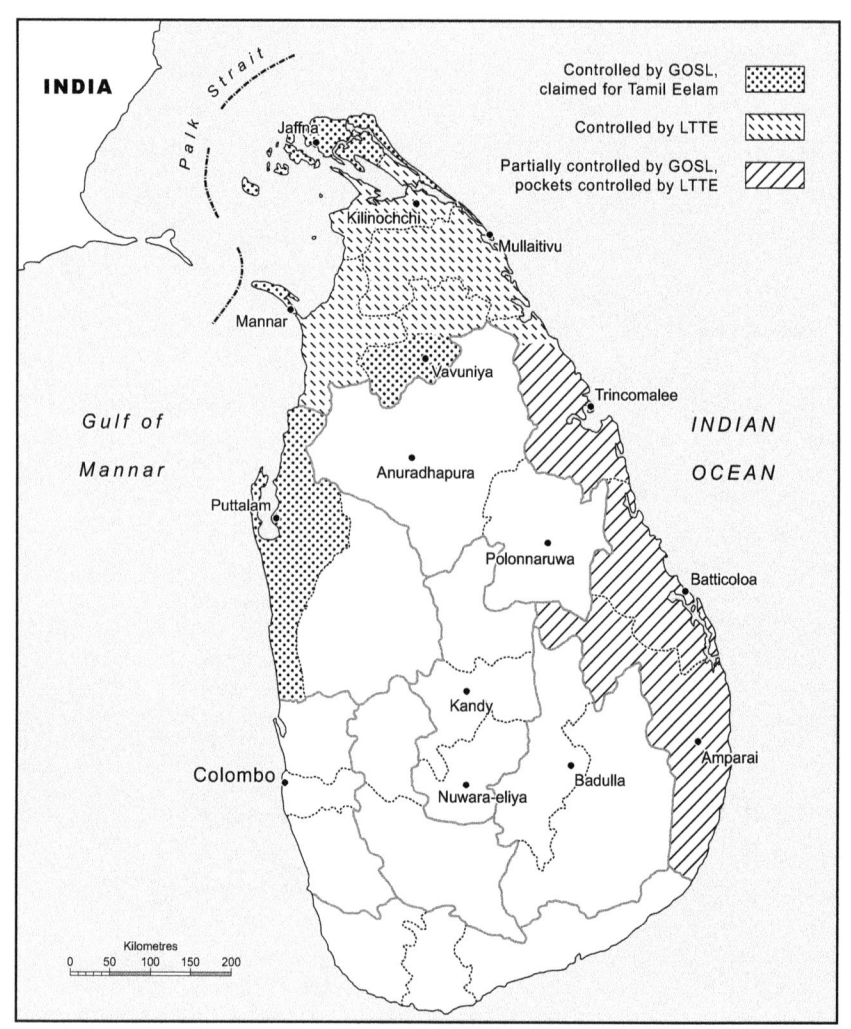

Map 3 Map of areas in Sri Lanka controlled by the government and the LTTE (2005).
Source: European Union Report (2009)

1

The beginning of the end

Everyday violence

On 19 May 2009, the government of Sri Lanka defeated the LTTE (Liberation Tigers of Tamils Eelam) in a brutal and bloody final battle ending a civil war that has ravaged the island of Sri Lanka for almost three decades. The conflict has affected all communities living in Sri Lanka; however, the north and the east of the island – the areas historically inhabited by the Tamil-speaking communities – have borne the brunt of the violence. Thousands have been displaced, often many times over, and social and physical landscapes have been scarred by the brutality and tragedy of war. Whilst engaged in armed conflict with the government forces, the LTTE – which emerged as the most powerful of the Tamil militant groups – has also unleashed tactics of terror on its own people, and Tamil-speaking populations throughout the north and the east have become the victims of the sheer savagery of conflict. In turn, the state forces have been involved in the arbitrary arrest, detention, torture, disappearances, and deaths of thousands of Tamil men and women from these same areas. It is the experiences of Tamil-speaking people who have lived through and continue to face conflict and violence in Sri Lanka on a daily basis that is the main subject of this book. Set within the context of eastern Sri Lanka, this book focuses on the years between 2005 and 2007, a distinctive time in the history of the conflict, when the country was facing massive change in the lead up to the defeat of the LTTE. At this time, while violence waxed and waned, intensifying at times and at others casting a dark shadow over daily encounters, people carried on with their lives, negotiating through and around the violence.

Much of what communities have endured in Sri Lanka has been characterised by the terms 'dirty war' and 'everyday violence', terms that speak in the abstract about the uses of violence to fragment, isolate, and destroy the lives of those caught up in fighting. A proliferating genre of literature describes 'everyday violence' as a lived reality through which the insidious and pervasive effects and mechanisms of violence and terror are made more visible (for example, Feldman 1991, 2000; Nordstrom and Martin 1992; Nordstrom and Robben 1996; Nordstrom 1994: 14, 1997, 2004; Scheper-Hughes 1993, 1996; Green 1999;

Robben and Suarez-Orozco 2000; Scheper Hughes and Bourgois 2004). 'Dirty war' (Rajasingham-Senenayake 1999: 59–60) meanwhile pertains to the ways in which constructions of terror and the absurd are used to contaminate or 'dirty' everyday life in order to gain and maintain control over a population.[1] Although small-scale compared to the grand attacks and counter-attacks that capture media attention, 'everyday violence' and 'dirty war' can be equally, if not, more terrifying. In fact, it is argued that because this kind of violence takes place often between known actors and through familiar objects and items of everyday experiences, it can be all the more disturbing (Nordstrom 1992; Green 1994: 41–2; Hughes forthcoming). Despite variation in cultural location and theoretical issues, thematically much of what emerges in the description of areas of conflict critically overlaps. Details of militarised towns, guerrillas or 'terrorists', rebellion, fragmented communities, broken families, displacement, trauma, and loss of trust, while manifested differently, are woven together as hallmarks of everyday violence. Within these distinguishing marks, ideas of the everyday and of violence are conflated to suggest spaces where fragments of a familiar everyday have been soaked through with violence, rendering them unsafe. In turn, it has also become integral to accounts of conflict and war to have the extraordinary acts of survival pitted against tragic reoccurring violence.

It was through the network of families, knitted by the informal human rights group known as the *Valkai* group and extending across the eastern border villages and towns, that I was introduced to the multiple strategies and spaces that people used in their daily routines to cope with the violence that surrounded them.[2] I met with mothers fighting to get their children back, men under threat, hiding in the shadows of darkened homes, and grandparents mourning the loss of children who had survived detention and torture by the army, only to be taken by the waves of the tsunami. The experiences these individuals and families faced were not new or uncommon under the prevailing conditions of protracted war and widespread violence in Sri Lanka. However, as much as people had come to recognise suffering and pain, this did not mean that their everyday experiences were defined by violence or that this was normal or ordinary in any way. The idea of ordinary violence (when ordinary is taken to mean banal and mundane) suggests a failure to recognise what is unacceptable. It also suggests that the totalising nature of violence prevents any understanding outside of a 'culture of terror' (see Sluka 2000: 22–3). Yet, for these mothers, fathers, grandparents, and grandchildren, it seemed that rather than allowing the situation to consume their sense of the everyday, people learned to negotiate and question, to work their lives around and beyond violence. Pushing at the small cracks and spaces in the continuum of violence, they created a sense of the everyday that was about violence yet also challenged the meaning of the everyday and of the ordinary, opening up meaning to encompass other possibilities and imaginations. What emerged in the spaces between the accepted understandings of ordinary and extraordinary was a sense of the *endurance* of everyday life. The term endurance, which lies at the heart of this book, captures the sense that something happens beyond the self, that is protracted violence that endured. Exploring what it means to endure violence, rather than say to resist, be resilient to, or even to contain, this book is set apart from many of the other works on violence in Sri Lanka and the anthropology of everyday violence more generally.

The way in which the topics in this book flow reflect my journey of research and the various issues that became important along the way. Thus, in following my experiences through the conflict and the tsunami, I aim to build up a larger and richer picture of life in Batticaloa that moves between accounts of everyday violence and suffering, and dwelling more on the particular people who are actively making it possible to endure and invest in a more humane future. Using ethnographic experiences and narratives collected over twenty-two months between 2004 and 2007, this book argues that to look to the moments of hope and imagination as well as the everyday endurance which drives people forward must constitute a core element of anthropological representations of violence and suffering. This includes highlighting the non-violent spaces or parts of daily life, which are less dramatically framed by violence, and are often lost in contexts of conflict, faded out as weak shadows to the more forceful violence.

Sri Lanka's conflict

The Sri Lankan conflict has been well documented, and as a popular setting for research, including numerous anthropological case studies and political studies of ethnic conflict, terrorism, and peace, has been represented in many different ways. Countless scholars and journalists have written about the conflict, commonly through constitutional issues such as human rights and refugees, and identity-related issues of ethnicity and nationalism. While some have explored topics outside of the conflict, the majority either have focused on conflict-related issues or have found their subject area inextricably linked to the conflict in some way. As would be expected, particular events in the country's past have received more attention than others, and journals, newspapers, and country-situation updates have contributed to identifying what are regarded as significant events or times of intervention. Many of the effects of violence on civilian populations in the north and east are described through the hallmark topics of Sri Lanka's conflict – mass internal displacement, land disputes, child-recruitment, and trauma. Given the competing and often contradictory versions of events and claims made about the 'truth' of the past, it is difficult to set out in simple terms the background and roots of conflict. At the same time, it is also important at the start of this book to provide a sense of what has taken place, why, and how. In particular, I want to highlight the recent significant shifts and developments in the country, to provide the context of escalating tension and violence in which my fieldwork was carried out, and which precipitated the paths to the final war.

Therefore, while what follows does not purport to be a comprehensive analysis, it outlines some of the significant moves and shifts on the timeline of Sri Lanka's conflict and introduces some of the key players.

Landscapes of suffering

What is often referred to as an 'ethnic conflict' in Sri Lanka can be benchmarked as having started with a militant attack and subsequent widespread anti-Tamil rioting in July 1983 and ended with the defeat of the leadership of the LTTE in May 2009.

Although the conflict has discursive and mythical roots in ancient Buddhist chronicles, its direct roots lie in the ethnic bias that entered Sri Lanka's nation-building practice in the run-up to Independence from the British in 1948. The Tamil population – located mainly in the north, the east, and the hill country – is the island's largest minority (18.2 per cent) while the majority of the island's people (74.0 per cent) are Sinhalese (Department of Census and Statistics 1981). Muslims (Moors) comprise 7.4 per cent. The remaining 0.4 per cent of the population is composed of Malays, a small community descended from troops and exiled royalty, brought in by the Dutch and British colonial administrators from what is now known as Malaysia and Indonesia; Burghers, descendants of unions between Europeans and inhabitants of Sri Lanka and others including the indigenous Veddas, who are generally considered the aboriginal population of Sri Lanka (see also Chapter 2, page 34).[3] Sri Lanka's last complete census was held in 1981. Although an all-island census was attempted in 2001 and 2006, they have been unable to provide a comprehensive picture since it covered only eighteen of the twenty-five districts across the island, excluding many areas in the Northern and Eastern Provinces due to the effects of armed conflict in the areas. Given these caveats, I have used census data from the 1981 census only as indicative estimates. Although literature on Sri Lanka often makes reference to Tamils and Muslims as though they form a unified social body, they are, in fact, historically, geographically, and politically diverse and fragmented. Of the Tamil majority, Sri Lankan Tamils, located mainly in the northern and eastern regions, make up 12.6 per cent, while Tamils of Indian origin, who are mainly labourers in the hill country tea plantations, occupy 5.6 per cent. Muslims and Tamils are identified as the Tamil-speaking community, but have their own distinct religious identities in which Muslims practice Islam and Tamils mainly identify with Hinduism. The Sinhalese are separated by language and religious affiliation, mainly identifying with Buddhism and speaking Sinhala, which under Sinhalese-dominated national politics became the official language of the state in 1956. Christians can also be found in both groups and a number of religious practices adopted by 'Sinhala-Buddhists' and 'Tamil-Hindus' reflect the multiple influences of the different religions upon one another (Gunaratna 2001).

When, in preparation for Independence, the colonial government introduced universal suffrage, politics (which until then had been the preserve of a small elite) became dependent on large numbers of votes. Where earlier the main ethnic group had received equal representation, group size suddenly became directly linked to access to power, thus posing a threat to overrepresented minority groups, such as the Tamils, and an opportunity for the underrepresented Sinhalese. Tamils, at this time, were in particular heavily represented in the civil service and at the professional level (due to their access to good missionary schools in Jaffna). Therefore, attempts at achieving proportional representation of Sinhalese were easily construed as anti-Tamil actions by Sinhala and Tamil ethno-nationalists alike. However, it was the 'Sinhala only' language policy of 1956 implemented by newly elected S.W.R.D Bandaranaike that put fuel to the Sinhala nationalist fires and underscored the fears of non-Sinhalese in the country. This policy made Sinhala the official language of the country (except for the administrative areas of the north and east), and in doing so effectively barred Tamil speakers from entering public service in the rest of the country. At this time and also two years later in 1958, anti-Tamil riots broke out. These were met with an increasing ethno-nationalism amongst Tamils, which began as campaigns of non-violence but were met with brutality and increasing violence from the state. Simultaneously, the Sinhala-majority government also embarked on projects of resettlement of Sinhalese communities from densely populated areas in the south and west to areas known as the 'Dry Zone', which for centuries had been predominantly inhabited by Tamil-speaking populations (see Chapter 2, pages 60–1). For Tamil nationalists, this was seen as another deliberate attempt to undermine and destabilise Tamil claims to land and territory (Senanayake 1985 [1935]).

In 1972, an overtly Sinhala and Buddhist constitution was adopted, and exclusionary practices, such as restricting university admission against the Tamils, particularly Jaffna Tamils, increased. Frustrated with the failure of the older generation of Tamil leaders to accomplish change in the political process, Tamil youth began to form militant groups. A new model for political activism had been set by the originally Maoist (and largely Sinhala) Janatha Vimukthi Peramuna (JVP or People's Liberation Front) in 1971 when in response to specific grievances with the state and influenced by other socialist and communist youth protests across the globe JVP launched an insurrection against the state (see Hoole *et al.* 1988). From the late 1970s, a large number of Tamil militant groups emerged. The most powerful of these groups was the Liberation Tigers of Tamil Eelam (LTTE), popularly known as the Tamil Tigers or the Tigers, which was formally established in 1975 and led by Velupillai Prabhakaran (also written as Pirabakaran). Graduating from small attacks and ambushes on the police and the government forces to wide-scale violence including terrorist attacks and counter-attacks, the LTTE developed into a tightly structured and strictly controlled organisation with a two-tier structure: a military wing and a subordinate political wing, overseen by a central governing committee and several subdivisions. These included the Sea Tigers, the Air Tigers, an elite fighting wing, a suicide commando unit (the Black Tigers), a highly secretive intelligence wing, and a political office. Children also featured prominently in the makeup of the LTTE throughout the conflict.[4] International law prohibits the recruitment of children under the age of 18 by non-state armed groups, and all participation of children in active hostilities (Human Rights Watch [HRW] 2004), and therefore the LTTE's strategy of recruiting children into their ranks has been widely reported. However, as the University Teachers for Human Rights

(Jaffna) (UTHR) (2002: 8) has noted, child conscription is 'a reflection of the whole society being conscripted.[5] The question of choice, whether child or adult does not arise.' It is important to note that throughout this book I use the terms 'recruitment' and 'abduction', in reference to children made to join the LTTE, interchangeably. This is because the lines between the two are not clear-cut. While many children opted to join the LTTE, this was often due to a number of pressing factors such as poverty, fear, loss of family members, or the force of the recruitment campaigns used by LTTE cadre in schools and youth groups. Furthermore, many parents testify (as the stories in this book reveal) to their children being forcibly abducted – often snatched on their way to tuition classes and town.[6]

In 1976, the Tamil Liberation Front (TULF), a Tamil nationalist coalition of political parties, began to advocate for the establishment of a separate state for Tamil people, known as Tamil Eelam.

State violence and youth militancy

In July 1983, following an attack by the LTTE on a military convoy, killing thirteen army personal, large-scale anti-Tamil riots broke out in Colombo. The riots lasted a week and spread to other parts of the country leaving up to 3,000 Tamils killed, and thousands of Tamil homes and businesses destroyed. The role of the government in orchestrating the pogrom, which became known as 'Black July' is no secret and played a role in driving up the numbers of recruits for Tamil militant groups, in particular the LTTE. While many Tamils fled to the north of the island, roughly around 500,000 Tamils are thought to have sought refuge in countries such as Britain, France, Canada, and Australia. Thus amongst the widespread Tamil diaspora, the LTTE became a romanticised symbol of hope and survival for the Tamil communities playing out in collective rituals of remembrance and loss (see De Mel 2007: 18). The diaspora also became a critical support base for the LTTE from which much financial backing was derived. However, the spectacle of memorialisation and longing for a homeland that did not exist also hid the reality of the lives of those surviving under the Tigers. For those living in the north and east of Sri Lanka, the LTTE dictatorial *de-facto* state ensured that support was given in multiple ways, including the 'giving' (often forced) of one child per family (and often more than one), limited and often prohibited travel to the south, and a crippling taxation system. Following the violence of Black July, a state of emergency was imposed, and, by 1984, the armed conflict between the government and Tamil militant groups escalated into what is called the 'First Eelam war', taking on the proportions of a civil war.

In the course of dealing with violence, the Sri Lankan state has resorted to large-scale extra-judicial killings against Tamils from the early 1980s and also against Sinhalese youth during the two JVP-led insurgencies in 1971 and again in the late 1980s. The second insurgency and its brutal suppression by the state forces during the period 1987–90 is known simply as 'the Terror' (*Bheeshanaya*), and was a time of deliberate and systematic terrorism on the part of both the JVP and the United National Party (UNP) government of the time.[7] Between 60,000 and 100,000 people, mostly youth died, the vast majority gruesomely killed by forces linked to the state (Chandraprema 1991; Gunaratna 2001; Hughes forthcoming). Such violence critically highlights the interplay of marginalisation, discrimination, and state brutality inflicted on both Sinhala and Tamil communities, particularly in non-urban and poorer backgrounds thus complicating the often simple portrayal of 'ethnic conflict' in Sri Lanka. *Bheeshanaya* along with Black July were not simply tragic periods of violence in themselves, but can be seen to reveal the ways in which those who govern Sri Lanka enforce control and deal with dissent (see Manikkalingham 2002).[8] Therefore, although it cannot be denied that ethnic discrimination is a particular aspect of the suffering experienced by Tamil people, at the same time it is important to recognise that the violence in Sri Lanka is part of a much wider story with political and socio-economic class dimensions (ibid.; see also de Silva 1994).

No war–no peace

The deployment of the Indian Peace Keeping Force (IPKF) in 1987 to patrol the north-east of Sri Lanka and to disarm the Tamil militants brought its own set of problems. Having previously offered military training and support to Tamil militants who had set up camps in Tamil Nadu, the Indian government aimed to enforce a programme of devolution of powers (as agreed in the Indo-Sri Lankan Accord or ISLA) to the provincial level. In the east, the arrival of the IPKF brought more suffering, particularly for women as the Indian soldiers became notorious for sexual abuse and rape (Amnesty International [AI] 1990a). While the state took on the second JVP insurgency in the south, the LTTE took on the IPKF, rejuvenated at the last minute by a government that also wanted to see the Indian soldiers leave. By early 1990, the IPKF were forced to abandon its mission. With the withdrawal of the IPKF, the now well-armed and revitalised LTTE moved into their vacated camps, and its hegemony in the north became further entrenched as it banned all other Tamil political groups, killing many of those who did not disband. The government's counter-insurgency strategy, meanwhile, made use of former Tamil militant groups such as the People's Liberation Organisation of Tamil Eelam (PLOTE) and the Tamil Eelam Liberation Organisation (TELO), realigning with them against the LTTE (UTHR 1991; International Crisis Group [ICG] 2011a). In June 1990, the Second Eelam war began with hundreds of unarmed policemen in the east, mainly Muslim and Sinhala, being murdered by the LTTE, and, for the next decade, the two sides battled for control over various areas in the north and east, especially Jaffna and Killinochchi (see map 1: page xx).

While there had been successive attempts to develop a political solution to the conflict over the years, including a brief ceasefire between the government and the LTTE in 1990 and in 1995, all ended in escalations of violence and a return to war. Thousands of Tamils, mostly men but also women and children, disappeared during this time as a culture of impunity led by the government forces reigned.

The LTTE also evicted an estimated 70,000–100,000 Muslims from the Northern Province, giving them a maximum of forty-eight hours to collect their belongings and leave (see UTHR 1995). In 2002, amidst an economic crisis, which badly effected the government of Sri Lanka (GoSL), and the post-9/11 'war on terror', which impacted negatively on the LTTE's international reputation and funding channels, a new ceasefire was declared. Facilitated by the Norwegian government, the Ceasefire Agreement (CFA) was signed between the UNP led by Ranil Wickremasinghe and the LTTE. The Memorandum of Understanding (MoU), monitored by the Sri Lankan Monitoring Mission (SLMM) made up of experts from Norway and other Nordic countries, led to the ban on the LTTE, which had been in place intermittently since 1978 being lifted in August 2002. This paved the way for the resumption of direct negotiations between the two parties.[9] Although the CFA was heralded as the most successful of its time, a breakdown of negotiations in April 2003 and the consequent stalemate allowed the violence to escalate once again.[10] This period took on what has been referred to as a 'no war–no peace' impasse, and the north and east in particular faced a 'shadow war' as attacks and counter-attacks continued on a daily basis.

Two disasters: The LTTE split and the tsunami

In 2004, two major events occurred, both of which had profound affects in the east and which in their own ways altered the course of the conflict. The first, which affected the east specifically, occurred in April 2004 when a renegade LTTE eastern commander, Vinayagamoorthi Muralitharan, mounted a military challenge against the LTTE. Defecting with around 5,000 militants in the eastern district, Colonel Karuna, as he was more popularly known, claimed to represent the political aspirations for autonomy of the Tamils in the Eastern Province (AI 2005). Resentment escalated from the fact that, while the higher echelons of the LTTE were dominated by northern Tamils, many of the young cadre fighting on the front lines and losing their lives were taken from this east. However, although Karuna initially made a show of releasing around 2,000 children and young adults to distinguish himself from the northern LTTE, he quickly began his own campaign of child-recruitment and abductions, political killings, assaults, and extortion. Despite being militarily much weaker than the mainstream LTTE (which became known by Batticaloa people as the 'P-party' or 'Vanni party'), the Karuna party ('K-party'), which developed a political arm known as the Tamil Makhal Viduthalai Pulikal (Tamil People's Liberation Tigers or TMVP), was successful in claiming control over the town of Batticaloa and other areas along the east coast. Known to be working in collaboration with government forces, Karuna's actions negated many of the more positive developments that had followed the 2002 ceasefire (HRW 2007a).[11]

The second major event was the Indian Ocean tsunami, which hit the Sri Lankan coastlines on 26 December 2004. It was by far the most devastating catastrophe in the recorded history of Sri Lanka and caused a death toll of approximately 35,322 with 21,411 injured. According to official estimates,

558,287 people (3 per cent of the total population) were displaced, and between one million and two million (10 per cent of the population) were affected through loss of homes, businesses, and community structures (Asian Development Board [ADB], Japan Bank for International Cooperation [JBIC] and World Bank [WB] 2005a, 2005b;WHO 2005: 1). The north and east coastal belt of the country were the worst affected areas, with in the Batticaloa district approximately 3,177 dead or missing and 255,000 affected (Department of Census and Statistics Special Enumeration 2008). Around 12,494 families and 55,974 individuals were displaced (ibid.).[12]

The stories of what people encountered that day accomplished what the tragedy of the conflict had not managed to do, putting Sri Lanka on the global map and triggering donations from millions of people across the world. The enormity of the disaster was thus matched by the international response, with total aid pledged to Sri Lanka passing one and a half billion dollars by mid-January 2005, by far exceeding the tentative reconstruction budget (WHO 2005). Accordingly, this led to an influx of International Non-Governmental Organisations (INGOs), local Non-Governmental Organisations (NGOs), foreign workers, and volunteers into Sri Lanka. In Batticaloa, they arrived in addition to the dozens already present in the east who were focused on either conflict-related and development programmes, or both (Fernando and Hilhorst 2006: 297).[13]

It has been argued that the spontaneous and rapid reactions of care and support that emerged in those first few days following the tsunami would have been an ideal basis for building up mutual trust and more long-term peace, especially given that the immediate aftermath was also characterised by 'good will' from the leadership on both sides and marked by spontaneous cooperation between the government and LTTE forces (Uyangoda 2005).[14] However, the failure of the Post-Tsunami Operational Management Structure (PTOMS), a mechanism designed to liaise between the government agencies and the Planning and Development secretariat of the LTTE in June 2005 meant that initial hopes were destroyed.[15]

Instead, disagreements over the distribution of aid to Tamil regions under LTTE control and strong opposition by predominantly Sinhala political parties – the JVP and Jathika Hela Urumaya (JHU) – and by the Muslim political parties led to new disputes and a deepening of hostilities (see Pirani and Kadirgamar 2006). The attempts of the JVP (who left the government in protest) to block the P-TOMS through the Supreme Court ensured that the agreement could not be implemented (Goodhand and Klem 2005). This was followed by a hardening of the government's post-tsunami policy stance *vis-à-vis* international involvement in domestic politics. Furthermore, the international humanitarian response, following the tsunami, suffered from poor coordination and control, and was shaped by feverish and competitive claim-staking among INGOs which Jock Stirrat (2006: 11) has branded 'competitive humanitarianism'.

A plethora of analyses and critiques have emerged since 2004, mostly highlighting the failures of many of the international organisations to pay attention to

Plate 1.1 A woman sitting outside her tsunami-destroyed house, Kallady (Batticaloa) (2005)

local nuances and political sensitivities (see Fraser 2005; Uyangoda 2005; Goodhand and Klem 2005; Fernando and Hillhorst 2006; Harris 2006; Stirrat 2006; Bohle and Fünfgeld 2007; Ruwanpura 2009; Hasbullah and Korf 2009; Korf et al. 2009).[16] What has been less commented on, however, are what those few days after the tsunami meant for locals in terms of the broader picture of the overlapping effects and vulnerabilities created by the disaster and the protracted conflict. The importance of understanding these two events is explored further in the next chapter where I provide a closer reading of the LTTE split and the tsunami in relation to the spatial politics of the east. In particular, I look at how this distinctive time led to the formation of the *Valkai* group, who were able to use the post-tsunami space to reach families in ways they had not been able to before.

Fragile calm

In 2005, against the backdrop of an unravelling ceasefire, failed talks, P-TOMS, and the chaotic tsunami response, the political situation, which had experienced a temporary reprieve after the tsunami, was once again worsening day by day. The instability caused by the two events of the LTTE split and the tsunami had enabled abductions, extortion, and killings to continue and to escalate. When asked of his fears of war returning, one fisherman told me, '(I)f the tsunami comes I can climb a tree, but if *they* [referring to the armed groups] return with their guns, no tree will save me or my child.'

My fieldwork in the east, therefore, began in a period of what could be described as fragile calm, a sharp contrast to the raging and indiscriminate violence of the 1990s. That said, despite the town being less affected by direct army repression and open paramilitary violence, there was still a strong military presence, and clashes between militants and the army were not infrequent. Killings were still happening, and not just of soldiers and cadres but also of those who lived in the towns and villages, and who through simply living in the east were implicitly knitted into webs of violence. Peace talks that had been held intermittently after the signing of the ceasefire agreement had broken down in April 2003 with both the government and the LTTE accusing one another of carrying out covert operations and preparing for a return to war. Therefore, despite the ceasefire still being in place and an apparent decrease in body counts and reported atrocities at this time, in areas of the north and areas of the east such as Batticaloa the reality for locals was quite different. In fact, the lack of clarity and the resumption of everyday 'normal' activities hid much of what was happening under the surface. It also allowed violations of the ceasefire and of human rights to be pushed even further, a clear example being that the number of children abducted by the LTTE during the ceasefire escalated despite their pledge to cease all child-recruitment (HRW 2004).

The tensions between militant groups meant that Batticaloa experienced many *harthals* (general shutdown of everyday activity) called for by either the LTTE or TMVP. At such times, business would be brought to a standstill and streets would be silenced, edged with fear and threat. Even the army, who seemed to stand back at such times, would appear agitated and tense. With more than one master in this context, people were essentially trapped. To obey one side was to automatically defy another. Similarly, if support were shown to one faction, even if it had been in the past, then a person would be immediately under threat. Children too, became trapped, sought after by both sides. Often families were forced to give one child to the LTTE and another to the TMVP and mothers captured the confusion and desperation created by this when they favourably compared the LTTE taking their children to the TMVP. The LTTE, they noted, were better controlled and structured and so the mothers knew where to go and search for their children, while the TMVP in comparison were far less organised, leaving the mothers unsure of what to do next.

The final offensive

In November 2005, the United People's Freedom Alliance (UPFA) candidate, Mahinda Rajapakse, won the presidential elections on a hardline Sinhala-nationalist ticket.[17] A number of significant and controversial factors were seen as responsible for Rajapakse claiming victory over the Prime Minister Ranil Wickramasinghe, including the boycott of the election by the LTTE in the north and east and thus banning 300,000 Tamils from voting after allegedly having been bribed by the Rajapakse camp.[18] This was seen to mark a fundamental change in the future of Sri Lanka and particularly in the handling of the conflict. Since the Tigers would have gained little from re-engaging with peace talks, they were seen to have actively encouraged the election of Rajapakse, who advocated a military solution to the conflict and would allow the LTTE to pursue their differences by military means. From the moment of his election onwards, Rajapakse's government became increasingly anti-LTTE, to which the LTTE responded with ever-more attacks and provocations.[19] Tragedies such as the killing of Joseph Pararajasingham MP in Batticaloa on 24 December 2005, the disappearance of Raveendranath, the Eastern University Vice Chancellor (whose fate is not known, except that the State is involved), and the murder of five young students in Trincomalee at the dawn of 2006 marked a degeneration into a deeper climate of unlawful killings, terror, and everyday fear (see UTHR 2007).

Throughout 2006–07, government forces battled to take control of the entire LTTE-controlled territory in the Eastern Province and in July 2007 announced a 'New Dawn to the East' after almost a year of military action and the displacement of thousands of civilians. The lack of protest from the international community to this military offensive can be put down to a number of factors including the assassination of the Sri Lankan Foreign Minister, Lakshman Kadiragamar in August 2005, allegedly by the LTTE.[20] Also, the general silence from the Tamil diaspora at this time can be linked to the continued grip and threat by the Tigers internationally, which meant that it was seen as safer to remain silent than to overtly criticise the LTTE.[21]

Amid escalating violence, the government announced it would be withdrawing from its ceasefire with the Tamil Tigers in January 2008, formalising a return of the conflict. In light of the government's decision, the Sri Lanka Monitoring Mission, set up to monitor the ceasefire and its violations, terminated its operational activities. Looking back now, it is possible to recognise a pattern during the period I carried out my research that led to the build up of the final stages of conflict. However, at the time the train of events was far less obvious given that the LTTE had never before been militarily defeated, and many locals in Batticaloa expressed disbelief that this was possible. An elderly gentleman called Daniel, who had lived in Batticaloa all his life and had a keen interest in updating me on the conflict, summed up people's frustration and confusion when he told me:

> They fight and then they stop fighting, then they talk about peace but they never *do* peace. I don't know what peace is anymore but everyone is suffering. What do we Tamils own anymore? What can we say is ours other than the graves where we bury children? Now those Tiger fellows are getting chased away from the east. But will that bring peace? I don't think so because there are always more problems.

Between 2008 and 2009 the army advanced through the north towards the LTTE *de-facto* administrative capital of Kilinochchi (see map 1: xx), which they took in January 2009. What took place in those final months of offensive in 2009 when the LTTE found themselves trapped on a small stretch of land in

Mullaitivu, along with tens of thousands of civilians who they used as human shields, remains unclear. In their military push, the government closed off the north and prevented international agencies and medical supplies from getting through to the trapped civilians. Very little information was forthcoming as the government maintained strict censorship of any information that filtered out. While the UN had estimated that 6,500 civilians were killed in the three months from February to April, no official figures are available and some speculate that the figure could be three times this number (HRW 2009a). The International Crisis Group's report, 'Reconciliation in Sri Lanka: Harder Than Ever' (ICG 2011a) states that although no accurate figures exist for the number of deaths – civilian or combatant – in the final four years of active insurgency and counter-insurgency, it is possible that between 65,000 and 70,000 lives were lost. This amounts to almost the same number as those killed since fighting broke out in 1983 and brings the total number of lives lost over the decades of conflict in Sri Lanka to an estimated 100,000 (ibid.: 1). What is known, however, is that in its rush to exterminate the Tigers, the army showed little regard for the Tamil civilians, reportedly firing shells within the designated 'no-fire zones' (NFZs), while the Tigers, in turn, blocked escape routes for civilians in a desperate bid to win international sympathy (HRW 2009a).[22] Those who tried to escape or resisted fighting alongside the Tigers were fired at and killed (UTHR 2009a, 2009c).

Some of the harrowing details of the brutality, suffering, and death that occurred on that small stretch of occupied land in the north in the final days of the war are vividly captured in *The Cage* by Gordon Weiss (2011), a UN spokesperson in Sri Lanka at the time of the end of the war. Weiss's documentation of serious violations of international humanitarian law and international human rights law committed by both the GoSL and LTTE echoes significant concerns raised in the report released by the UN Secretary General's Panel of Experts.[23] However, other than Weiss' book, reports by human rights organisations (such as UTHR, HRW, and ICG) and journalistic reports as shown in the Channel 4 documentaries ('Sri Lanka's Killing Fields' (2011) and 'Sri Lanka's Killing Fields: War Crimes Unpunished' (2012)), there is still no substantial academic analysis of what took place in those last days of conflict. Furthermore, even less has been said about what happened in the east as the final offensive to the conflict began. An end to fighting in Sri Lanka has not brought peace, and although the country has moved from one embroiled in protracted war to a country claiming to have 'defeated terrorism', the situation continues to be extremely volatile, and communities in the north and east remain trapped by violence, threat, and fear.

Ever-changing realities

It is clear that since the period that I carried out my fieldwork during the years of 2005–07, the situation in Sri Lanka has undergone dramatic changes. However, in planning this book I decided that rather than update my research and keep adding the ever-changing realities to the content, I would stay within the context in which the data were collected, while acknowledging that much has happened since. This is primarily because less has been written about the distinctive years in the run up to the end of the war, particularly in eastern Sri Lanka, which in hindsight can be seen as when the fabric of Tamil Eelam began to unravel and the end of conflict came into sight. It is also because my focus is on the experiences of people whose lives have not, as yet, significantly altered as a result of the changed circumstances in the country. Many continue to live in fear, with loss, and with violence in their daily lives, and the unanswered questions and absences created by past atrocities continue to shape paths, despite being flattened out by the rhetoric of post-conflict and change. While I expand on these issues in the conclusion, it is the intention of this book to draw attention back to the period of uneasy everyday life and unforgettable everyday ruptures in eastern Sri Lanka during 2005–07 to highlight the importance of understanding what has come to pass and continues to be faced. Furthermore, with the changing contexts and passage of time, the lives and stories that are told in the following chapters take on new significances. Experienced during a context of protracted conflict, they now must adapt to a post-war context, in whatever guises that takes in the east. Therefore, in considering how people inhabit unfinished pasts and work towards uncertain futures, the realities of everyday violence, risk, threat, and hope, which underline the main themes of this book, take on a new urgency.

The *Valkai* group and 'active living'

The *Valkai* group

It was in the aftermath of the tsunami that the *Valkai* group came together in Batticaloa to try and find ways of supporting families and individuals affected by the escalating violence. The group was composed mostly of Sri Lankans and people local to the north and east but also a few foreigners (such as myself) who were living in Batticaloa and concerned about the suffering and climate of impunity. The group met weekly to discuss the current situation (mostly the kinds of violence occurring, fear, and threats) and bring together information gathered by members from different areas across the east. The main focus of the *Valkai* group was to reach out to the families directly affected by the ongoing violence and to offer support – emotional and practical – where possible. Emotionally, the intention was to create space where families could speak openly of their fears, their grief, and their concerns, while practically the group sought to help with basic needs such as locating the body of a loved one, visiting army and LTTE camps to find a missing person, or obtaining a death certificate.[24]

Where the group sought to act in marked ways to reach out to families and connect people with one another, they also did this in a low-key and extremely careful way, the intention being to minimise risk by drawing as little attention to themselves and others as possible. Members of the group emphasised the fact that their roles were defined by the choices they made, based on a set of practices of what could be done in the present context. Where they pushed at boundaries and opened spaces, they also embedded their work in the crevices of life already present, making it a form of what I call 'active living', rather than what might ordinarily be labelled as 'activism'. Furthermore, while the *Valkai* group intentionally tried to create change through their networking, at the same time this was done in accordance with the roles that individuals and families across the east were already carrying out rather than new forms of activism. This is an important point to highlight because the *Valkai* group did not emerge out of or exist in a vacuum, rather it grew from the seeds of work already being done with the intention of strengthening and widening the spaces for alternative thought and action. In this way, the work of the *Valkai* group also challenges the perspective of the majority of academic debates and literature on informal networks and non-violent action in which the dimensions of collective politics as subaltern subjection to domination become the principle underlying aspect of analytical discourse.

Throughout this book, the role of the *Valkai* group is revealed in terms of their connections with families, particularly women across the east, and the activities they carried out such as tree-planting ceremonies and mother's meetings. In Chapter 2, I discuss the formation of the group in detail through an understanding of the spatial politics of the east. Considering how the group used space and worked around the shifting politics of control and power in Batticaloa, I explore two of the group's activities. The first – tree-planting ceremonies – was carried out for families whose loved ones had been killed and the second – parents meetings – was for (mostly) mothers whose children had been recruited by the LTTE and/or the TMVP.

Women and war

Although the *Valkai* group was predominantly made up of women, and it was primarily women from whom the group collected information and stories, one of the most important messages they conveyed was that they recognised that men also suffered irrevocably through conflict. This was not just as fighters, but also as grandfathers, fathers, uncles, brothers, and sons. Men also grieved for their loved ones, sought out strategies to survive, and imagined a different everyday. Lawrence (1997) points out that during the 1990s in Sri Lanka a disproportionate share of men between twenty and forty-five years of age lost their lives. Although this age range is the prime fighting age, it does not mean that most men died fighting; the simple fact of being within that age range and, therefore, possibly a fighter made men suspect and at risk of arbitrary arrest, torture, and disappearance throughout the war. Men, therefore, had to learn to minimise their movements and visibility, avoiding checkpoints and the market in order to reduce the risk of being arrested; instead, women took on these tasks. Concurrently, the role that militarisation – as the mobilisation of resources for war, employed by both the state and the LTTE – has played in shaping women's lives, in particular in determining their security, economic opportunities, and vulnerabilities, cannot be ignored. As Jacklyn Cock (1994: 152) has pointed out, militarisation uses and maintains ideological constructions of gender which widely cast women in the role of 'the protected and defended' while men are the aggressors.

The role of women in Sri Lanka, throughout the decades of conflict, has attracted much scholarly attention, raising some interesting questions about gender identity. The number of armed women combatants who have taken the path of violence, for example, has challenged the often-assumed link between women and peace-building that places women as 'natural' creators and nurturers of life.[25] Furthermore, the increasing number of women as the primary income generators and heads of household defies the assumption that women are always the helpless victims of violence. While widows and female-headed households are not an uncommon phenomenon in Sri Lanka (see Weerasinghe 1987; Perera, M. 1991), they have increased in large proportions due to the decimation of the male population in the north and east. In particular, during the period 2005–09, when hundreds of Tamil civilians and combatants were killed in the east, as fighting between the government and LTTE escalated, the vast majority of victims were men.[26] This has left thousands of new 'war widows' and female-headed households in the north and east, and while estimates vary, the government has referenced up to 90,000 'war widows', with over half in the east.[27] The social stigma that surrounds widows in all three communities – Sinhala, Tamil, and Muslim – has not made these women's tasks any easier, and the many vulnerabilities that women face in daily life are further exacerbated by their widowed status (Rajasingham-Senanayake 1998: 10; Samarasinghe and Galappatti 1998: 6).

For many, the ability of women to endure and work through the effects of everyday violence has been encapsulated within the dichotomy of 'suffering' and 'resilience', in which the struggle for women, particularly Tamil-speaking women, through conflict is translated in terms of the 'empowerment' of women's lives (Coomaraswarmy 1996: 10, de Mel 2002). This is contrasted with the traditional role of the Tamil woman in which she is seen as circumscribed by gendered norms rooted both in Tamil culture – and in Sri Lankan society more broadly (cf. Thiruchandran 1999). This has been capitalised most effectively by the LTTE through the incorporation of the language of women's liberation into the movement in which they have claimed to 'free' women from the constraints of traditional Tamil culture (see Balasingham 1983, 1993, 1998; Coomaraswarmy 1996, 2002; de Mel 2002: 215).

Despite the presence of counter-discourses (encouraged by women's movements and globalisation) and the fact that access to education and jobs in the public domain, including as doctors, lawyers and teachers, have been opened to women, the ties of the gendered ethnic discourse of 'the good Tamil woman' have remained tightly bound in many communities and areas. Subsequently, women have remained largely defined through their relationship with men (Schrijvers 1999: 329).

Based on research with Tamil women in refugee camps during the 1990s,

Schrijvers notes that between the two extreme images of the Tamil woman as soldier and suicide bomber on the one hand, and the poverty-stricken, dependent refugee, on the other, new identities have emerged. These new identities embody, what Schrijivers suggests, are 'ideals that come very close to the Sri Lankan feminist discourse' (ibid.: 307) according to which women assert themselves in the public and the private sphere, renegotiate gender power relations, and increase their autonomy and self-esteem. While Rajasingham-Senenayake (2004a) deals with this debate by stressing that these new roles for women create a sense of 'ambivalent agency' in war-time situations, I suggest that this counters the realities of war in which women suffer intolerably through displacement, widowhood, sexual abuse, and marginalisation (see ICG 2011b). This is illustrated most powerfully through Meena's story in Chapter 5. Meena's account of her experiences of growing up in the east and living through conflict illustrates the multiple forms of violence faced, such as extreme poverty, deprivation, lack of education, access to employment, poor health, and the risks and loss brought by the presence of militants and the state forces.

Women's activism

Given this reality of life under conflict for women in Sri Lanka, there is a long history of women's activism and the formation of various coalitions, organisations, and forums to address women's issues (see de Alwis 1997, 2009a; Manchanda 2001; De Mel 2001, Tambiah Y. 2002; Barry 2005; Samuel 2003, 2006). Some of these organisations and forums have been formal and structured, such as women's NGOs and local forums; others have been based on informal and, therefore, less visible ties of connection (see Samuel 2006; Emmanuel 2008). In the mid-1980s, the Mothers' Front (following the example of the Mothers of the Plazo de Mayo – *Madres de Plaza de Mayo* in Argentina) formed, first in the north and then the east of Sri Lanka. According to Samuel (2006), this was at a time when women were increasingly joining the ranks of 'freedom fighters' within the LTTE while simultaneously focusing on their role as mothers in response to increasing state repression. Women activists, notes Samuel, claimed that the use of the identity of motherhood was a 'necessary form of "protection" in a climate where state repression was at its height and opposition to military presence and military activity was fraught with danger' (2006: 27).[28]

However, despite repeated attempts to demonstrate, protest, and demand the return of their children, the increasing threat and violence directed at the Mothers' Front led to its overall weakening as an organisation for political change. In contrast, de Alwis (2002) points out that the formation of a Mothers' Front in the south of the island in 1990 to protest the disappearance of their male kin during the 1987–90 uprising was more successful than its northern and eastern counterparts. Despite being founded and funded by the main opposition party at that time – the Sri Lanka Freedom Party (SLFP) – and therefore implicated in political patronage, the group managed to occupy 'an important space of protest at the time when feminist and human rights activists were being killed with impunity' (ibid.: 685). By forcing the political sphere to address what was represented as the non-political and natural issues of motherhood, the movement continuously put the political into question (de Alwis 2002).

The fate of the northern and eastern Mothers' Fronts reflected a pattern of decreasing space for many women's organisations that attempted to challenge patriarchal norms of war and conflict, and sought to replace these with ethics of dialogue, negotiation, and consensus (de Alwis 2009a; Samuel 2006: 59). There have been many other examples of the work of women and feminist groups and the simultaneous loss of space and silencing of oppositional voices in Sri Lanka. Often the informal networks have grown out of the failures of formal organisations to adequately address the needs of the poorest such as widows, the elderly, and the landless, serving their own agendas instead (Goodhand and Hulme 1999: 27).

In light of this broader picture of women's peace work and activism, it is clear that the *Valkai* group has not been the only group focused on human rights in Sri Lanka or in the east and nor has it been the only group of women working together. However, the existing majority have tended to be defined by bureaucratic organisation, internal disputes, and reliance on donor funding. Providing a critique of feminist organisations in Sri Lanka, de Alwis (2009a) suggests that many have shifted from strategies of 'refusal', which include forms of non-cooperation, civil obedience, strikes, etc., to strategies of 'request' such as signature campaigns, charters, and petitions. This, in turn, has rendered many feminist projects often indistinguishable from projects of governance (ibid.: 6). This understanding is based on the fragmentation of women's activism, where de Alwis argues intervention has often been diluted by NGO-inspired projects of 'women's empowerment' and 'gender sensitization' (ibid.: 85). She states that, '(t)oday, there exists no autonomous feminist peace movement in the country, and the voices of feminist peace activists are rarely heard nationally' (ibid.). She attributes this to the same groups of feminists being stretched to support the multiple campaigns on women's issues alongside the institutionalism and professionalisation of feminism. The latter, in particular, can be recognised as a 'sticking point' for feminist organisations through cooption and codification of local organisations by larger donor organisations and development aid. While providing funding, they also narrow frameworks forcing the recipients to devise strategies of 'request'. This has been noted not only in South Asia but also as an effect on women's groups globally (Cockburn 1998, 2007; Menon 2004). However, while recognising the critique of contemporary feminist groups, it is also important not to romanticise earlier feminist networks, who struggled precisely because of their lack of support and protection exposing women to the violence of the state (de Alwis 2009a).

Thus, between the vulnerability of the less-defined feminist networks and the overexposure and standardisation of women's feminist activism as a 'profession' (Menon 2004: 219–20), there is a lost sense of what can and is being done by women actively challenging violence and subordination. It is from this platform that I explore the work of the *Valkai* group in this book. Through the stories of women and men, and the meaning of their everyday experiences, I argue against the notion that activism by women is no longer happening or possible. I suggest instead that the way in which it is carried out – as everyday strategies and tactics of negotiation and risk – transcends the categories through which feminist activism has thus far been understood. While the 'lack of visibility and voice' identified by de Alwis is clearly palpable in the working sphere of feminist organisations and NGOs in Sri Lanka, it does not necessarily account for the networks of women (and men) in eastern Sri Lanka who are carrying out critical and vigorous work and in many ways align with the feminist peace movement. These networks do not have an obvious voice and they remain largely invisible. However, it is also these very factors that enable them to continue effectively.

In this sense, the story of the *Valkai* group is a gendered story, and one which I consider in this book in relation to women's experiences of war and women's activism. Yet, to only consider the group in these terms is to silence a much greater vision of the *Valkai* group, and to ignore the fact that both women and men worked in and beyond their capacities to push for change. Therefore, I explore the relationship between women, war, and, in particular, the effects of violence on women's strategies of endurance and networks. At the same time, I do not intend this to be a purely gender-based or feminist account. Where comment appears to be lacking on the ways in which men and women work together and strategically, in spaces of violence and fear, I hope to provide a new perspective from which creative activism and active living in contexts of conflict can be better understood.

Narrating violence and silence

The conversations, ideas, and experiences of the women and men that I lived and worked with formed my central frame of reference in eastern Sri Lanka, and their understanding of the world invariably came to shape my own understanding of life in Batticaloa. The particular spaces in which I moved also allowed me to alternate between the specific accounts of the women with whom I lived, and the linking passages of other people's lives. From there, I was able to generate many other levels of conversations which addressed questions about everyday living and loss, and how these hooked onto experiences of endurance and survival. Therefore, it is in the processes of listening to, extracting from, and participating in the world and stories of these women and men that the substance of this book is formed.[29] In this final section of the introduction, I want to briefly look at the processes of listening to and narrating stories of violence, and the climate of silence and fear that often surrounds traumatic and difficult pasts and uncertain futures.

The genre of narrative and oral histories have come to be recognised as an important part of historiography, particularly for learning how people negotiate the experiences and meanings of violence. Previously neglected in favour of a focus on state and hegemony, narrative analysis, as a method increasingly used in much historical writing today, is grounded in the phenomenological assumption that phenomena are ascribed meaning through being experienced (see Eastmond 2007). Furthermore, it contends that an understanding of another's experience is contingent upon the ways in which others express these experiences to us (Schutz 1972: 99–100). In the dynamic interplay between experience and expression, experience gives form to narratives while expression provides its own meaning and shape. Past experience is always remembered and interpreted in the light of the present, while the present relies on what we have learnt in the past. The narratives that are used in this book reveal to us that what are remembered, re-presented, and told are situational, shaped not least through the contingencies of the encounter between the narrative and listener and the power relationship between them (Skultans 1998). Gathering personal perspectives and 'private voices', oral accounts of the past and present, can provide the individual element of a private self to a broader, more social collective of people and their context (Mines 1994). Ross (2003: 77) argues that by uncovering the unspoken domains of experience, the nuances and sensitivities of narratives can ensure that subjects are not just presented as refugees, child soldiers, widows, or victims, for example, but can actually straddle different categories and transcend them as their life experiences are recognised outside of a specific label. Here, stories can challenge, question, blur, and transgress existing boundaries and categories to reveal in-depth and varied understandings of lives in areas of conflict. Furthermore, the continual creation, negotiation, and revising of strategies and approaches to everyday life as revealed throughout this book powerfully convey the ways in-which the past, present, and future is not only made, but encountered and lived. Pulling all of the threads together allows the many strands of the lived experience of conflict to be understood in a way that locates people both in their story and in relation to the reader. As such, the different relationships, temporalities, and spatial orientations that make up the political and social landscapes of everyday life for people in eastern Sri Lanka create a deeper and more revealing picture.

Writing violence

We also face the problem of how one writes an anthropological account of life amidst violence when, for a large number of contemporary sociological and anthropological studies into Sri Lankan everyday life, violence has become a primary entry point of understanding (Perera 1998; Jeganathan 1998).[20] Such a focus on violence as generated and legitimised in the Sri Lankan everyday has created a problem for the anthropology of Sri Lanka (see Jeganathan 1998) in which violence is an analytical phenomena in itself. In this sense, the everyday has become more about writing violence than the actuality of what constitutes daily life (ibid.: 12). In other words, the fact that the questions of the everyday, juxtaposed with historical, political, and social inquiry into the state's violent practices and counter-state agents of violence have created a specific form of academic writing on Sri Lanka, illustrates how the images of a violent everyday have become almost more powerful than the reality of everyday life itself. Criticising the particular writing styles that have emerged in Sri Lanka following the 1983 riots, Jeganathan suggests that violence has been considered as decoupled from political cause and explanation, thus categorising it as its own object of inquiry. Failure to moor violence to the particular social environment from which it emerges is to risk treating violence as self-evident, and also to assume that it is the defining lens through which all other aspects of life are considered. Jeganathan suggests that we should rather firmly locate violence within the social and political field from which it has ruptured, in order to pursue the ideas of violence without removing it from its context. I would add to the argument here by suggesting that more than simply locating violence within its context is the need to consider what else goes on as well as the violence in everyday situations – not just violent events as part of everyday life but everyday life that continues through, beyond, and despite of violence.

At the same time, in contexts such as Sri Lanka, where for many in the north and east, violence in its multiple and varying forms has become a daily reality, we also need to find a way to narrate the tragedies of loss and disruption. It has been noted by many scholars that the effects of violence and trauma on the ability to narrate pain and loss can be immense. The 'un-narratability' of terror is something that has captured much interest amongst those attempting to find ways of narrating the experiences of violence (see Daniel 1994). Pain resists and destroys language, as Elaine Scarry tells us (1985: 4–7); beauty, on the other hand, may resist language but always finds another form of representation, another way to carry on what could not be spoken. However, Skultans (1998: 101) disagrees with Scarry, and, in an account of narratives from sufferers of violence in Latvia, states that her informants were able to draw upon cultural resources like folklore and songs to recount their experiences, even though it remained an emotionally difficult task. Similarly, Das (1995, 1997), in an attempt to understand the silence of people who suffer, questions whether pain destroys the capacity to communicate or creates a moral communication between sufferers. Evoking 'critical events' that bring us closer to terror, Das finds, beyond bodily mutilation, the mutilation of language that is the 'essential truth' of terror. In these circumstances, language is struck a blow, falling into silence. Drawing on Ludwig Wittgenstein's example of 'feeling pain in the body of another', Das (1997) traces routes of acknowledgement and recognition – new constructions of speech and silence – through which social suffering might enter the body of language. This transformation occurs at the level of cultural paradigms for the expression of grief and the mimetic transactions between language and body by which 'the antiphony of language and silence' (ibid.: 67) performed in the genre of women's public mourning re-inhabits a world that has become uninhabitable in the face of desolating events of violence and loss. The complexities of the relation between pain, language, and the body are also found in Lawrence's study of Batticaloa's Amman temples where unspeakable violence and loss finds a voice through the body of an oracle, Saktirani. As Lawrence (1997: 10) argues, '[a]t the end of language, her [Saktirani] body became the agent, a site where truth is made public'. In Chapter 6, I explore the question of silence and the absence of words in relation to the experiences of a widow called Rani. I argue that while trauma's unspeakable dimensions are identified in silence, Rani's experiences demonstrate that silence should not necessarily be viewed only as a legacy of terror, but instead as an intimate and embodied strategy of keeping up routine while simultaneously questioning meaning. This is important precisely because it allows the ethnographer a means of representing experiences of the past, including pain, but without using representations of suffering and terror to build authority, and to 'speak for' the subject. Instead, by sharing speech, or the lack of it, the relationship between narrator and speaker can 'speak to' lived realities of the past. The significance of this kind of writing is that it also illustrates many of the less-visible effects of violence, which penetrate everyday life but are often hidden within the rhythms and routines of daily activity. Thus, a focus on fear, terror, silence, and suffering can actually illuminate the methods by which people cope and survive. If we follow Das's assertion that 'a discourse on suffering is worth having only if it helps the victim to live forwards' (1994: 164), then looking to the moments of hope and imagination, as well as the everyday endurance which drives people, must constitute a core element of anthropological representations of violence and suffering. This could include the non-violent spaces or parts of daily life, which are less dramatically framed by violence, but often lost to contexts of conflict. Kelly argues that 'non-violence is often as problematic as violence, and should not be seen as a default state that exists in the absence of conflict' (2008: 356). Das (2007: 3), for example, looks specifically to what can be recovered after violent experiences and argues that rather than through the transcendent, it is a 'descent into the ordinary' that allows people to live amidst devastation.

Hidden identities

Finally, before moving on to describe in greater detail the chapters in this book, it is important to highlight here the fact that the complexities of the situation in Batticaloa meant that in writing this book I faced a number of difficult decisions over the identity of various people and in exposing the work that they do. This was partly because the levels of violence and risk made it impossible to talk in detail about people, in particular the members of the *Valkai* group with whom I was working and on whom I was documenting. Moreover, my social context, set within a particular time and across and between particular spaces, which formed my 'ethnographic object', was slippery and hard to define. In other words, while my work developed from the kinds of experiences and stories that were extracted from, and made possible by, these interactions with certain people, at the same time the specifics of their lives and work could not be revealed. The decision whether to write about the group did not ever really feel as if it was mine to make, and, in the end, it was not so much a choice as an obvious conclusion. With the ongoing and increasing violence in the east and the ever-widening risk of saying or doing something to upset those who carry guns, I could not risk jeopardising anyone's life. Therefore, I had to fade the lives of my family and the *Valkai* members into the background of my writing, and instead focus on the fragments of stories and the lives of people that I could tell. As such, all names, places, and details where necessary have been changed and the stories and experiences that I do specify have been done so with agreement from those involved. However, I have not attempted to hide the identity of Batticaloa town for two reasons. The first is that anyone who knows the east of Sri Lanka would easily recognise where my work is based. Second, I feel it is important that Batticaloa is known as a place where people have sought paths forward and imagined futures amidst the devastation that conflict and violence have wrought. Rather than be known only through its dichotomous identity of a beautiful coastal town destroyed by bloody warfare, the reality is that Batticaloa is shaped by the habitable spaces that people forge in their everyday lives; lives that are both about violence and about so much more. As a result, this book constitutes what could be called an ethnography of process, for it is the processes, the articulation, embodiment, and imaginations that spun out from the social context rather than the context itself that have been captured in my work. Running throughout the chapters is an underlying attempt to grapple with these dilemmas. How to talk about the lives of a particular cast of characters who both structured my research yet cannot take centre stage; and how to give credit to a group of people who, in essence, co-authored this book, and yet cannot and most often do not want to make claims to what is produced? These questions are tackled throughout the book.

Outline of the book

This introductory chapter has provided a brief overview of the conflict in Sri Lanka and introduces the main key themes to be considered throughout the book. Chapter 2 maps out the east, providing some background information on the various ethnic groups present, their relationships, and how they have been affected by the conflict. It also situates the work of the *Valkai* group within the spatial politics of the east during the period of the LTTE split and the tsunami in 2004 which led to a temporary opening up of space for people to come together and reach out to others. Considering how the *Valkai* group came together during the period of the aftermath of the tsunami, the chapter describes how the activists sought out spaces to connect with others and pursued forms of 'active living' amidst risk and fear.

From setting the scene in terms of Sri Lanka and the east, Chapter 3 then provides a deeper sense of the author's journey of fieldwork in a context of unpredictability and violence. This reveals the many complexities of the research process, and of living and working in a place of conflict. In particular, it addresses the vicissitudes of fieldwork as shaped by the tsunami and escalating violence in the east, and questions what it means to carry out moral and ethical fieldwork in situations where risk defines everyday movements and interactions. Chapter 4 offers a theoretical framework for the book by taking the concept and basic meaning of the everyday to question the boundaries of what becomes demarcated as ordinary in situations of uncertainty and extreme risk. Relating this to a visit to a displaced family in 2007 close to where shells were being fired by the army, it questions how everyday violence is understood when it is neither ordinary (in terms of being banal and routine) nor extraordinary (in terms of an exception to the norm). Asking whether it is possible that other kinds of ordinary exist, the chapter suggests that locating the endurance of everyday life between the ordinary and extraordinary can allow space for imagination and hope. In doing so, an argument is made for an understanding of everyday life in conflict situations, which places narratives at the centre in order to illustrate how the meanings of the everyday and the ordinary, like patterns of violence, are fluid and variable.

Chapter 5 presents the life story of Meena, a widow who grew up in eastern Sri Lanka, experiencing the many ruptures and tragedies that living through a conflict brings. Given that Meena's narrative is a long and richly detailed text that starts in 1960 on the day that Meena was born and ends in 2006 when the interviews were carried out, the chapter is the largest in the book. It is also a central chapter as Meena's story provides a link between the 'grand narratives' of the history of the conflict in Sri Lanka and the 'small personal narratives' of history which are often less visible. Placed alongside or over a basic understanding of the main organising themes and events described in this chapter and Chapter 2, with their social and political contexts, Meena's story provides a reality of the lived experiences of war. Moreover, Meena's narrative powerfully represents life in the east during the decades of war, crucially allowing the past, present, and future to emerge as a living and fluid process that is being constantly negotiated and worked through.

Chapter 6 returns to a focus on what is ordinary in situations of violence through an exploration of two case studies, thus challenging conventional writing which relates 'normalcy' in violence-prone areas to peace and productivity. The first case study considers how a woman grieving for her son (and later, her husband), lost to the long-standing violence, copes with her grief through sustaining her routine life. Observing how she negotiates her bereavement, particularly through planting a tree in his name (during the *Valkai* group tree-planting ceremony), it draws attention to the importance of the quotidian sphere of daily life, social events, and cultural rituals. The second case study explores the experiences of a group of fishermen who had lost their livelihood to the tsunami in 2004 and continued to go out to sea everyday even though they returned empty-handed. Demonstrating the fact that daily ritual does not have to be purposeful, the chapter offers an understanding of the ways in which violence is understood and incorporated into the ordinariness of everyday domestic and economic life in areas of conflict.

The final chapter, Chapter 7, brings together some of the prominent themes of the book. These are themes that have emerged throughout, such as fear, risk, trust, and hope, which have been plaited through with both existential and political meanings and experiences in everyday life. This allows for a conclusion that asks questions about everyday living that unsettle our understanding of what it means to inhabit contexts where survival and healing do not necessarily take place outside of the realm of conflict, but are found at the juncture of cross-cutting networks of social tensions, relations of trust, and processes of grief.

Drawing upon Butler's (2004) emphasis on the power of grief and mourning, the chapter argues that there are different ways of experiencing and acting upon the past, present, and future that do not have to be about violence and suffering, but instead reveal a world of possibility and fragile hope.

Taken together, all of the chapters in this book grapple with the idea of ethnographic life stories as products of a complex collaboration between the past and present, narrative forms, historical experiences, and social settings. The overall focus of this book, therefore, is about dwelling in the myriad layers and spaces of everyday life that conflated being and surviving to a level of endurance. Throughout, I work from the premise that studies of conflict need to highlight non-violent times, not in opposition to violence, but as implicated within it. As vital as the voice of the remarkable and of survival is, the implicit ontology of suffering and agency, like the dichotomy of victim and perpetrator, tends to ignore the slipperiness of boundaries in less than clear distinctions. Therefore, where we gain a sense of victims and heroes, we perhaps lose a sense of what exists in that slippage between suffering and agency. This is the shade of grey where people suffer, survive, resist, and simply live, the endurance of the everyday. It is these shades that compose the substance and heart of the narratives in this book.

Notes

1. The term 'dirty war' is not unproblematic and I prefer to use Kalyvas's notion of 'intimate war' (2006: 330), which similarly describes ways in which everyday experiences become the specific targets of violence but without implying that there can be a form of war which is not dirty or that 'dirty war' contaminates every part of the everyday.
2. The term 'border villages' referred to the areas of shifting defence lines or 'grey zones' where political and military control was contested by the Sri Lankan military and the LTTE. In these villages violence was often at its worst. Land held by the military was commonly referred to as 'cleared areas' while land controlled by the LTTE was termed 'uncleared' (although this, of course, depended upon the perspective from which you were defining land – to the LTTE, for example, 'uncleared' referred to land controlled by the SLA and was, therefore, deemed 'unliberated') (Rajasingham-Senenayake 1999: 150). See map 3: xxii.
3. According to the 1981 census, the highest concentration of the Burgher population (about 72 per cent) lived in Colombo. There were also significant communities in Trincomalee and Batticaloa who spoke mostly a pidgin form of Portuguese (McGilvray 1982a).
4. It was estimated in 2004 that up to 60 per cent of LTTE cadres were below eighteen, with 40 per cent of them girls (Hoole *et al.* 1988).
5. The University Teachers for Human Rights (Jaffna) (UTHR(J)) was formed in 1988 at the University of Jaffna. Their aims were to challenge the external and internal terror engulfing the Tamil community as a whole through documenting the stories of ordinary people, holding perpetrators accountable, and creating space for humanising the social and political spheres of life in Jaffna. Throughout this book, I draw from their meticulous reports and publications, which document the many atrocities

experienced by all communities through the decades of war in Sri Lanka.

6 This is an important point to make as it challenges the context of books such as Margaret Trawick's work on childhood and play in Batticaloa, which claims that joining the LTTE is an 'important decision facing each child on entering his or her teens' (Trawick 2007: 2). In failing to acknowledge the existence of forced child-recruitment amongst the LTTE, Trawick dangerously misrepresents the full picture of life in the east.

7 Sri Lankan politics has been dominated by the UNP and the SLFP, and the alliances formed round these two. Control over the government has alternated between the UNP and SLFP since Independence. Sri Lanka has a cluster of smaller, but, at times, influential socialist and communist parties including the JVP. On the right wing, the Sinhala Urumaya (SU), a small but highly vocal Sinhala-Buddhist party, reformed to become the Jatika Hela Urumaya (JHU), a party of Buddhist monks who currently hold nine seats in Parliament.

8 The Presidential commissions established during the 1990s by President Premadasa found that over 20,000 people disappeared over the course of the second JVP insurrection and the 1990 war. Human rights groups, however, argue that this figure is two or three times higher (Hughes forthcoming).

9 The CFA, signed on 21 February 2002, had the stated objective to 'find a negotiated solution to the ongoing ethnic conflict in Sri Lanka'. The agreement set up modalities of the ceasefire, measures to restore normalcy, and created the Sri Lanka Monitoring Mission. The agreement is available at www.slmm.lk/documents/cfa.htm.

10 For a comprehensive account of Norway's role as a peace facilitator in Sri Lanka, see 'Pawns of Peace – Evaluation of Norwegian peace efforts in Sri Lanka 1997–2009' (Norad 2011).

11 It is worth noting that in October 2008 Colonel Karuna became a member of parliament and in March 2009 was appointed to the SLFP's cabinet.

12 These figures relate to those displaced in the long term, namely those who could not return to damaged houses and/or areas that were off-limits. Immediate and short-term displacement is thought to have been almost double this figure.

13 Together with traditional 'relief' work, humanitarian agencies have been increasingly undertaking activities such as reconstruction and rehabilitation, peace-building, and human rights monitoring and reporting, which has rendered the boundaries between emergencies, development, human rights, and politics far less decipherable (see Calhoun 2008; Terry 2002).

14 Many have made the comparison between Sri Lanka and Aceh, pointing out that in both countries the tsunami created the potential to deal with the pre-existing conflicts. Whereas in Sri Lanka the dynamics of conflict were exacerbated, in Aceh they were abated, and an end to the conflict was found within eight months of the tsunami disaster (Le Billon and Waizenegger 2007; Smirl 2008). De Alwis and Hedman (2009) explore the different political outcomes of the two countries through the primary issues of aid, activism, and reconstruction. In particular, they point to the differences between the ways in which the LTTE and GAM (*Gerakan Aceh Medeka* – Free Aceh Movement) sought to negotiate the terms of control in dealing with the state, humanitarian aid, and interventions (see de Alwis and Hedman 2009: 9–13).

15 The explicitly political nature of the P-TOMs must be noted here – the design would have allowed the LTTE enormous control over the post-tsunami resources even in areas of the north-east that were no longer under their control. Therefore, P-TOMs was far less a peace-building strategy than a strategic political move.

16 More than a year later, the Tsunami Evaluation Coalition (TEC) – a consortium of over fifty member agencies from the UN, donors, Non-governmental Organisations, and the Red Cross – published various reports, highlighting a number of failures in the delivery and practices of post-tsunami aid (Telford *et al.* 2006).
17 The UPFA is a coalition of former President Chandrika Kumaratunga's SLFP and the JVP.
18 See *The Sunday Leader* (2007) 'President's Tiger deal exposed', 8 July 2007. (www.thesundayleader.lk/20071118/archives.htm). More information has also recently come to light due to the Wikileaks phenomena (see Kurukulasuriya 2012).
19 In 2006 and 2007, for example, the United Nations Working Group on Enforced and Involuntary Disappearances recorded more new 'disappearance' cases from Sri Lanka than from any other country in the world (Lawrence 1997; Punyasena 2003).
20 Kadiragamar, a Christian Tamil who had been sharply critical of the LTTE, was highly respected internationally, and the blaming of the LTTE for his death led to their marginalisation by the international community (see UTHR 2005a).
21 Sunil Bastian (2009: 229–37) also highlights the nexus between the continuation of foreign aid and periods of extreme violence in Sri Lanka, which also played a role in the general lack of protest at the military offensive in the east.
22 It is still unclear exactly what took place in the NFZs. One perspective is that by declaring the NFZs and subsequently firing into them, the GoSL intended to 'engage in widespread and systematic attacks against civilians'. Furthermore, it has been pointed out that the NFZs were unilaterally declared by the Ministry of Defense (MoD) without the agreement of the LTTE and, therefore, had no legal standing. A counter argument, however, is that the NFZs were declared to protect civilians, and by entering and defending from the NFZs it was the actions of the Tigers rather than the GoSL that turned the NFZs into bloodbaths (see Groundviews 2011).
23 See 'Executive Summary of the Report of the Panel of Experts' (United Nations 2010).
24 A death certificate would be needed in order for a relative to apply for compensation for their loss. However, this was one of the most difficult processes as often families did not know the whereabouts of the bodies of their loved ones, and even if they knew they were dead, they could not always prove it.
25 See discussions by Manchanda (2001) and Coomaraswamy and Fonseka (2004) in which it is argued that although there is no intrinsic link between women and peace, women are often more likely to understand and identify structural inequalities, power relations, and oppression due to their daily experiences of injustice and structural oppression within and outside of overt conflict situations.
26 There have been a number of excellent articles, books, and reports with first-hand accounts of the challenges faced by widows and single women. See, for example Thiranagama, R. 1988; de Alwis 1997, 2002, 2009a; de Mel 2001, 2007; Samuel 2003, 2006; Tambiah 2005; Emmanuel 2008. The International Crisis Group's report 'Sri Lanka: Women's Insecurity in the North and East' (ICG 2011b) also provides a clear picture of the situation of women in the north and east post-war.
27 In September 2010, the child development and women's empowerment ministry said it had lists of 49,000 widows in the east and 40,000 in the north, and that of those in the east, 25,000 are from Batticaloa (approximately half below the age of 40 and one-third with three or more children) (see ICG 2011b: 19–20).
28 See Peteet's paper 'Icons and Militants: Mothering in the Danger Zone' for a comprehensive outline of the much-studied relationship between motherhood, militarisation, and resistance (2011: 103–29).

29 My ability to communicate in a Tamil-speaking area was made easier by the fact that the main members of my Sri Lankan family mostly spoke in English, sometimes also using Sinhala, which due to my year in the south in 1998 meant that I could manage at conversational level.
30 Anthropological work on Sri Lanka's political violence and ethnic identity as revealed through everyday experiences include Kapferer (1998); Gananath Obeyesekera's numerous writings on the social formations of Sinhalese Buddhist society (see 1964, 1974, 1978); Spencer's (1990a) *A Sinhala Village in a Time of Trouble*, and Stanley Tambiah's books which focus on the relationship between Buddhism, politics, and violence (1986, 1992, 1997). The latter two writers, in particular, have explored the ways in which ordinary men and women in Sri Lanka use crude public displays of support and resistance to engage with violent politics.

2

Mapping spaces and lives: Batticaloa and the east

A lack of space

One of the things that became most apparent to me during my time in Batticaloa was the lack of space: a lack of physical space, emotional space, space to think, space to talk and to act, space to relax – space to do what one wanted without premeditation, planning, and the expectation of disruption. Where physical barriers mapped out the town, militarisation and the anticipation of violence circumscribed behaviour and kept people tightly anchored to strategies of silence and protection. Checkpoints ran like tracks through people's daily lives, while the unseen eyes and ears of Foucault's panopticon power (1977[1975]) meant that, while a lot was known, very little was said. Whether in a line at an army checkpoint or queuing for tsunami rations, people experienced some form of restricted space and choice. One old man commented, as he waited to register his need for a temporary shelter: 'We cannot choose where we go, who we see, whom we talk to. Who are we?' Another person noted, 'It's not that we can't do anything but that we don't have the space to choose what we do. We can go out, and here and there but we always know where we can't go and what we can't do' [sic].

In this way, it appeared as if Batticaloa was constituted through its daily management of space, spaces that felt safe and spaces that posed risks, all subject to change on a daily, momentary basis. When a claymore mine exploded, for example, people would scatter in silence into the shadows of the back roads leaving the debris, and when cordon-and-search operations began, messages jumped from house to house as if on a live wire, warning people to leave the area.[1] When husbands and sons were arrested and detained, mothers crowded the entrance of police stations, acutely aware that the sooner they could locate their loved ones, the more chance there was of saving them. Thus, an awareness of time and space was imperative to enduring life in the east.

Alongside the lack of space, I also became aware of the ways and means in which people, particularly those with whom I lived and worked, negotiated around and challenged this context of decreasing space in order to create networks of support. As I discussed in the previous chapter, the *Valkai* group came together in the aftermath of the tsunami as violence was escalating. Invested in an understanding of their everyday realities, mapping out what could and couldn't be done in relation to fluctuations in violence and risk, the members of the group worked accordingly through strategies of 'active living' to meet the basic needs of others. Moreover, by carefully observing, listening to, and experiencing the ways in which spaces were being claimed and militarised, the *Valkai* group sought to push open spaces within and against everyday violence and control.

The focus of this chapter is, therefore, on space; specifically on an understanding of space and activism or 'active living' in relation to the *Valkai* group. This is done through an exploration of the spatial politics of the east and, in particular, the landscape during the distinctive years of 2005–07 when I carried out my fieldwork. Considering how the *Valkai* group was formed in the turbulent and increasingly violent aftermath of the 2004 tsunami, I look at how this unique group of people, focused on human rights, were able to come together and work effectively by pushing open spaces of support and non-violence.

The first part of this chapter briefly sketches out the east of Sri Lanka in terms of the ethnic makeup of the area and some of the particularities of kinship patterns, caste, and marriage. However, since these are subjects that have been well covered in academic scholarship, I look instead to the ways in which all communities in the east have suffered intolerably through the decades of conflict as those with arms have fought over claims to land and people. In particular, I note how the distinctiveness of the east in terms of the multi-ethnic communities and its social and political history, which has both played into and separates it from that of the north, critically complicates and challenges the taken-for-granted notion of a monolithic and homogenous Tamil identity. Focusing on life in the east during the 1990s, I describe the thousands of deaths, disappearances, and daily atrocities committed within everyday spaces of intense fear and control due to the presence of the elite commando police unit, the Special Task Force (STF), and strategies by the LTTE and the state to incite violence between Tamil and Muslim communities.[2] This contrasts sharply with the situation in Batticaloa when I arrived in 2005. Placed alongside the details given by Meena in Chapter 5 of growing up through times of intense conflict and widespread fear in the east, my intention is to emphasise the central importance of the east as a lesser-known theatre of violence throughout the decades of conflict. It is a region that has seen and felt some of the worst effects of fighting and fragmentation of everyday lives, and, yet, has often been overlooked in relation to the north of the island.

The second and third sections of the chapter look more closely at the 2004 events of the LTTE split and the tsunami, and consider the kinds of spaces that were opened up in the advent of chaos and confusion, but then rapidly shut down (controlled and militarised) once again. Accordingly, I describe how the *Valkai* group used this initial open space to reach out to families affected by the ongoing conflict and to carry out forms of 'active living' to create support networks. I describe two activities that the *Valkai* group carried out: tree-planting ceremonies and meetings for mothers whose children had been forcibly recruited/abducted by either the LTTE or TMVP. In so doing, I suggest that the work of the *Valkai* group problematises the boundaries that have been drawn around the work of women and activists (as discussed in Chapter 1), and challenges the notion that there are no longer people, particularly women, who actively engage in opposition to militarism and war in Sri Lanka. While there may be a lack of formal organisations actively participating in conflict issues in the north and east, the story of the *Valkai* group shows that work is being done within and through everyday experiences and spaces of violence and fear.

Mapping the east

As one of the nine provinces in Sri Lanka, the Eastern Province is divided into three administrative districts, forty-five Divisional Secretary's (DS) Divisions, and 1,085 *Grama Niladhari* (GN) Divisions, also known as *Grama Sevaka* (GS) Divisions. Together with the Ampara and Trincomalee disticts, Batticaloa district forms the Eastern Province. The Batticaloa district is composed of fourteen DS divisions (many of which I refer to during the course of this book – see map 2: xxi) including Vaharai, Valachchenai, Eravur, Kattankudy, and Kiran (Department of Census and Statistics 2007). The first elections of the Provincial council were held in 1989, when the Eastern Province was temporarily merged with the Northern Province to form the North-East Province. This council became dysfunctional in 1990, and instead a Chief Secretary and his administrative staff, who were answerable to the provincial governor, ran the North-Eastern Province. In 2007, the Northern and Eastern Provinces were demerged following a long battle by Sri Lankan nationalists who opposed the idea of the combined province, which occupied one-third of the island being under the control (either directly or indirectly) of the LTTE. In March 2008, the TMVP (who broke away from the LTTE in 2004) won local council elections in the Batticaloa district while President Rajapaksa's party, the UPFA, which campaigned with the TMVP, took control of the municipal council. An alliance of the parties won local elections in the Eastern Province the following May.

Inter-ethnic communities

The east has, in the past, been noted for its distinctiveness as a multi-ethnic, multi-religious province, with particular spatial mapping of juxtaposed Muslim and Tamil communities along the coastline. With Sinhala, Tamil, and Muslim populations having almost equal presence within areas of ethnic concentration, this ethnic demography of the east stands in contrast to the Northern Province, where Tamils are the dominant group (McGilvray 1982b, 2008; Kearney 1987). The littoral in the Eastern Province is often referred to in poetic terms as *Eluvaankarai* or 'shore of the rising sun', and the spatial interspersion of Tamil and Muslim villages along the coastal strip has prompted people to evoke imagery of a *puttukkulal* or pittu bamboo, where the flour and coconut are closely packed together in layers (see Schrijvers 1998). The historical residence patterns of Muslim, Sinhalese, and Tamils in the Eastern Province is subject to much contention and debate, reflecting the wider arguments of nationalist discourses claiming the north-east of Sri Lanka as originally Sinhala-Buddhist or Tamil-Hindu (see, for example, Kearney 1987; Arasaratnam 1994; Samaraweera 1997; McGilvray and Raheem 2007). However, what appears more significant about this is the ethnic mixing and intimacy embraced by the east, which challenges nationalist assumptions, but also reveals ways in which the east has specifically suffered, particularly during the first two decades of conflict.

It has been reported that by the time the Portuguese arrived in Batticaloa in the first half of the seventeenth century all three major ethnic groups were living in the east; the Sinhalese were scattered in the interior and the Tamils and Muslims were living along the coastal belt and around Batticaloa lagoon. This spatial pattern of ethnic distribution continued largely unchanged in subsequent years. The Sinhalese population in the former Sinhalese area, however, increased rapidly due to the government post-independence colonisation schemes described in the next section (Kearney 1987). The ethnic balance at the time of the 1981 census for Batticaloa points to 80.5 per cent Sri Lankan Tamils living in the Eastern Province, 8.6 per cent Muslim, 5.1 per cent Sinhalese, 0.8 per cent Indian Tamil, and 4.7 per cent Burgher (Department of Census and Statistics 2007).[3]

With a heterogeneous mix of communities, the Eastern Province also lays claim to a cultural distinctiveness, with the *Mukkuvar* people (a Tamil caste of Kerala origin) forming the majority of the population with their own customary laws, matrilocality, and practicing of the *kudi* system of inheritance and naming (Yalman 1967; McGilvray 1982a). Tamil rootedness in the east is linked through the notion of a self-contained autonomous system of villages, presided over by the *ur pōtiyār* – the large landowners, elected from among the *podiyars*. Most *podiyas* were originally *mukkukar* and *vellalar* (the two dominant castes in the Eastern Province) cultivators, although by the end of the nineteenth century Muslim traders had begun to significantly control large areas of land (Whitaker 1999: 9–13; McGilvray 1998b).[4]

Marriage patterns among Tamil (and Muslim) population of the eastern region have been well studied and documented.[5] According to McGilvray (1982b: 43), they follow a 'sort of shifting matri-uxorilocal pattern', with the bride and groom tending to live in the bride's natal house for a period of between six months and two years. The transmission of family property from parents to daughters in the form of dowry, constitutes what McGilvray, following Goody, calls a 'pre-mortem matrilineal inheritance' (ibid.) with most of the wealth of the natal house (including the house itself) generally making up the dowry of the elder sisters, and with brothers obligated to acquire wealth and build 'dowry-houses' (*ciitanam vittu*) for younger sisters.[6] The most distinctive aspect of east coast matrilineany, however, lies in the exogamous sub-categories created within the endogamous caste category by a system of dispersed named matriclans known as *Kuti* (see McGilvray 1973: 9, 1982b). Simply put, *Kuti* is a clan system which has forged strong bonds between Tamil-speaking people, including Muslims but with the exception of Christian groups in some places on the east coast, including the Portuguese Burghers and other Catholic inhabitants of Batticaloa town, and is based upon the importance of the *tay vali* (mother way) (ibid.).

Muslims and Tamils: cooperation and conflict

While the Muslims and Tamils in the east view themselves as separate ethnic groups, different from one another, they also view themselves as distinct from the Tamils and Muslims living in the rest of Sri Lanka (see McGilvray 1998b). Although the Tamils constitute the overwhelming majority, since the 1980s the demography of the area has unquestionably been altered in the course of protracted conflict. Much has been written on the Tamil-Muslim/Moor identities (as distinct and similar) and their relationships (see, for example McGilvray 1997, 1998b; Schrijvers 1998). It is clear that both groups have suffered immensely over the many years of conflict, often due to deliberate provocation of intercommunal violence including massacres and displacement of entire villages by those seeking to prevent any form of Tamil–Muslim alliance. In the 1950s, the appeal of a unified Tamil state envisaged by Tamil politicians in the north and south caught on rapidly with a large number of Muslim adherents. This Tamil ideology, however, was rooted in Jaffna and the north, and revolved around a northern leadership that seemed to marginalise Tamils in the east and overlook their unique and separate identity (McGilvray 1998a and b). Over time, Muslims also distanced themselves further from the Tamil cause. They claimed that an independent Tamil Eelam was generally not in the interests of the Muslims as they would be a minority there, which would, in turn, reduce the bargaining power they held in Sri Lankan politics. Recognising that their interests would not be represented by Tamil organisations or by the two national parties catering mainly to the Sinhalese electorate, the Muslim political activist M. H. M. Ashraff founded the Sri Lanka Muslim Congress (SLMC) with its base in the east.[7] This aggravated not only Tamil political groups but also the Colombo-based Muslim leadership and the national parties who had garnered support in the east. Over the course of the 1990s, the SLMC became dominant among the Muslim electorate, although its electoral heartland was always confined to the Eastern Province.

Indian Tamils

The Muslims of Sri Lanka were not the only large minority of the Tamil-speaking community that revealed a glaring blind spot in the concept of the Tamil nation as encouraged by the LTTE. Another Tamil-speaking minority group were the Indian Tamils (known variously as 'Estate Tamils', hill country Tamils, or 'Plantation Tamils'). Brought over by the British during colonisation to work on coffee, tea, and rubber estates in the plantations in Ceylon in the 1860s, from the moment of their arrival in Sri Lanka they were discriminated against and exploited by the British colonial establishment, Sinhalese, and Tamils alike (Kearney 1987; Daniel 1996). Soon after Sri Lanka's independence in 1948, they were disenfranchised, which instantly reduced almost a million of them to the rank of stateless persons (Hollup 1994; Daniel 1996). Since then, almost half a million have been expatriated to India under various agreements between the governments of India and Sri Lanka, while over a million have been granted Sri Lankan citizenship. In 1975, under sweeping land reforms by the Sri Lankan government, the tea estates were nationalised and many of the Indian Tamils lost their jobs and land. A reduction in rice rations, which caused starvation, and the violence of the 1977 riots also drove thousands of Indian Tamils from the hill country to seek safety in the north-east (de Silva 1986).[8] With assistance from a number of NGOs, several thousand families were housed in a string of settlements spanning the north-east. Even though various castes are represented among the Indian Tamils, many Sri Lankan Tamils treat them as belonging to one low-ranking caste (Kearney 1987: 576).

Other minority groups, which add to the heterogeneous mix of people in the east, and who complicate the nationalist notion of a 'Tamil-speaking' nation, are the Veddas and the Burgher communities (see Thangarajah 1995: 191). Found primarily in small coastal villages from the eastern areas of Trincomalee to Batticaloa as well as in some southerly Batticaloa villages, the Vedda community composes a distinct aboriginal ethnic group considered to be partly descended from the indigenous Vedda people. They have intermarried with Tamils, generally speak Tamil (as well as other mixed dialects), and are identified by local communities as '*Vedar*' (Tamil for hunters). Most are Hindu Saivites and combine worship of a plethora of folk deities with the main Hindu deities such as Murugan, Pillaiyar, and Amman (see Seligmann and Seligmann 2003 [1911]: 331–40). The Veddas tend to identify themselves in terms of caste amongst Tamils rather than as a separate ethnic group, claiming superior *vellalar* status within the caste structure of the region (ibid.). The presence of east coast Veddas has influenced discourses of both Tamil nationalism and Sinhala nationalism, both of which have endeavoured to assimilate the Veddas into their own communities. However, Thangarajah (1995) notes that in reality the Veddas as a community have faced much discrimination and marginalisation, and, like other groups in the east, have faced much loss and poverty as a direct result of the conflict. Jon Dart (1985 cited in Samarasinghe 1990) notes that due to the proximity of Vedda native villages to areas where both the LTTE and government forces have fought and carried out atrocities against civilians, this group of people has been particularly vulnerable. The same can be said for the Sinhalese and Burgher communities. While to the Tamils of the north-east these minority groups are recognised as part of the wider Tamil-speaking community, the attitude by the Sri Lankan army, and, particularly the STF, has been to respond with greater terror. Burghers and Sinhalese, for example, are seen as 'traitors' to the Sinhala nation for settling among Tamils, and are harassed simply because they do not belong to a 'clear and easily distinguishable category' (Thangarajah 1995: 193).[9]

Sinhalisation of the east

The history of the Sinhalese in the east is important because it illustrates the complex and intertwined relationships of all three ethnic communities in the east. Moreover, it highlights the deliberate attempts by the state to tap the agricultural potential of the region for Sinhalese settlers as playing a significant role in creating tensions and unease between communities (Peebles 1990: 34). Although many of the Sinhalese in the eastern region were brought in through the government colonisation schemes, a proportion of Sinhalese would have populated the region long before this. Sinhalese coastal settlements in the east, for example, have extended links to the region since deep-sea fishing is dependent on the weather patterns of the monsoon and thus migration between the south-west and north-east is commonplace creating interaction and co-existence in the fishing community (Ruwanpura 2006: 74). Like Tamils in the eastern region, Sinhalese communities primarily depended on farming and agriculture, either paddy cultivation or *chena* (slash-and-burn) cultivation, and were also involved in trading, particularly in Batticaloa town (ibid.). As Meena's narrative in Chapter 5 (page 106) describes, many Sinhala traders had close relationships with their Tamil and Muslim counterparts, and saw them as much as an integral part of the local community as themselves. Meena notes how sad people were when the Sinhalese started leaving after 1983 as they had been running schools and shops, and were central to many trades such as bakeries and the paper mills in the east.

Based on post-Independence Sinhalese chauvinist politics, the schemes which were implemented from the late 1940s onwards were designed to shift populations from the overpopulated Wet Zones of the south primarily to the sparsely populated eastern Dry Zone, in what Tamils and Muslims viewed as an attempt at a 'Sinhalisation of the east'. One of the most contentious projects was the irrigation system development of the 'Mahaweli System L'. Thousands of Sinhalese were moved to this area under the guise of the development and yet it has been noted that hardly any investment was made in the irrigation infrastructure; most of the land remains unirrigated (UTHR 1993b and 1995; Hoole 2001: 206–12). The development was however successful in drastically altering the ethnic composition in the east and causing much alarm amongst native Tamil populations (ibid.). In response to the encroachment of Sinhalese settlers, the first significant massacres of Sinhalese civilians by the LTTE took place on Dollar and Kent Farm, two small farming settlements on the border between Trincomalee (in the east) and Mullaitivu (in the north) in 1984. The former Tamil inhabitants had been chased away several months before the massacre by state forces, and replaced by Sinhala ex-convicts, and it is reported that the LTTE attacked men, women, and children with knives killing up to sixty of them (see UTHR 1993b; Hoole 2001). This was just the beginning of the atrocities committed against Sinhalese civilians by the LTTE. In May 1985, for example, the LTTE shocked the nation when it massacred 120 Sinhalese civilians, including women and children at worship in a sacred Buddhist site in Anuradapura. This massacre was seen as retaliation for the killing of seventy Tamil civilians by the Sri Lankan army in Valvettithurai in the north a few days earlier, and triggered an orgy of tit-for-tat killings and massacres (UTHR 1990b).[10]

Around this time, the state began arming Sinhala settlers (it is important here to distinguish Sinhala settlers from long-term Sinhala residents in the east) as a form of 'self-defence', and from 1985 onwards Sinhala settlers were provided with weapons and training in three 'frontline' areas in the north-east.[11] Simultaneously, the army built up a permanent and growing presence in the area (Gunaratna 2001; Hoole 2001).[12] The Sri Lankan armed forces and STF also began arming and training Muslims as Home Guards. Home Guards were officially known as the Sri Lanka Civil Security Service, an armed militia established to serve as a front line of defence against attacks by Tamil militants. As volunteers, the Home Guards fell under the authority of the police, and, hence, by extension enjoyed certain police powers. This also meant that the army and, particularly, the STF were able to create scapegoats out of the Home Guards by attributing much of their killings and destruction of homes to them, thus increasing communal tensions. Furthermore in 1984, some of the youth initially inducted as Home Guards broke away to form their own organisation (still supported by the state) operating under the name *jihad* (UTHR 1990b; see also Gaasbeek 2010: 210). Accordingly, the LTTE blamed the Muslims for being agents of the Sri Lankan state, India, and the IPKF, and felt justified in carrying out ruthless attacks on Muslims in 'defence' of the Tamils (ibid.). Between July and August 1990, for example, the LTTE carried out a string of calculated massacres in Muslim areas to destabilise the Batticaloa district (Hoole 1995). On 3 August 1990, the LTTE entered mosques in Kattankudy killing over 120 Muslim men and boys and seriously wounding a further seventy-five. Many of the victims were praying at the time, and it is reported that the Tigers had entered the Mosque dressed in Muslim attire. They then escaped by boat (UTHR 1993a; Hoole 1995).

As noted in Chapter 1, in 1990 all northern Muslims were forcibly evicted from the five districts of the Northern Province by the LTTE. This has been described as an act of ethnic cleansing of the north and has been attributed to the LTTE's frustration with the Muslim community for their lack of support in the conflict (see UTHR 1991, 1995; Hoole 1995; Thiranagama 2011). Despite agreement by the LTTE after the 2002 ceasefire to allow Muslims to return home, many remain in Internally Displaced Persons (IDP) camps in Puttalam and areas in the east. It has been pointed out, however, that at the same time as attacking Muslims in the north and east, the LTTE in the east were able to survive the IPKF offensive primarily due to Muslims keeping supply lines open through Muslim areas to feed Tigers who were in the jungle (Taraki 1991[1990]: 71). This intervention is also mentioned by Meena in Chapter 5 (pages 113–14), illustrating that although Muslims and Tamils were pitted against one another in the east they also found ways of cooperating and negotiating through and around the everyday violence. However, with armed Sinhala settlers fearful of the LTTE; Tamil civilians fearful of the army, STF, Muslim armed groups, and

Tamil militant groups; and Muslims fearful of Tamils and the LTTE – the east became an area of wanton killing, indiscriminate attacks, and massive losses.

A final point to be made in relation to the extreme violence and series of atrocities committed in the east during the 1980s and 1990s concerns the focus of the LTTE in claiming a hegemonic rule in the east. As previously noted, given the diverse mix of communities in the east, the LTTE struggled to assert full control. In fact, before 1986, the point at which the LTTE decimated all other Tamil militant groups, the east had been mostly dominated by the eastern-based groups TELO, Eelam People's Revolutionary Liberation Front (EPRLF), and, to a lesser extent, PLOTE (see Chapter 5, pages 108–9, for Meena's discussion around Tamil youth involved in PLOTE and TELO in the east). After callously disposing of all opposition, and with the fear of the IPKF and ambiguity and fear about other Tamil militant groups (often conscripted and backed by India), the LTTE's propaganda machine began to work effectively and support shifted towards them.[13] It is noted by the UTHR that the many attacks by the LTTE against Sinhalese settlers were also part of a calculated move to elicit revenge attacks against Tamils which would then allow the Tigers to re-establish themselves as 'protectors' of the Tamil people in the east. However, in light of the 2004 split in the LTTE as described below, it is clear that the legitimacy of the LTTE in the east has never been fully accepted or unquestioned.

In the next section, I look at the period of the 1990s in relation to the work of the American anthropologist Patricia Lawrence.

Batticaloa: continuity and change

While Batticaloa has faced successive occupations by the Sri Lankan Army, IPKF in 1987, and the LTTE, no single armed group has maintained stable or full control of the eastern areas (Internal Displacement Monitoring Centre [IDMC] 2006: 24). The last three decades in the Batticaloa district have been characterised by widespread displacement of the civilian population. Because of their geographical concentration in these regions, the Tamil population has experienced by far the greatest displacement. According to a census of all IDPs in Sri Lanka conducted by the Ministry of Rehabilitation, Resettlement and Refugees in 2002, 80.86 per cent of the displaced population was Tamil, 13.7 per cent Muslim, 4.56 per cent Sinhalese, and other 0.88 per cent. Many of these IDPs have suffered multiple displacements during the course of the conflict (AI 2005: 2).[14] These figures, however, provide only a snapshot of displacement at that time and do not account for waves of displacement, followed by resettlement in the 1980s and 1990s. In 1990, following the murder of around 600 unarmed Muslim and Sinhala policemen by the LTTE (and the start of Eelam War II), the SLAF carried out a massive counter-offensive in the north and east, forcing almost a million Sri Lankans (overwhelmingly Tamil) to flee their homes as villages were razed to the ground. At this, time around 80 per cent of Batticaloa's population was displaced due to fighting and during the late 1980s and 1990s approximately 14,000 disappearances are estimated to have occurred in the Eastern Province, the majority attributed to the government security forces (UTHR 1990a and b; Lawrence 1997; British Refugee Council [BRC] 2002: 17–21).

Batticaloa district is connected to Colombo by a single train link and, until recently, a dusty main road that the army had redirected to snake its way around their isolated military camps, which cut through the dry scrub landscape. These military encampments regularly came under attack, and convoys of buses ferrying security force personnel were often the targets of remote-controlled claymore mines laid by the LTTE. Both the cleared and uncleared areas were buffered by the extensive system of inland lagoons with their abundance of prawn resources, which separated the (cleared) coastal zone from the (uncleared) hinterland (Bohle and Fünfgeld 2007). Throughout the years of conflict, by means of innumerable checkpoints, roadblocks, and bunker systems, both the army and the LTTE sought to control the strategic access route into the coastal zone of Batticaloa, meaning that the lagoons became arenas of intense fighting. Although travel to the east improved after the 2002 ceasefire and people began to move in and out more frequently, the increase in violence meant that far fewer people felt able to take the risk, and, thus, the east felt virtually cut off from the rest of the country. This loss of movement added to the severity of the east coast's economic hardship and created stark socio-economic disparities between the economically paralyzed Tamil population and the cosmopolitan Western-educated Tamil and Sinhalese elite of Colombo (Lawrence 1997: 33). While there has been a noted increase in movement to and from the east since the end of the conflict, many locals have observed that they continue to feel disconnected from the south. Trade has increased yet most economic development has not benefited the eastern communities, particularly the Tamils, as almost all of the large companies doing well are Sinhalese or, to a lesser extent, Muslim.

Mapping Batticaloa

A landscape of wild open beaches hugging discrete villages along the coastlines which shelter the busier and more robust town of Batticaloa, the eastern district confounds beauty with devastation. With a first glance, one can take in the crowded markets, the squatting fishermen with bloodied boards of fish guts, lit by the glow of a single kerosene flame, shopkeepers hanging up the latest fashions outside their stores, and the school children in white uniforms, shouting from their school buses. The Cathedral, the Catholic churches, the Jesuit schools, and the library form simple colonial structures washed with the traditional Batticaloa blue, and a series of bridges connect parts of the town across the lagoon. A second glance allows the indicators of conflict to sharpen into focus. Streets and roads are cut through by checkpoints, barbed wire marks off army camps and political offices, and army tanks take on the traffic.

Before I arrived in Batticaloa, much of my understanding of life in eastern Sri Lanka was based on the work of other anthropologists and researchers who had spent time and written extensively about life in the east (see for example

McGilvray 1973, 1998a and b; Lawrence 1997, 1999, 2000; Whitaker 1990, 1996, 1999; Trawick 1997, 2002). Patricia Lawrence, for example, an anthropologist who had spent a number of years doing fieldwork in Batticaloa in the 1990s, had described life there in terms of the consequences of extreme political violence for families living in the district (see Lawrence 1997, 1999, 2000). Considering ways in which families coped, Lawrence explored the role of local temples during annual propitiation rituals for local goddesses as providing the only well-attended collective social events in a war zone, where movement and sociality were severely constricted. Her study of the role of female oracles as a coping mechanism during the violence powerfully conveys the sense of hopelessness that existed, and the lack of choices people had for survival at a time when dissent was impossible for families caught in the region (Lawrence 2003: 105). The distinct lack of hope in Batticaloa was reflected in the stagnant peace-talks and the inability of any government or the LTTE to find a working solution to end the violence. Lawrence's documentation of everyday life in Batticaloa, including disappearances and massacres, is framed within what locals described as a 'slow genocide' (ibid.). Most of the terror is associated with the presence of the STF in the east, as previously noted. Having been involved in the brutal counter-insurgency campaign against the JVP in the South during the period of 1987–9, the STF transferred their 'terror tactics' to the east after the resumption of hostilities between the government and the LTTE in June 1990. Subsequently, the numbers of people reported to have been 'disappeared' or killed in the custody of the Sri Lankan security forces reached thousands within months (see AI 1990b). As the stories told by Meena in Chapter 5 testify, the majority of victims were young Tamil men suspected of belonging to or associating with the LTTE. Most of them 'disappeared' after being detained following cordon-and-search operations (known locally as 'round-ups') conducted by the army, often in conjunction with the police and particularly the STF. Due to the declared state of emergency, the government security forces were able to commit serious violations with impunity under the draconian 1979 Prevention of Terrorism Act (PTA) and 1982 Emergency Regulations (ER) (Nissan 1996).

The majority of the stories Lawrence tells, therefore, are of summary and extrajudicial executions, massacres, and disappearances of non-combatants in eastern villages, overwhelmingly at the hands of the state. One of the most significant was the Sathurukandon massacre in 1990 in which 184 Tamil men, women, and children from three villages in the Batticaloa district were killed and burnt by army personnel from the Sathurukandon army camp. The list of victims included sixty-nine children below the age of twelve, and sixteen men and women above the age of seventy, most of who were women (see Lawrence 1997).[15] Although the government instituted two investigations, no alleged perpetrators were ever prosecuted. In Chapter 5 (page 111), Meena also refers to another massacre in Kokkadichcholai in which 120 civilians, mostly women, children, and the elderly, were killed and burnt by government troops. Many women and girls were also brutally raped and wounded (see UTHR 1991). This was one of the first massacres to receive widespread publicity in Sri Lanka, and, although such terror was not new in the east, it brought attention to the lawlessness and brutality of the Sri Lankan troops at that time.

Civil society groups

Many of the incidents that Lawrence describes have been erased from official histories in Sri Lanka, as the battles for the north, and, in particular, the most recent decade of conflict, have taken precedence. However, as I note throughout this book, it is vital that accounts of horrors of everyday life through conflict, particularly during the first two decades of war, are acknowledged and remembered. I have accessed these accounts though the narratives given in this book, tying together what was happening at my time of research with what had occurred beforehand. However, it is important to also acknowledge that there are many scholars and activists who have courageously worked throughout the first two decades of conflict, providing detailed documentation of the everyday challenges and losses faced by those in the east. These include the Batticaloa Peace Committee (see Chapter 5, page 109), INFORM, the Civil Rights Movement and the government Human Rights Task force. Their efforts to publicise and condemn the atrocities of those years in a climate of extreme fear and threat must not be forgotten. Like Lawrence, they conveyed an overall sense of the east as a place where all familiar movement, speech, and relationships had been halted by violence, a sense of everyday violence similar to the processes of terror and dirty war which have come to define many other places across the globe.

The work of these groups and organisations also needs to be placed within a wider picture of 'civil society organisations' and INGO/NGOs in Sri Lanka during the 1990s.[16] This is an area that has been well documented (see, for example, Goodhand and Hulme 1999; Keenan 2003; Orjuela 2004, 2005; Walton 2010). Orjuela (2004) notes that 1994 was the dawn for increased 'peace aid' in Sri Lanka, when peace talks held between the People's Alliance (PA) coalition government and the LTTE brought a whole new perspective and fresh hopes for peace. Elected on an unprecedented platform of reconciliation, human rights, and anti-corruption, the government pursued a cessation of hostilities and negotiations with the LTTE, and the whole island was caught up in the euphoria of impending peace. This led to a rise in the number of INGOs and NGOs focused on peace-building and other projects, such as language reform, devolution of power, and government campaigns for 'national integration' (ibid.; Burke and Mulakala 2011: 150, see also Chapter 5, page 122).[17] As with the escalated focus on aid and conflict at the time of the 2002 ceasefire, the emphasis on 'conflict-resolution' and 'peace-building' often overshadowed and undermined the work of local groups operating with far less funds, less protection, and yet greater access to the realities of 'everyday violence'. It is important to note that the peace euphoria in 1994 was short-lived and despite many auspicious circumstances, three months after the ceasefire, negotiations collapsed as the LTTE resumed the battle. As a result, the government was damaged and disorientated, and saw little choice but to retaliate militarily and a controversial 'war for peace' strategy emerged (Nissan 1998; Rupasinghe 1998, 2006).

Twelve years on from the start of Lawrence's work, at the time when I began my fieldwork in 2005, the situation in Batticaloa and the whole Eastern Province had undergone many changes. Much of what had been described by Lawrence seemed far less identifiable. The most obvious change was the calming of political and military action precipitated by the most recent ceasefire. The CFA drawn up in 2002 still held, despite many shortcomings and continued disagreements on both sides. One of the most contentious issues was that the LTTE had continued recruiting children from the east into their ranks, and in August 2002 commenced compulsory recruitment on a wide scale in the Batticaloa district under the slogan of 'one child per family' (HRW 2004). This was a response to huge losses for families in recent years and increased resistance from parents in the north to handing over their children. Although parents complained to the Sri Lankan Monitoring Mission (SLMM) whose role in Sri Lanka was to ensure adherence to the terms of the 2002 ceasefire (which included no child-recruitment), they found them effectively redundant in their role since they were there to 'monitor' rather than 'take action'. Mothers, I spoke with in Batticaloa, were very clear about the ineffective role of the SLMM, UNICEF, and other international agencies in protecting families from recruitment and providing support to those whose children were taken (HRW 2004).

At the same time, the ceasefire had allowed for a slow steady opening up of areas in the north and east of the country with a number of significant and far-reaching effects. Roads were reconnected between the north and south, and trains from Colombo were running regularly as far as Vavuniya in the north and to Batticaloa in the east. This meant that travel was much easier and as a result businesses could prosper. There were fewer military impediments in terms of checkpoints, and the number of STF commandoes in the town had been reduced along with the number of round-ups and arrests taking place. People talked about having more freedom of movement and generally being less scared. The ceasefire had also given the LTTE more legitimacy, thus allowing them to operate in a less clandestine way and move about between camps and offices more freely. Therefore, in planning to move to the east in 2005 from my original research site of Vavuniya, I encountered few problems and my plans to stay were relatively simple to work out. The next section looks at some of the specific events during the years of 2005–07, which dramatically shaped the east and also framed my time of fieldwork.

A distinctive space and time (2005–07)

Although I did not realise it at the time, this period during which I lived in Batticaloa (2005–07) marked a distinctive and unusual time for the eastern region due to the two major aforementioned events of the factional split in the LTTE in April 2004 and the tsunami on 26 December 2004. Arriving in Batticaloa in January 2005, I found people still upset and confused by the horrors of the

December disaster. Batticaloa people talked relentlessly about the waves, both the destruction and the subsequent incoming traffic of aid workers and 'experts' who had taken over the town. The hive of activity and the constant arrival of vehicles, supplies, and people stood in stark contrast to the isolated patches of barren land, of the coastline deserted by those who had fled the wave. Relying on the aid brought by local organisations and INGOs, people were forced to play a waiting game as the government and other main stakeholders quarrelled over issues of rebuilding and resettlement.

Before the tsunami, an increase in the INGO presence had taken place after the 2002 ceasefire when 'peace' became a buzzword for unlocking funding opportunities (Orjuela 2004: 4). This meant that when the tsunami struck in 2004, there were already a number of established organisations in eastern Sri Lanka ready to respond and expand in accordance with the overwhelmingly generous response of the international community to the disaster. As the number of organisations expanded, a much larger network of expatriates moved into the town, bringing with them a phenomenon of feverish and competitive claim-staking among INGOs (described as 'competitive humanitarianism', see Chapter 1, page 9), squeezing out local organisations, and driving up of the costs of living, including rent for homes and offices (ibid.). Though many of the new organisations professed commitment to working in partnership with local groups and coordinating their work, local NGOs claim to have found it very hard to implement their own tsunami-related activities.[18] Meanwhile, individuals and local groups, such as a group of fishermen that I worked alongside (see Chapter 6, pages 137–46), described how they could not gain access to funding to rebuild their own boats and houses. Instead, they felt they were being forced into positions of dependency whereby they could not control how they were helped and instead had to either wait for handouts or find ways of making themselves an attractive cause to one of the thousands of organisations. The competition to stake claims over villages and camps, to emblazon temporary shelters with INGO branding, and to decide the futures of communities became frenetic and created what could be termed as a toxic discourse of giving (cf. Korf 2007). Malathi de Alwis has also described this confluence of aid and conflict in terms of exacerbating and heightening existing fissures between and within communities as a 'double wounding' for affected communities (see de Alwis 2009b: 121).

While the tsunami response has been well documented, what has been less considered is the way in which many local organisations experienced the loss of space to carry out even the roles they were doing before the tsunami.[19] In the rush to help, the climate of protracted conflict and unrest was ignored and misread, and newly opened space that needed to be dealt with carefully and slowly was shut down. Moreover, those who best knew how to deal with such situations and those who had learnt to live with and through everyday violence and now faced increased vulnerability after the tsunami were generally overlooked. Elsewhere I have argued that this misreading of spaces by the humanitarian agencies played a part in the undermining of local responses (see Walker 2013). While a number of complex factors come into play here, and no one actor is to blame, I suggest that had a recognition of local space and actions been better understood and harnessed a stronger agenda for interactions and cooperation could have been pushed, thus weakening the chances of a return to war.[20] That having been said, the discussion is much larger than the capacity of this chapter, and my interest here is how this particular distinctive time from 2005 onwards led to the coming together of a unique group of people – the *Valkai* group. I come to this point in the next section of this chapter.

Karuna and the TMVP

The one-track focus on the tsunami also directed attention away from the earlier disruption to Batticaloa life caused by the factional split in the LTTE in March 2004 as discussed in the previous chapter. The factional split had come just a month before the governmental elections of April 2004 and dramatically altered the political landscape of the east, increasing levels of violence and fear. It should be noted that an LTTE commander, Karuna, had an extremely negative reputation amongst Tamils and Muslims. It was well known, for example, that he had been involved in organising pogroms against Muslims, and had, thus, acquired the nickname of 'the Butcher'.[21] However, by distancing himself from Prabhakaran and the LTTE's ethnic cleansing of Muslims from the north, Karuna sought to re-establish relationships and gain support (Hariharan 2004).

Following the initial clashes with the LTTE in April 2004, Karuna's eastern forces were beaten back and forced to disband. In fierce fighting that took place at the Veragul River, which divides the Batticaloa and Trincomalee districts, scores of cadre, many of whom were children, were killed. The exact numbers of those killed are not known, however, Human Rights Watch (2004: 24–9) cites witnesses who reported that large numbers of cadre were killed or wounded. Those who died were burned or buried by either the LTTE or local villagers (ibid.). The fact that following this defeat Karuna gradually reasserted influence in both government and previously LTTE-controlled areas in the east not only points to the support he enjoyed from government forces but also suggests that the LTTE hegemony was far-less powerful in the east than the north. The very existence of the Karuna group also complicated the 2002 ceasefire agreement as Karuna asked to be formally included under the ceasefire agreement, which would have obligated his forces to abide by the terms of the ceasefire but also given him a seat at further peace talks. The LTTE rejected this and instead demanded that the Karuna group be disarmed under the ceasefire agreement as a 'Tamil paramilitary group' (ICG 2006: 9). Karuna rejected this on the grounds that this provision did not apply to his forces, which had been part of the LTTE under the peace accord.

Simultaneously, the confusion caused by the split, in catching people off guard and unsure of what would happen next, meant that spaces were opened up. These were spaces where people could suddenly move, speak, and act in ways that had not been possible under the tight controls of a unified LTTE. Many children, for example, who had earlier been forcibly recruited were able to escape as confusion spread throughout the Tiger camps, and it was reported that parents and grandparents (particularly mothers and grandmothers) beat back LTTE cadre to gain access to and release their children from the camps where they were residing (see HRW 2004, 2007c; de Alwis 2004b: 12–14). One fifteen-year-old girl described to me how her grandmother had stayed outside the LTTE camp for days during the split, waiting for her. Finally, with a change of clothing for her under one arm and a food packet in the other, the grandmother had marched past the LTTE cadres declaring that she was taking her granddaughter home.

While opportune in this way, the confusion also caught some, such as the international organisations mandated to work with vulnerable children, off guard. Locals described to me how, despite there being a large number of organisations working closely with child soldiers in the east, they were totally unprepared for the split in the LTTE and, therefore, had nothing in place to help and protect the young cadre who were flooding out of the camps and onto streets and buses.[22] Although the *Valkai* group had not officially formed at this point, a number of local residents involved in human rights works, such as Anuloja, Krishna, and Kamla (the women I lived with), were already working in these spaces trying to find ways of helping the families of returned children. In particular, they had warned UNICEF and other INGOs that there was a need to implement programmes that followed up on, and protected, children who had been returned, and who otherwise remained incredibly vulnerable to re-recruitment (see endnote 8).

'Clearing' the east

Both the LTTE split and the aftermath of the tsunami played into a weakening of the LTTE as a whole and helped to set the scene for the military offensive to follow in 2005 (as noted in the previous chapter). When an LTTE suicide bomber attempted to assassinate the Army Commander, Sarath Fonseka, the combined armed forces initiated an extensive bombardment of LTTE-controlled areas in the east close to Muttur. At the checkpoints on the boundaries of these areas, soldiers prevented civilians and NGOs from taking any significant quantities of goods into LTTE-controlled territories, and, consequently, tsunami rehabilitation projects came to a standstill. Furthermore, when the LTTE blocked the Mavil Aru sluice gates in Verugal in the east in July 2005, denying irrigation water to the Sinhalese farmers in government-controlled areas, the Sri Lankan government responded with a massive offensive to capture not only the Mavil Aru but also the entire LTTE-controlled territory in the Eastern Province.[23] Promising the restoration of democracy, devolution of powers to local and provincial politicians, and development of the Province, a year-long campaign to 'clear' the east of the LTTE saw large-scale destruction and the displacement of almost 200,000 mostly Tamil civilians (HRW 2008b).[24] Karuna's group, the TMVP, became valuable allies to the security forces during this time, although there also seemed to be a deliberate attempt to keep Karuna's power limited, most probably due to the campaign by international NGOs to take Karuna and the government to task for their collaboration in human rights violations.²⁵ In Batticaloa, intimidation, abductions, and extra-judicial killings intensified with the climate of fear and violence. Large numbers of displaced people flooded into the Batticaloa district where they stayed in IDP camps run by the government and INGOs. Most who moved to the east coast came from the interior areas of Batticaloa: the first wave in January and a second wave of IDPs in April (2006). Reports at the time also suggested that many IDPs were being forced to return to their homes by government agencies and the security forces, and that the majority of these homes had been damaged, destroyed, and looted by government forces (HRW 2007d; ICG 2008: 2).²⁶

During this time, the TMVP was also able to strengthen its grip on the east, controlling many of the IDP camps, and, like the LTTE, using displacement as an opportunity to recruit more children and young adults (HRW 2007d). As a crucial factor in the government's counter-insurgency campaign, the TMVP were given full access to the camps and allowed to screen incoming refugees for their links with the LTTE. On one occasion, when attempting to deliver underwear and sanitary items to women in a temporary camp close to Batticaloa, I was turned away by a group of TMVP cadre who told me in no uncertain terms, 'this is our area and we are managing. We don't need outsider help.'

Understanding space and activism

It was in the aftermath of the tsunami that the *Valkai* group came together. Most of the members had worked individually and together on human rights issues in the north and east of Sri Lanka for the majority of their lives, focussing on work with torture victims, support for abused and war-affected women, and advocacy work for women's and human rights. As noted earlier, the tsunami literally washed away demarcated space and lines of control by creating confusion, chaos, and the need for immediate action. Spaces that had been fought over, restricted, narrowed, and shut off became chaotic and vulnerable in a matter of minutes. Claims to space were lost as military actors and others lost their bearings, and although it did not take long for the order and control to be re-imposed, there was a short time, a particular moment and pocket of space, where it did not exist. One of the *Valkai* group members described the experience to me in the following way:

> There were no clear lines anymore. No clear indication of the power groups. The chaos gave us the ability to do things that we could not do before. Well, it's like the clear power dynamics are not there and so a type of energy comes from the chaos. (Member of the *Valkai* group 2005)

Another noted:

> It's like there was a loss of consciousness of differences. There are the army who had to pull Tamil children from the waves, some who died themselves and the LTTE who at that point immediately rushed to help with the army. It's funny, it's like, in that crisis everyone becomes human ... but then that was lost. (Member of the *Valkai* group 2005)

This kind of networking between locals and between locals and foreigners affected by the tsunami has not gone unnoticed. Nigel Clark, for example, notes the small acts of kindness and unconditional generosity as 'a kind of give without take, generosity without expectation of any return, hospitality without limits and conditions' (2005: 385). If we relate the behaviour Clark describes to the discussion of the concepts of space and place below, we can see that in those initial days after the tsunami, unfamiliar and unrecognisable spaces were opened up, and Batticaloa presented a context of open spaces of opportunity and potential. These spaces could be entered, engaged with, and, possibly, widened through a local response that drew on experience and knowledge of the area. As a local priest commented to me, 'everyone was helping everyone. There was no problem to go over to your Muslim or Tamil brother and help – the fears that were there before were gone.' Such a transformation had something to do with local sensitivities to a time, place, and space that allowed change to happen without claims being made for that space. This does not mean that locals worked together without differences or conflict or that people were not in a state of desperation and pain.[27] At the same time, it is important to acknowledge the lack of claims over space for that short time which enabled community involvement through an engagement with a 'local' experience that encompassed a wider sense of humanity. This local experience of space was powerfully shaped by a past, present, and foreseeable future of conflict in a community deeply divided and where there was a need to push for greater space for change and hope. Unfortunately, and as the statement from one of the *Valkai* members about the 'los[s]' of this space makes clear, the space that had been suddenly opened up by the disaster was rapidly closed down. As the numbers of international agencies, NGOs, and volunteers flooded into the east, those unique spaces became even more fragile.

Open spaces, narrow places

As we have seen so far, a cursory examination of the east's past in terms of violence and contests of control reveals a picture of narrowing spaces, spaces that throughout the years of conflict have squeezed the life out of the Tamil communities in the east, throttling the ability to move and speak freely. This can be considered as claims over space and the profound insecurity generated by those who hold spaces in suspense (cf. Korf *et al.* 2010). Space can, thus, be seen in terms of landscapes of social differentiation, and, as both the site and stake of struggles of power, which reflectively alter the social and physical space in which negotiation continues.

In common concepts of space and place, space is most often seen as unpredictable, insecure, and unknown in comparison to place, which is demarcated as fixed, stable, and known (cf. Massey 1995; de Alwis 2004a: 12). In Batticaloa, however, this interpretation does not quite fit, and actually can be turned on its head. Where people talked of places, for example, they described control, restriction, and oppression, which in relation then opened up the idea of space as a more flexible and free concept. Their comments suggest that in areas that were constantly contested and posed most risk, the sense of confusion and lack of definitive control meant they could do more. While danger and risk remain, and in some ways may heighten when unknown spaces are entered, it is better to keep spaces open than to put claims on them and thus turn them into places. If the known world of place can be experienced as a site of fear and intimidation, then the emptier experience of space can be seen as an opportunity to escape the dangers of the familiar world, as is supported by de Certeau (1984) in *The Practice of Everyday Life*. Analysing space and place in terms of everyday actions and movement, de Certeau regards place as a fixed site of stability in which elements are distributed in distinct and ordered locations. He conceptualises place as a kind of order in which only one thing can exist at one time in a location, and that location is fixed. Two things cannot be in the same location and other elements have to come next to one another, each in its own location. In contrast, space is a site of strategy, which allows for multiple different actions and people in the same site. As de Certeau notes, 'Space is composed of intersections of mobile elements. It is in a sense actuated by the ensemble of movements deployed within it' (1984: 117). The concept of space, thus, emerges through the actions or operations that orient, situate, or temporalise it.

Therefore, while working with the well-known distinction between space and place, in relationship to the complexities and ambiguities of the situation in Batticaloa with many different intersecting levels of control, I also try to rethink the values attached to both. I have, therefore, developed my understanding of space and place to accommodate the idea that in highly contested zones, where visibility and deliberate action are risky, less defined and more ambiguous spaces can actually provide a greater sense of freedom and opportunity. In other words, to shape space and keep it open is to allow a process to occur. The processes, I suggest, can thrive in an environment that is more ambiguous and shaped by competing claims of control. The unfamiliar thus offering an opportunity to escape the fears of that which is known for something different. When considered in relation to how the *Valkai* group came together after the tsunami and used space, as I will go onto argue, this interpretation becomes clearer.

The vulnerability created by this vying for control is underlined by Kalyvas's (2006) argument about patterns of violence in which he suggests that rather than territorial control it is the *lack of* territorial control that makes contexts of conflict more dangerous. Kalyvas notes that violence is predicted to be lowest in territories in which one party has total control and highest in territories in which control is only partial. Such high levels of violence and terror cannot be sustained for long periods of time without authority being lost. Therefore, a certain level of 'everyday violence' is maintained in which different actors control various spaces, and levels of fear and threat fluctuate. In Batticaloa, this could be seen particularly after the split in the LTTE and after the tsunami when claims to territory were not clear-cut, and were regularly contested and fought over. These ideas, which relate to how space can be perceived and encountered, can also help to paint a more realistic picture of the blurred fault lines and interlocked lives and feelings amongst Tamil-speaking people in Batticaloa. Where protagonists in war zones are represented as binary pairs of victims and perpetrators, terrorists and state actors, Batticaloa, like many other places of conflict, represented a mosaic of intricately woven lives and histories with allegiances and opinions sutured across critical boundaries and spaces. The nature of people's mottled identities and the narrowing of spaces through the conflict and the tsunami were revealed particularly in the ways that the LTTE and other armed actors would catch people up and take their lives on the basis of their pasts. Therefore, people were not given the space to redeem themselves, or could not escape their histories. The fate of many in this situation was tragically captured in the body of a man shot dead just outside our house in Batticaloa in 2005. He had recently returned from the Middle East. He had gone to escape threats against his earlier involvement in one of the Tamil militant groups, and returned to attend the funeral of his only child who had been killed in the tsunami. Days after the funeral he was cycling with a friend towards the lagoon, when the quiet of the afternoon was shattered by the piercing bang of a gun. Lying face down, legs sprawled, and the bicycle wheels still spinning, his life seeped into the sand. He was a victim of his complex political history. This was a history shared by many men and women, across the north and east, who became involved, often without choice, in Tamil militancy. Despite building a new life elsewhere, his present and his imagined future had not been strong enough to dilute the potency of his past. It was lives such as these that the *Valkai* group were involved with and committed to. They were not lives that were outwardly militant, but the inner views and sentiments, which locked away active pasts and muddied presents, were less clear. As such, these lives became even more vulnerable as spaces for connection and support were rapidly shut down in the aftermath of the tsunami, and the relief and rehabilitation effort expanded to include more international actors and organisations than local ones.

The *Valkai* group

Recognising that the moment of the tsunami emergency had passed and that the aftermath meant a long process of reconstruction, rehabilitation, the politicisation of aid and squabbling over the share of the tsunami funds, the *Valkai* group came together as a group of individuals concerned about what was happening around them. Krishna, one of the main female members, for example, described her shock at seeing a body of a man who had been shot in Batticaloa a few days after the tsunami:

> I was horrified to see another killing. I thought people had learnt. Was the tsunami not enough? But no – somewhere, somehow people are managing to regroup and continue to kill. I asked others, 'Didn't we learn anything from the tsunami?' What is this?

As described in Chapter 1, the group was composed of mostly local people and a few foreigners living in Batticaloa and the east at that time. Most of the locals were women, including Anuloja, Krishna, Kamla, and Ranjini, whom I lived with, but there were also a number of men involved, including Anuloja's husband, Rajan. A number of the group members had previously worked with international organisations such as Quaker Peace and Peace Brigade International (PBI), which had a presence in Sri Lanka until the late 1990s. These organisations had worked with similar ideas of widening spaces in order to support the most vulnerable and at risk. PBI, for example, provided unarmed protective accompaniment to Sri Lankan individuals, organisations, and communities threatened by violence, and regularly publicised the deteriorating human rights situation in the country. However, in 1998 PBI was forced to shut down its work in Sri Lanka following unreasonable demands made by the Sri Lankan government for access to their reports, and to the names and addresses of their contacts.[28] During the years of 2005–07, the *Valkai* group was also linked with the Non-Violent Peace Force (NP), one of the only international organisations that worked to protect civilians and individual rights in the north and east of Sri Lanka at that time.[29]

The *Valkai* group would meet every weekend to discuss the situation, and, in particular, to try and make sense of the intersecting violence of the tsunami and the conflict that was closing in around them. Activities such as tree-planting ceremonies and meetings for mothers whose children had been abducted were planned and organised. Sometimes family members from the east needed to go to Colombo to seek news of a relative who had been detained by the security forces or had disappeared. This was a risky and frightening process for families as many did not know Colombo, and travelling was not easy with all the checkpoints and surveillance. The *Valkai* group would try to help by linking the family members with contacts in Colombo who would provide support during their trip. This was always done on an informal basis and with careful attention to the security risks. On one occasion, Anuloja and others accompanied a group of women, whose husbands had been abducted or killed by the LTTE, to Kilinochchi, the LTTE headquarters in the north (see map 1: page xx), where they demanded information about their husbands and signed statements reporting their cases. This was a perilous move on the part of the mothers and Anuloja. Normally one would do anything to avoid being noticed or known by the LTTE; however, by challenging the LTTE in this way the women were making themselves highly visible and vulnerable to a group who were well known for callously disposing of anyone who opposed or appeared to oppose their totalitarian rule.

One of the key concerns of the group was not to be classed as an NGO or organisation in any way. This was a reaction to both the dominance of the NGO structure in the areas, and the recognised need for something more open and fluid that could 'quietly move and share information without a visible leader and control' while at the same time 'show families that there are continued relationships, support, and trust' (said by Anuloja in 2005, a member of the *Valkai* group). One woman in the *Valkai* group explained to me that she felt many people's roles have been 'undone' by violence, meaning that many people had tried to organise and to support others but the threat against them and the fears they faced had prevented them from continuing. Recognising this reality, and knowing that working as a formal organisation and seeking funding would bring unwanted attention, the *Valkai* group saw it necessary to work quietly and through small spaces to reach out to others. This also reflected the need for fluidity and ability to work with an unpredictable and uncertain everyday.

The purpose of the *Valkai* group, in this context, can be seen as a way of finding spaces, as understood as opportunities, to move into and open up, and furthermore of finding common points, shared feelings, and thoughts that could straddle the cracks of fear and violence with relations of trust instead. This form of 'active living' is perhaps best illustrated through activities such as the tree-planting ceremonies and also meetings for mothers whose children had been recruited and abducted by the militant groups.

Tree-planting ceremonies and mother's meetings

The idea of tree planting developed from a desire to bring families who had lost loved ones together in a non-threatening way with a focus on life, nurturance, and growth, creating a space where they could share their stories. During the ceremony, photographs were placed in the middle of a room surrounded by small oil lamps. Over them, the silky leaves of young coconut tree saplings bowed. One tree for each life lost. The families themselves had decided upon the idea of planting trees, and had wanted coconut saplings because of their multiple uses in everyday life. The tree was to be an active and 'growing' reminder, and one that could be tended into the future. Tree planting is not an unusual form of memorisation in Sri Lanka (although it is also not commonly a part of Tamil funerals) and it does not necessarily stand apart from the rituals and routines of everyday life. During 2005 and 2006, in a culture of suspicion and mistrust where every action was watched and differences marked, it was crucial for the families to remain within the boundaries of what was seen as 'normal'. Yet, at the same time, the tree-planting ceremonies were unfamiliar and thus marked a disjuncture from the violent disruption to everyday life and routine.

Deaths and disappearances in Sri Lanka created absences and voids that could not be filled, those that were oversaturated with affect. The tree planting presented an action that marked absences rather than simply death, and opened up a raw space where questions could be asked and pain felt. While in Chapter 6, I describe the tree-planting ceremony in greater detail, at this point I look at what these absences meant in terms of the experiences of the families and of the *Valkai* group. I consider how they can be understood as a different form of activism, as 'active living' that questions the past, the present, and future while finding ways in which to work through and reorder the spaces of the everyday.

It is interesting to note that tree planting has also been used as a regular form of memorialisation by the Tamil Tigers. In their commemoration of death on their annual *Maveerar Nal* (Hero's day) on 27 November, for example, the honouring of fallen heroes and paying homage to them was often carried out through the planting of trees. Mass ceremonies would be held at the cemeteries of cadre, and the LTTE, family, and friends would gather around the headstones and lay flowers and offerings to their loved ones and comrades. The careful orchestration of such ceremonies can be seen as a motivation strategy harnessed by the LTTE to transform the feelings of grief and loss amidst the families of those killed to a form of pride over their participation and role in the movement. The intention can be seen as bringing the families of the dead fighters closer to the LTTE rather than estranging them from it, thus ensuring their continued support at a time when it could easily be lost. In the harnessing of the grief of the families, the LTTE intended to guide and create a celebration of life that glorified and justified death for the sake of the movement (see also discussion in Chapter 7 titled 'The currency of grief', page 151). This glorification of loss also sought to shut down space to question the reasons behind death and instead expected families to simply accept loss as a sacrifice that was necessary (according to LTTE rhetoric) for the future.[30]

Yet, the meaning of a tree to symbolise life and remember death for the LTTE in comparison to the *Valkai* group, although similar in practice, could not be more different in intention, meaning, and symbolism. As much as the *Valkai* group sought to mark loss, they also sought to mark a disruption in everyday life – a disjuncture that recognised what was not acceptable or explicable – and in doing so asked questions and demanded new ways of thinking and connecting. This is illustrated most powerfully in Chapter 6 in relation to Rani who participated in one of the tree-planting ceremonies for her son who was killed in 2004. The tree that Rani and her husband planted in their compound, known as '*kutti annar maram*' (older brother's tree) became a marker not only of life lost, but of a present that was being continuously endured and worked through, and of a challenged and questioned future (see pages 132–6).

An illustration of how the tree-planting ceremonies organised by the *Valkai* group challenged everyday life rather than keeping it tightly in check can be seen in the reaction of a father who came to one of the first ceremonies. The father's only son, a fourteen-year-old, had been shot by the army in the market place in Valachchenai (in the Batticaloa district) as he tried to help a friend, injured minutes earlier in a grenade attack. He had been shot through the stomach from behind and died almost immediately. The father came to the tree-planting ceremony with his two daughters and granddaughter. He was clearly still distraught, and while he sat quietly through the ceremony, at the end he had got up and started talking. He began with the story of his son's death and ended by asking questions. He wanted to know why had they killed his son when he was just a young boy, why the army had arrived on the scene just after the attack. Who had called them, who had told them to shoot his son and why was no one being prosecuted? As he talked and grew increasingly agitated, so did the other families in the room. It was not that they did not understand what this father was saying; many of them probably shared the same feelings and questions. But these were not questions that one shared with others – even family members and close friends – as the risk that pervaded every aspect of their daily life was far too great.

However, the reaction of this father during the ceremony demonstrates his feelings of relative safety in the 'safe space' created by the *Valkai* group, and with other families, all who had lost in one way or another. The space allowed absences to be felt at their most raw and to push people to ask questions and demand answers. While the answers could not necessarily be given in this space, at least they could exist, be shared, and be heard – something that the context of militarisation and control had long shut down in eastern Sri Lanka.

Mothers' meetings

Another way in which a relatively safe space was found was in the meetings for families, particularly for mothers and grandmothers whose children had been recruited and abducted. The meetings were not initially created only for mothers; however, as I have already mentioned, most often in the context of risk and violence it was safer for women to travel and to meet together than it was for men. Therefore, most often mothers and grandmothers attended. What was most significant about these meetings was that rather than being organised by the *Valkai* group for the mothers to come and participate, the mothers themselves actively organised the meetings, set the agenda, and led the discussions. The group members would take part alongside the mothers, sometimes facilitating if discussions became heated or confused, but mostly listening to and learning from what the mothers had to say. The *Valkai* group's main responsibility would be to organise a safe space to meet (often in a local NGO building) and would provide tea, lunch, and help with the cost of local transport since many women had to take a day off work and travel long distances to come to the meeting. Much of the meeting would be spent sharing stories and discussing particular problems, such as dealing with the army or crossing through checkpoints, etc. The women would also spend some time lighting candles next to photographs of family members they had lost during the conflict and sit in silence to remember them.

To provide a sense of the meetings, I turn to one particular meeting that I attended in 2006 when a mother chose to tell her story to all the other women. The mother began her story by describing how her child was forcibly taken from her when he was on his way to school and kept in an LTTE camp in Kokkadaichcholai, an LTTE-controlled area in the east (see map 3: xxii). Since she knew where he was, the mother began daily visits to the camp, travelling the long distance from her home and over the lagoon to the gates of the camp guarded by young LTTE cadre. 'I would plead with them for my child back', she stated, 'I would sit on my legs like this [demonstrating how she would kneel in a praying/begging position] and ask again and again for my son.' The mother was eventually able to get her child back, and in telling her story, she had berated the other women in the group for willingly negotiating with those who were holding their children. She insisted that they should not negotiate but rather keep pushing and finding ways to move forward. She said they should not listen when they were told to come back the next day or to pay money to certain people. The mother went on to explain in detail her daily trips to the camp and how she eventually decided to threaten to commit suicide in front of the LTTE if her child was not returned. She described:

Plate 2.1 Mother's meeting, Batticaloa (2006)

I went to that camp every day – I insulted them so much that they would have had fifty lorry loads of my saliva!

For nine days, I did not eat, did not go to the toilet – how could I if not eating? Then I went there with a knife – it was actually so blunt that it would not pierce my skin but they [the LTTE] did not know that. I waited at the camp and told them I would kill myself. They said I wouldn't but I told them I had only my son so it did not matter what happened to me. Then they [the LTTE] told me they would see me the next day and sent me to stay with a family close by. The family was told by them [the LTTE] to take the knife from me when I went to bathe so that I could not kill myself. I left the knife under my dress when I went to bathe but I saw them do this [take the knife] and I told them, 'I will not cause you any trouble – I am not here to trouble you but only to get my child.'

The next day at the camp I refused to leave until they [the LTTE] gave me my son and said I would kill myself if they did not. In the end, they came to me and they said, 'If we give you your son, do you promise to go far away from here and not come back again.' I told them that I would because I did not chose to be near them but that they had brought me by taking my son. Then they said, 'If we give you your son, do you promise not to come back and shout at us again?' and I told them that, if I had my son, I wouldn't need to shout at them. Then they put my son in front of me and told me to take him. Then I took him and he told me that in the camp they [the LTTE] would talk about my shouting at the camp gates and they told him about a letter I sent them. They said the words had scared them.

This mother's story powerfully demonstrates how she had to map out the landscapes of risk and violence, and push against the boundaries of restrictive spaces (literally in terms of the LTTE camp and metaphorically in terms of her own fear) to find her child. Like Meena's life story in Chapter 5, the significance of this anecdote is that it is not framed as the narrative of a victim or a heroine, but reveals the realities of everyday life as a mother in eastern Sri Lanka. Furthermore, located within the space of the mother's meeting and alongside the work of the *Valkai* group, the story illustrates the sharing of experiences as a means to strengthen everyday activities and strategies, and for women to challenge those who took their children and husbands.

Given these two activities of tree planting and mother's meetings, it can be said that the role of the *Valkai* group, although less defined and specific, was hinged upon its ability to creatively map the socio-spatial realities of the particular context in which it was working. Strategically, the women and other members needed to push wider specific spaces and create new meanings within that space while theoretically, a focus on such spaces offers a deeper understanding of 'women's ways of remembering, recording and articulating their struggles, and of the nature, content and meaning of their political actions' (Nagar 2000: 360). However, the immediacy of violence and fear in Batticaloa and the desperate needs of individuals such as mothers seeking their children and fathers asking questions about the death of their children meant that the work of the *Valkai* group had to remain outside of the organisational/project structure. Thus, it was defined more by what it was not, than what it was.

However, the paradoxical nature of being ephemeral yet dependent on ties of trust meant that the group was constantly in tension and reliant on the willingness of individuals to challenge space. This, naturally, created problems. Relationships and connections amongst members were not inherently fixed and virtuous; they were also fractured from within, in terms of individual interests, the need to protect one's family and fear of others, all within a constantly changing context. This was captured in the words of one woman, who had joined with the mothers and the *Valkai* group to discuss child-recruitment: 'If I get my child back, I will not let go. Nothing else will matter then. I just want my child.' Although when explicitly asked in a group setting, most mothers confirmed that they would continue to support others even if their child was returned, the levels of risk and fear woven through their everyday contexts, and their ultimate concern for their own child's safety, meant that they could not make promises or fixed decisions. Furthermore, within the *Valkai* group itself, intentions to keep membership open and remain a 'non-group' were strongly tested when new people came to meetings. On one particular occasion, one of the *Valkai* members brought along a woman who was not known to the other members. During the meeting, I noticed that a number of women were unusually quiet. When I asked them about it afterwards, they replied, '[w]e weren't sure about that other lady. We don't know where she is coming from and who she is connected with. So we are scared for her to know us.' On another occasion, one of the members had spoken at length about a situation in a village where all the men were leaving at night to sleep in the jungle to escape threats from the TMVP. It was much later that I discovered that he had, in fact, been talking about his own village and his own experiences. This illustrates the intense fear in Batticaloa, which meant that even in contexts where trust had been established and connections formed, people still held back, remained cautious, and questioned every word and action. Bähre argues that in situations of extreme poverty or violence, 'ambivalence' must be acknowledged as part of social relations and interdependences. He notes, '[r]eluctant solidarity encapsulates that help, particularly under conditions of destitution and hardship, does not result in extensive unifying bonds of comradeship, but in small bonds fraught with social tension' (Bähre 2007: 52). This is an important point to make, as Bähre notes that the prevailing assumptions made by the World Bank, the UN, and other NGOs of disadvantaged communities in the developing world, as well as urban centres in the West, are based on perceptions of solidarity and social cohesion amongst the poor (ibid.). Echoing the argument I have made throughout this book about how experiences of everyday violence are understood through the dichotomy of suffering vs. survival and resilience, the emphasis on the creative, supportive, and uncomplicated agency of poor people, particularly women, plays into a romantic notion of solidarity and social relations in general. To then apply Bähre's argument to the *Valkai* group, we can see how it is vital to recognise that nothing about the group is simply cohesive. Rather, tensions, fears, risks, and ambivalence weave throughout their everyday activities and interactions. For Bähre, it is the 'fierce disputes over inclusion, respect, and mutual support' that in the end form 'the materials of solidarity' (ibid.: 33).

The disputed and the undisputed

In summing up the work of the *Valkai* group, Anuloja explained to me that one way in which the group sought to work with silences and fears both between themselves and, more broadly, with the communities they worked in was to delineate 'the disputed and the undisputed'. That is, that in situations of violence there is always disputed and undisputed factors. The disputed are those such as the identity of the killer, the motive, and reason for killing and related unanswered questions, while the undisputed is the simple fact that a life has been taken and that those connected to that life feel grief and pain. So, in looking to the simplicity of loss, the group sought to connect people through their undisputed grief and suffering, which in some ways minimised risk as it avoided asking questions which could lead to further threat and violence. In Anuloja's words:

> [I]n bringing more people together with shared feelings, we can then create trust because there is not that risk and so then you get more space to connect. So you are doubling your space all the time. But in that space you need to have the energy, back and forth, from one to another, between all the people.

For families whose loved ones had disappeared or been killed, the focus was on the undisputed sense of loss and the absence it created rather than on the disputed factors of who was responsible, how, and why. In reality, however, even focusing on the 'undisputed' reason could not evade risk, and it was noted that on many occasions when families who had lost loved ones were brought together to share their grief, fear and threat were palpable. Yet, the fact that there were also small fragments and signs of hope, trust, and friendship that emerged from such occasions led the *Valkai* group members to argue that such work had to continue. For example, an older widow, whose son had been recently killed, expressed concern about a young woman she had just met, who had not been able to get the death certificate for her husband. The widow had suggested that she could perhaps help the young widow to get the certificate. This way, we can see such moments as a foundation to building trust between people and as providing glimmers of hope for change in the future. Subsequently, new possibilities for shaping and creating spaces could emerge. Recognising that many viewed the role played by the *Valkai* group as unrealistic and overly dangerous, Anuloja would often return to the following argument:

> No one knows fear and death better than these families, than the *ammas*. If we don't take a risk and see our lives with their lives, see ways of, at least, trying to break closure and fear with openness and trust, then why are we here?

Anuloja's argument outlines the foundations of the vision of many of the *Valkai* group members – to break through the spaces that have been claimed and closed down, and to find ways of (re)opening them to create relationships of trust and support. In doing so, these challenged spaces represent a process of 'active doing' in the deliberate attempt to stay outside of the theatre of INGO/NGO politics and women's projects, and, therefore, to look directly at the fear and violence isolating communities. In other words, 'active living' attempted to take the social and political landscape of conflict as a problem, but without becoming a part of the problem itself. At the same time, the reality of the environment in Batticaloa ensured that 'active living' could never be completely effective, nor could it avoid the risks and fear that drove its purpose in the first place. However, the intention to draw on strategies of endurance ensured that a creative edge was maintained that sought to work with what was at hand and 'work towards preserving life not the dead' (said by Ranjini in 2006, a member of the *Valkai* group). This is evoked throughout the stories in this book that link the way in which families have dealt with the multiple losses that everyday violence brings to the work of the *Valkai* group.

Having mapped out the spaces and the work of some of the people living in the east in this chapter, I turn next to a consideration of how the vicissitudes of fieldwork were shaped by the tsunami and escalating violence in the east. Thinking through my own journey as a researcher trying to form relationships and understand networks, I address questions such as what it means to carry out moral and ethical fieldwork in unstable and changing situations. This, in turn, reveals the many complexities of my research process, and of living and working in a place of conflict.

Notes

1 During cordon-and-search operations (also known locally as 'round-ups'), the security forces would block off an area, and move from house to house checking identification. They would then either detain people or seize their documents and request that they report to the army camp or another location to collect their IDs. In both scenarios, some people who went to collect their documents never came back (HRW 2007a).
2 Formed in 1983, the STF received specialist training by the British Special Air Service (SAS), and specialised in counter-terrorism and counter-insurgency operations. As the most highly trained police organisation in Sri Lanka, the STF has led operations against the LTTE, and has been mostly stationed in the Eastern Province. Over the years, it has become notorious for its widespread human rights abuses, including extra-judicial killings, torture, and disappearances (Human Rights Watch [HRW] March 2008a).
3 In 2007, the Department of Census and Statistics released a preliminary report of basic population information on the Batticaloa district based on special enumeration. The stated objective of this enumeration was to provide the necessary basic information needed to formulate development programmes and relief activities. Given the timing of the data collection, when large numbers of families were being displaced, the accuracy of the report is highly questionable.
4 For a more detailed description of *podiyars*, see Canagaratnam (1921: 60–5), and for landownership patterns on the east coast, see Herring (1972: 99–124).
5 There is a large body of comparative kinship analysis in Sri Lanka and South Asia more generally. For example, see Dumont (1957, 1966, 1970, 1983); Leach (1961); Yalman (1967, 1975); Tambiah (1973); Good (1980, 1981, 1991); Trautmann (1981, 1987) McGilvray (1982b and c, 1998b, 2008) and Agarwal (1990, 1996). For a detailed examination of the practices of kinship and household structures in eastern Sri Lanka, see McGilvray (1982b and c, 2008); Ruwanpura (2006).
6 The preference is for bilateral cross-cousin marriage (Tambiah 1973:127).
7 Ashraff later died in a helicopter crash just before the elections of October 2000, leaving the SLMC disintegrated. Rauff Hakeem then took over the leadership of the party, but very soon Ashraff's widow, Ferial split off and formed her own party, the National Unity Alliance (NUA). In 2003, further splits followed, and, by 2007, the bigger Muslim towns on the east coast were like small town republics, each with its own dominant political party.
8 The communal riots in 1977 were the most serious since 1956, killing over 100 people and displacing about 25,000 (de Silva 1986; UTHR 1993).
9 Thangarajah (1995) provides a fascinating study which chronicles the transformation of the ethnic identity of the east coast Vedda over time *vis-à-vis* Tamils. He looks at how the communities have maintained an ethnic consciousness as Veddas, despite pressure to integrate, particularly with the affects of the conflict impacting on their livelihoods and security.
10 Valvettitura, also known as 'VVT' was the birthplace of the LTTE leader Prabharkaran.
11 Gunaratna (2001) points out that a plan for arming Sinhala settlers had existed earlier, however, it was only after the farm massacres that this move was seen as politically acceptable. Thus, in 1985 weapons were distributed amongst colonists and training provided.
12 In response to a massacre of Sinhala civilains in April 1987, many of whom were long-term residents in the east, the state characteristically reacted with punitive aerial

bombardment and shelling in Jaffna, thus setting the stage for the Indian intervention (see UTHR 1990a: Chapter 7).
13. After disbanding and claiming to give up violence, the EPRLF are alleged to have worked with the IPKF and Sri Lankan Army. In Batticaloa in 2005 and 2006, many locals connected the *Razeek Group*, composed of former EPRLF cadres and working along with the SLA, to killings and disappearances in the Batticaloa region.
14. There has been no comprehensive comparative study of IDPs since 2002.
15. It is important to note that Lawrence provided vital information to the 'Commission of Inquiry into the Involuntary Removal or Disappearance of Persons in the Northern and Eastern Provinces' on the Sathurukandon massacre in which she listed the names of all those killed (see Lawrence 1997).
16. Here I use the broad definition of civil society as 'an arena of uncoerced collective action around shared interests, purposes and values' (Walton 2010: 184). This definition incorporates a range of organisations such as NGOs, trades unions, religious groups, and the media, while also recognising that the distinctions between 'civil society' and the state are not always clear-cut.
17. For an interesting discussion on the role of donor funding in the Sri Lankan peace-process, see Burke and Mulakala (2011: 150). For a more general critique of the escalating role of aid agencies in conflict-resolution and peace-building activities, see Terry (2002: 245).
18. Not ignoring the fact that many local NGOs (which often expanded beyond their own capacity) were also unclear in their approaches. This made it difficult of INGOs to find sound local partnerships (see Harris 2006).
19. One exception is the work of Timmo Gaasbeek (2010) which draws upon first-hand experience to document the local tsunami response.
20. In 'Taking a back seat: The uses and misuses of space in a context of war and natural disaster' (Walker 2013), I explore the spatial politics played out between international organisations and local actors in the aftermath of the tsunami. I argue that by failing to understand the local spaces that opened up and by competing for control, the humanitarian approach adopted by international organisations missed an opportunity to help keep new spaces open.
21. Interviews with Muslim families, 2006.
22. In June 2003, the LTTE and the Sri Lankan government agreed to a formal Action Plan on Children Affected by War, brokered primarily by UNICEF. Under the Action Plan, the Tamil Tigers agreed to end their recruitment of children and to release children from their forces, either directly to the children's families or to new transit centers that were constructed specifically for this purpose and funded by UNICEF, the International Labour Organisation (ILO), and Save the Children. However, this was done in partnership with the LTTE-controlled TRO which essentially meant that LTTE controlled all the information on and had access to the children they had purportedly released. It is, therefore, no surprise that UNICEF figures showed that since the Action Plan was signed, the LTTE recruited more than twice as many children as it released (HRW 2004).
23. The GoSL created the Mavil Aru reservoir to benefit the state-sponsored Sinhala settlements in the region. The reservoir had changed hands twice during the course of the conflict. In 1991, during Eelam War II, the LTTE failed to capture the reservoir but blew up the sluice gates, and then in 1997, in Eelam War III, the armed forces captured it and lost it again. After the ceasefire in 2002, Mavil Aru came within the LTTE-controlled area but continued to water the fields in government-controlled areas.

24 On the same day that Muttur in the east was taken by government forces, seventeen local staff members from Action Against Hunger (Action Contre la Faim, or ACF) involved in post-tsunami relief were summarily executed by forces linked to the state (see UTHR 2006).
25 The EU and the UN repeatedly took up the issue of violations, although the government continuously denied involvement with the TMVP. In 2008, Karuna was assisted to travel to the UK on a diplomatic passport, which saw him imprisoned by the British Authorities for carrying a fraudulent passport. In his absence, Pilliyan took a leader role in the TMVP, and following success in the eastern provincial elections entered an alliance with the current government.
26 This was in violation of the UN Guiding Principles on Internal Displacement, to which the government pledged its adherence (IRIN 2007; HRW 2007b; CPA 2007).
27 It should be noted that I have not come across any stories of the TMVP and LTTE working together after the tsunami, indicating one boundary that seemed impervious to change.
28 See 'International Human Rights NGO Forced to Leave by Sri Lankan Government' (1998), www.peacebrigades.org/archive/lanka/slp98-5a.html).
29 The important work of NP during the years of 2005–06 was carried out by a number of dedicated and courageous individuals within the organisation. These individuals, who were also part of the *Valkai* group, recognised the importance of working with local human rights activists to understand their strategies and ideas, and offer forms of support.
30 Benjamin Schonthal (2011) offers an interesting discussion around the role of LTTE commemoration practices and how they seemed to straddle both religious and non-religious interpretive possibilities. He notes that the ambiguous language of Heroes Day speeches could be part of a 'deliberate discursive strategy' employed by the LTTE to appeal to both religious and non-religious families in a way that does not compromise its stated official 'secular' position. On the other hand, however, Schonthal suggests that such practices could also be part of a wider appeal to militaristic ways of controlling memory in order to valorise and justify loss (see Schonthal 2011: 544–54).

3

Living and learning in Batticaloa

'Do[ing] something at the time'

One March afternoon, at the height of the dry season, a group of us were sitting around in a circle in the main room of the house where I stayed. We had deliberately positioned ourselves in the centre of the room beneath the ancient dusty fan, which reluctantly whirred over our heads like a low-flying helicopter. Slouched on woven mats, our sleepy bodies melted onto the cool floor as the blades of the fan cut through the still air as they picked up pace and found their rhythm. Freshly squeezed lime juice had been passed around along with a plate of very yellow sponge cake in the hope of reviving us, while the front doors stood open allowing the lagoon breeze to drift in. Outside, children were playing in the lane. School had finished for the day. Some of the boys shouted to one another as they raced up and down on bicycles, while others played a rather disorganised game of cricket, frequently interrupted by the motley crew of mangy stray dogs who kept running off with the ball. The group I sat with was composed of the family members with whom I lived, friends who often stayed over at the house, two women from a local NGO, and two researchers from Colombo. The researchers had dropped by as part of a routine, but, infrequent, visit to the east. It was common for academics, researchers, and other interested parties to do this, spend two or three manic days staying in the infamous guesthouse overlooking the lagoon. They would eat fresh prawns and curry, and visit designated 'insider' people whom they could quiz about the situation in Batticaloa, before climbing back into their vehicles and disappearing back to Colombo. While a few did keep contact and would return to visit occasionally, the majority would never be heard from again.

As a group, we had been discussing an event that had happened a few weeks earlier when a number of Tamil-speaking men and women had been rounded up and taken to police stations across the east. Although most had been released after a few hours, a few remained unaccounted for. While discussing what could be done about this situation, one of the Colombo researchers noted that they planned to write a report on this particular incident at some point in the near future. Sitting upright, one of the local NGO women, a good friend of mine, looked at her and countered, 'You researchers all say that you will look at something *after* it happened. That is not what we need. Then it's too late. You are supposed to do something *at the time*.'

Although this comment was offered with a mix of humour and irony, the murmurs of agreement and vigorous nodding of heads indicated that this was a sentiment shared by most of the group. Having spent a lot of time with the individuals present, I knew their cynicism towards 'experts', researchers, journalists, and people outside coming in to collect information. I knew it was not an uninformed perspective either, as many members of the group had spent years documenting and raising awareness of the issues in Batticaloa, and most had, at some point, been involved in research projects themselves. They were also very aware of all the money that had poured into Sri Lanka after the ceasefire for conflict and peace-related studies. I also knew these sentiments were not confined to the room in which we sat either, but that such feelings echoed through the homes, communities, and work places across the east. It was frequently noted how many 'outsiders' (not local to Batticaloa and the east) visited the district as if it was a laboratory where interesting data could be collected and taken away for analysis. People pointed out that despite the amount of research done, little change occurred, and what most frustrated them was that those who told their stories, and were encouraged to bear witness to the climate of violence in which they lived, got very little, if anything, back. On one particular occasion, I had listened as a woman told a UN Special Rapporteur the story of how her son was abducted by the Karuna group. The rapporteur had specifically asked mothers to come and tell him their stories, and, in turn, the mothers had asked that he bring up their cases with the government and head of the army. After sharing her story, the woman had left in floods of tears, scared to return home, in case she had been noted talking to a member of the UN. The mothers never heard back from the expert and the woman's son was never found.[1]

I was, therefore, not surprised when my friend uttered this comment. However, I also uncomfortably had to admit that, despite my long-term stay in Batticaloa and relationship with the family, I was one of those researchers who had come into Batticaloa temporarily and then would leave to write something back in the UK. As much as I did not want to see myself in this way, the reality was that I had arrived in Batticaloa to do research, and did plan to leave eventually. Yet, the boundaries seemed far from clear-cut since I had found myself personally engaged in ways that I had not foreseen, and was committed to people and life in the east far beyond my researcher position. Nevertheless, at the end of the day, I would leave, and would take away stories and fragments of lives with me to turn them into an academic exercise, detached from the tumultuous everyday reality of violence and conflict in which they were embedded. My friend's comment touched on many of the moral and ethical dilemmas I grappled with in my research, and, by extension, that all researchers in conflict situations face at some point in their fieldwork. In the context of thinking through some of the issues triggered by my friend's comment, the many difficulties I faced in my research experience become known. Reflecting on the situations and the various emotions brought up by my time in the field, it is possible to start to look at the complexity of the role of an ethnographic researcher trying to live in an environment of conflict and violence. This, in turn, brings out aspects of everyday living in the field that sharpen into focus because of the role the researcher is taking on in attempting to understand and empathise with the lives of those around her. Similarly, it is within the study of the perceptions, emotions, meanings, and interpretations of those who experience violence that the separate and indistinguishable subjective and objective components of the research process can be highlighted. By bringing attention to these experiences, the theorising of the anthropologist and the anthropologist's interlocutors in their dialogic encounters in the field provide a greater sense of life and accountability both in research and in the field. These amount to fragments of conversations that are overheard, pages of field notes written under the gaze of curious children, informative discussions after an interview has finished, and even previously written ethnographies which impinge on what we know and what questions we as ethnographers might ask. It is at this juncture, of how the individual and collective ideas and emotions are formed, that we can render more visible the everyday experiences of living through violence.

This chapter is shaped by three basic convictions: the first, that a focus on the reflexivity of the researcher as author reveals how his or her relationship with the research subjects is formed, as well as with the subject of violence itself. The second, that stories and encounters emerging from ethnography not only illuminate the lives of the people studied but also the shape of the relations formed between themselves and with those who study them. Third, the ethnographer's position and location (professional and personal), and the significant shifts occurring therein, profoundly shape the contours of the ethnographic process. Therefore, through these three themes I trace my journey in terms of the specific situations and problems I encountered, which, in turn, reflect on a number of key ideas that run throughout the book. These include configuring social and cultural relationships with others, negotiating fear and violence, making moral and ethical judgments, learning how and who to trust, and learning how to listen – to the silences as well as the words being said.

Being, becoming, belonging

> Being is never some fixed or intrinsic attribute; in so far as being is being-in-the-world – tied to the contexts of interactions with others – it is in continual flux. (Jackson 2002: 13)

Being in Batticaloa

In many ways, the methodology of my research emerges during all of the chapters in this book. However, there is also something more specific that needs to be brought out here which attests to the personal and private journey of a field-worker trying to 'find' herself in the field, and the ways in which research becomes, not a separate space out of life, but an integral part of life at that time. An ethnographer's biography is evidently an intricate and complex story with multiple strands and layers, and any undertaking in a context of war creates constraints, risks, and concerns, which have to be dealt with as particularly difficult ongoing factors in everyday life. Feelings of fear and anxiety are common to researchers of violence (see Kelly 1988; Hearn 1998; Campbell 2002), even though few openly discuss the experiences of dealing with this. Mo Hume (2007: 153) reveals that during her research in El Salvador, she struggled with admitting to fear as she viewed it as a sign of 'weakness', and suggests that such feelings extend from considerations shaped by gender-norms in terms of what is 'appropriate' research, and also the fact that fear is so rarely talked about. Moreover, there can be a reluctance to be labelled a 'thrill seeker' (Lee 1995: 5) or to cause concern to those back home. These were concerns that I shared and felt very aware of. There can be a certain kind of 'attraction' to dangerous and tragic situations. People talk about the 'exhilaration' of war; when danger is close, every object, every feeling seems more alive and relationships more real. While I may have touched on such feelings during my fieldwork, especially in terms of the work I did post-tsunami, I think that time inevitably dims the intensity of such feelings. Instead of exhilaration, you feel exhaustion and rather than feeling more alive you feel burdened by the heaviness of the situation and the reality that the line between the risks to yourself and others is permeable. Acknowledging such feelings does not have to be about drawing attention to one's own plight or indulging in the art of 'navel gazing', rather it can be a balanced reflexive means of addressing the risks and difficulties of doing research in areas of conflict without denying that there is a measure of cost to *all* those involved.[2] To ignore the range of our own ethnographic stories and emotions that ethnographers carry is, Narayan argues, 'to miss a precious resource in a situation where we already have privileged insight and rapport' (1992: 7).

During the first few months that I was in Batticaloa, I convinced myself that before I began any 'real' research, I had to understand the many factors and issues that made up life at that time. Yet, in hindsight, my research began the very day I arrived. It was not in a systematic structured format and nor did it necessarily make much sense to me at the time, but from the moment I stepped off the Batticaloa train into the dark cool hours of the early morning, I was learning about life and taking in far more than I could ever write down. Climbing down from the rickety carriage onto the station platform and walking through the gate partly blocked by soldiers whose faces and guns were obscured by the dark, I became part of the landscape that I was to inhabit.

Eager to start feeling I was actually doing something, I spent many hours worrying about whom to talk to, and how to approach them, as a way of clocking up the interviews and fieldwork data. These 'fieldwork blues' as Wood (2007) describes them are important to identify as they frame some of the initial ways of coping in the early stages of research. Moreover, they also demonstrate how easily we construct connections and categories as a focus of research when they are not necessarily a priority for the people at the heart of our studies. While planning research before arriving in the field can be a way of establishing confidence and being grounded, it can also, if not destabilised, reduce research to a weak shadow of what it could potentially be. Around three months into my time in Batticaloa, I abandoned all sense of a timetable or specific research activities, and let my daily routine be set by my local family and the daily realities that happened around me. Based on what emerged at the time, my research began to find shape of its own, and direct me in ways that I had not initially expected or imagined. It also allowed me to recognise spaces and openings in the fabric of daily Batticaloa life, which I may have missed otherwise. While this did not necessarily reduce my anxiety about doing *real* research, and if anything it actually heightened my insecurities, it did mean that I was able to explore my own awareness and experiences in the field while allowing the awareness of those I was writing about to guide me.

Subsequently, where most people talk of their 'methods' of research, I regard the word 'tactics' as more relevant to the ways in which I dealt with the process of fieldwork. Where the former suggests orderly and systematic procedure, which can be designed before entering the field and followed through to an outcome, 'tactics' seems to allow space for malleability and flow according to the situation. De Certeau's (1984: 480) use of the idea of 'tactics' in contrast to 'strategy' describes ways in which everyday practices allow people to overcome their situations. He interprets a 'tactic' as something which 'insinuates itself into the other's place, fragmentarily, without taking it over in its entirety, without being able to keep it at a distance'. In this way, a tactic is interdependent on the context from which it emerges and relies upon opportunities presented in that moment; 'the place of the tactic belongs to the other' (ibid.). 'Strategy', on the other hand, is the outcome of 'force-relationships' and becomes possible when a subject of power can be isolated from an environment. My understanding of tactics is less tied to the idea of power than de Certeau implies. Rather than using tactics to manipulate events in order to turn them into opportunities, I regard them as working with what is at hand, and constantly adjusting to unanticipated events in order to deal with the changing realities of everyday life in a conflict environment.

Becoming in Batticaloa

While an increasing interest in the everyday nuances of conflict has made more visible the complexity of relationships and exchanges in the field, the position of the researcher has become even more ambiguous, and the shape of fieldwork less defined. In a collection of articles titled *Fieldwork under Fire*, Nordstrom and Robben (1996) explore some of the experiences and problems faced by ethnographers working in situations of violence. In demonstrating that violence is a cultural phenomenon, taught, remembered, transferred, exchanged, and mimicked within groups and across boundaries, they highlight the intersections of violence with 'expressions of everyday life' (ibid.: 6).

> For too many people everywhere in the world, violence is an all too human reality ... To understand their [the perpetrators] plight and to try to begin to

forge solutions, we must confront violence head on, place it squarely in the center of the lives and cultures of the people who suffer it, precisely where they themselves find it. (ibid.: 3)

By asking us to engage with all who are involved in violence, even those who are perpetrators, Nordstrom and Robben seek to put a human face to violence. Even those to whom we may have strong moral objections are seen in terms of their emotions and understandings rather than condemned by our own. 'It is this kind of confrontation', argues Mahmood (1996: 270), 'which is not only about "culture" but about lives and deaths, many of the borders around ourselves that we construct as ethnographers simply fall apart.' However, despite the new avenues explored by Nordstrom and Robben, their contribution has also left unanswered some fundamental questions about the methodology and ethics of doing fieldwork in violent places. They present the ethnographer, for example, as someone who, in skilfully moving between truth and lies, right and wrong, safety and risk, is unquestionably able to extract untainted and representative data from areas of violence.[3] In their introduction, Nordstrom and Robben (1996: 4) describe what they believe are the 'number of responsibilities' that anthropology, on the level of doing fieldwork under fire, involves, such as responsibility for one's own safety and the safety of one's informants. The issues they raise address strategies of survival and negotiation within a traditional framework of ethnographic research, which suggests that it is still possible to engage effectively with informants to elicit impartial data. While in some situations textbook ethnographic methods drawn from common sense – such as avoiding situations of military warfare, not putting interlocutors at risk, or misusing sensitive information – are useful, there are many times when things are far less clear, and previously learnt strategies of fieldwork can fall short. We do not always know what or where the violence to be confronted is. Knowing when to be silent and whom you can trust, for example, can be a vital part of coping in situations of extreme tension and violence, but is not an obvious methodological strategy (cf. Green 1995: 118–19, and this chapter, pages 78–81). Moreover, many contexts in which research takes place are not explicitly 'under fire' but rather comprise states of subtle everyday tension, and ebbs and flows of violence. Often, it is the burgeoning sense of anticipation and expectation of violence, the not-knowing and the silent questioning, rather than anything tangible, that weaves through a context of conflict. In such situations, how does one know how to find people who will talk, and learn the best tactics for surviving without unsettling or endangering the self or others? *Fieldwork under Fire* encourages recognition of all areas of violence, and advocates a closer reading of the perpetrators of violence, especially those whom we might feel uncomfortable with or repulsed by, in order to better understand the dynamics of violent contexts. However, I suggest that we perhaps need a more specific sense of how we might begin to do this in situations that are not cleanly divided into violence and non-violence, victim and perpetrator.

Belonging in Batticaloa

Being is thus not only a belonging but a becoming. (Jackson 2002: 13)

My sense of inclusion and ability to re-negotiate my research project largely relied upon people around me, and those to whom I turned for guidance and support.

I had previously met the family that I lived with on a visit for tsunami project work in the weeks after the disaster. Introduced to them by a friend with whom I was working, they invited me to stay with them until I was able to find suitable accommodation. Six months later, I was still there, and had been warmly welcomed as a part of their family. Although I was the youngest woman in the household, the majority of others, like me, were single and independent. While Anuloja, her husband, Rajan, and their young son, Selvam composed the nuclear unit of the household, the only thing that distinguished them from the rest of us was the fact that they slept in a different room, separated only by a flimsy curtain. The other family members included: Krishna (who had lived with Anuloja for over fifteen years), Ranjini (who was a few years older than me and had moved in a few months prior to my arrival), and for the first few months of my stay, Kamla (who had worked with Krishna in the past). Krishna's cousin, who was a student at the Eastern University, also stayed but slept and studied in the upstairs part of the house. When I first moved in, I was given a mattress to sleep on in a separate room on the second floor (as the family thought this would be more comfortable for me). This lasted for only a few weeks, however, as I soon found myself joining all the others downstairs, where we all slept together on mats, side by side in the cooler front area of the house. Although this meant I had little privacy and all sense of personal space pretty much disappeared, it also brought me much closer to the other family members and deepened our connection with one another. Often in the early hours of the morning, Selvam (the young son) would crawl, heavy with sleep, from the space where he slept with his parents, and curl up next to me for the last few hours of sleep. Once dawn broke, he would return to his mischievous questioning self, never giving me a moment's peace. However, for these precious few hours, his actions assured me that I was an accepted part of *his* family.

My ability to integrate into family life in Batticaloa was aided I believe by the fact that I was young (often assumed to be younger than I was) and, therefore, seen as needing support and care. I was happy to fill a role in the family as an older sister (*akkal*), and younger sister (*tankaicci*), daughter (*mahal*), and friend (*nanban*). People, especially women, would often express surprise and worry that my parents had allowed me to travel in Sri Lanka on my own, and, therefore, I acquired a plethora of surrogate *ammals* (mothers) desperate to take care of me. This enabled me to feel that I had a home in Sri Lanka while gaining a perspective on everyday life from a local family perspective. Yet, it was also the fact that I could never fully belong that allowed me insight. Being among many other women in the household meant also that I had the advantage and privilege of being able to access the intimacy of women's friendships and everyday lives.

Living and learning in Batticaloa 67

Incorporated into their world, I became involved in their activities, and party to their concerns and passions. My link to the *Valkai* group was also through the family, and this provided me with a space where I could watch, learn, and document in a way that I may not have been able to do had I joined the group from the outside. Jackson's sense of 'being', as drawn from Arendt's (1958) view of existence, articulates the importance of the web of connections and interactions that tie us to a particular context, permanently in flux. From this, we develop our own sense of being in relation to those around us, drawing from experiences past, which help to make sense of those in the present and future. As such, it was my various contexts in Sri Lanka, which set my experiences and sense of 'being' and 'becoming' at that time.

Being safe: ethical and moral issues

Living with people who worked on a daily basis to meet other people's needs and to listen to other people's stories meant I never felt it was my 'duty' to write. On the contrary, I actually found myself thinking that I should not write and that it should be left to those who knew the situation best, such as the *Valkai* members. This was partly because those around me were much better placed to write, given that it was their stories and their lives that needed to be told. Also, in seeing the little benefit and change that people experienced from any kind of writing (or relaying of stories to UN officials and others), I also questioned whether it was right to 'take' people's stories for my own purposes. Instead, I spent time encouraging those around me to document their experiences in hope that the women of the *Valkai* group and others would do for the east what Rajani Thiranagama and the University Teachers for Human Rights (Jaffna) had so courageously done in the north through their book, *The Broken Palmyrah* (1988), and regular reports and bulletins.[4] However, as Butalia (2000: 10) notes, '[f]or those caught in the maelstrom of the conflict, the business of living is much more important than that of writing'. That is, the immediacy of the fear and risk for people meant that people did not always have the luxury of space to stop and write, but instead had to concentrate on staying alive. In Batticaloa, documenting details and stories in writing could also be a risky business given that the army would regularly search houses or stop people at checkpoints. In the previous chapter, I highlighted the work of the Batticaloa Peace Committee and many other local scholars and activists who sought to publicise the situation in the east during the 1980 and 1990s and many who have continued to do so since. However, given the climate of intense risk and fear, it is also understandable that people have grown silent or sought other means by which to highlight the atrocities. Moreover, I noticed that in the east, it seemed that even if there was space to write, experiences were so intense that words often failed to capture the overwhelming grief and sorrow that seeped out from so many lives and stories. After a day of visiting families with the *Valkai* group, we would often return to the house, have a wash, drink tea, and eat dinner in silence. It was largely a comfortable silence, but it was also burdened with the unspoken emotions of other people's suffering and loss. At such times, these small rituals and chores played an integral part of coping with the intense and, often, fractured experiences of daily life in a conflict zone. Watching over the other women as they worked or slept late in the evenings, I quickly came to understand why writing was not a part of their daily lives.

It is equally important to highlight the fact that while those around me occupied spaces of considerable risk, they also provided me with a sense of security and safety upon which I became dependent, and which may have, in turn, increased their own vulnerabilities. Knowing how to operate in a landscape of different and rapidly changing boundaries and spaces meant that my ethical basis, or the grounds from which I attempted to make sense of my position, was equally contingent on the boundaries and spaces of the particular social context within which I moved. In many ways, this was one of the hardest realities in the field for me: that there was no room for heroics or grand gestures, even when meant well. Learning to live in Batticaloa with a group of people engaged in human rights work meant that I not only saw first-hand the ways in which people were managing, but became aware of the many complex issues that people faced – issues which rendered ideas of simply helping or 'empowering' people (a common term associated with NGOs) as naive and misguided. Moreover, I also became acutely aware of the extent to which I relied on others for protection and support, and, therefore, found that in my social context, I was like a child learning how to conduct myself in a new and strange environment. In this environment of conflict, however, small mistakes could cost lives.

Writing 'against terror'

Given the context of risk and violence in Batticaloa, the ethical position that I embraced is far more complex than being able to simply claim to take a moral and ethical stand 'against terror' (Sluka 2000: 12). While there has been an overall reluctance of anthropologists to take a critical, let alone activist or political stance *vis-à-vis* the communities and events concerned, an increasing number have supported the emerging 'anthropology of state terror' (ibid.: 13). This, Sluka argues, takes the form of 'a relevant and politically engaged anthropology that observes, witnesses, and records, but also seeks to confront, expose, and oppose human rights abuses'. Building on the call by Nancy Scheper-Hughes (1995) for anthropology to take a more extreme militant position, and arguing for a politically committed, morally engaged, and ethically grounded anthropology, Sluka (2000: 13) argues that anthropologists, who write against terror, 'step outside the boundaries of standard anthropological practice'. However, where Scheper-Hughes argues that 'cultural relativism, read as moral relativism, is no longer appropriate to the world in which we live, and anthropology, if it is to be worth anything at all, must be ethically grounded' (1995: 409), I want to question exactly what ethical grounds are being supported. As attractive as the notions of 'politically committed' and 'morally engaged anthropology' sound, in reality the questions of which politics we are supposed to be committed to and which morals we must engage with make any practice of such anthropology far messier than implied. As Hallisey (2010) suggests, the large-scale challenges of investigating the diverse and ambiguous moral cultures and ethical traditions of South Asia take us far beyond what we might comfortably and conventionally call ethics or morality. Emphasising the discrepancy that can exist between our own understandings, whether taken from our Euro-centric perspective or extracted from the cultural contexts of South Asia, and the scope of our new environments, Hallisey's subtle argument provides a sensitive and realistic structure. This stands in stark comparison to the militant and more fixed position postulated by Scheper-Hughes, Sluka, and others who vociferously call for anthropologists to 'write back against terror' (Taussig 1987: 4). Hallisey suggests that research should consider the connection between different conceptions of ethics, while keeping the differences in tension to allow for a kind of theoretical ethics that is implied by the gap between what we feel should be done and what actually is done in the story. In other words, there is a need for a 'moral creativity' that goes beyond simple language and conceptual categories to 'achieve a desired ethical end when one is living with and for others'.

Placed within a context such as Batticaloa, where politics of any kind is entangled with risk, Hallisey's argument speaks more closely to an environment where stepping out of line and making explicit one's opinions are aspects of everyday life that cannot be toyed with and negotiated. To put one's head too far above the parapet in Batticaloa equals certain danger and possible death. The moral creativity, therefore, is hinged upon a grasp of how far one can go and in what situations. In examining and learning from local strategies, strategies for an ethical and moral approach can be adopted, and, thus, to adhere to the practices of a specific social context is to recognise those spaces of overlapping control and subversion. This does not imply sitting back and watching the violence unfold without comment or intervention. Instead, it means to look for the implicit, intricate, and intimate spaces through which people connect and make change. Such spaces are not only the underlying focus of this book but also define the way in which I was able to carry out research into the lives and active living of those with whom I moved in Batticaloa.

Social relationships and negotiating identity

Learning to identify threat and live with fear were dual lessons that were enlightening for me in terms of understanding the situation but also frightening given that there were no specific guidelines and you had to rely on your own sense and understanding in the moment. The fear that builds up with the threat of violence cannot be underestimated; like a dramatic thunderstorm that follows increasing humidity, only the anticipated outcome was not always a relief but far more tragic and final. At times, I found myself wishing something would actually happen, if just break the mounting tension. In such situations, every movement and noise would be interpreted in terms of violence and threat. One particular afternoon, for example, Krishna and I were in the kitchen when we heard loud banging noises coming from outside. Thinking these were gunshots, we both crept quietly out of the house, our minds invaded with thoughts of what might be happening and what we should do. Tentatively moving across the compound, we arrived at the gate and peered out only to find two men loading bricks onto a cart, each brick landing with an explosive bang. It was more relief than our own foolishness that saw us collapse into fits of laughter in the garden sand. This was one of many situations, which, although ultimately amusing, induced fear that was not quick to leave us, and that edgy feeling was something that would follow me around for days at a time. There were also many times when I was caught off guard, to be left feeling extremely vulnerable.

One incident was when a claymore mine exploded just a few minutes after I had passed under the tree where it hung. Looking back over my shoulder as I struggled to keep my balance on my bike following the blast, I had seen a number of soldiers on the ground and watched as civilians scattered in every direction. Another occurred when I was crossing the main town bridge, again on my bicycle. Here I became trapped between an army truck and a 'buffel' armoured vehicle – both were stationary, leaving little room for me to get past. Knowing that mines and grenades were being targeted at army vehicles at that time, I knew this was a precarious and frightening situation to be in, and the faces of those around me also seemed to mirror my fear. Desperate to get away I was unable to move past the vehicles for about ten minutes.

In both situations, I was extremely lucky not to get caught by any direct impact of the violence. As Sluka (1995) suggests, such luck in settings of political violence should not be underappreciated. Yet, the situations also revealed to me the vulnerabilities of life in Batticaloa and the extent to which circumstance can overtake you and induce much fear.

Insider–outsider

Given the context of the post-tsunami rush of international aid and the influx of foreigners working for INGOs and NGOs, when I first arrived in Batticaloa I spent a lot of time trying to differentiate myself from others and establish my identity. Trying to understand my 'insider–outsider positionalities' (Pickering 2001: 492) meant, for me, confronting many of the complexities of fitting into multiple roles and contexts. This dilemma was captured in an amusing encounter with a curious old man in the street in Batticaloa:

> Old man: 'Which international agency are you with?'
> Me: 'I'm not with any international agency.'
> Old man: 'Which local NGO do you work for?'
> Me: 'I don't work for a local NGO.'
> Old man: 'Which church are you here with?'

And so it went on with the old man working through all the various groups in the area until he finally asked, somewhat exasperated and baffled 'Why *are* you here?' This was a question I struggled to answer a number of times. In many situations, I was not sure how to present myself, or what my role was. I was aware that in a highly fragmented and violent field, assuming a particular identity in certain situations could be a practical necessity. At the same time, I knew that any association with one particular group could have meant that I was bracketed in certain ways that would close the door on many other associations and networks. My aim was to talk to as many people in the field as possible and hear voices from all sides; as such, I did not want my association with one group to hinder my chances of connecting with others. Equally, however, I did not want to spread myself so thin as to prevent strong relationships forming between others and myself. Therefore, at times I felt I had to negotiate multiple identities, to allow different relationships to form in different situations. The strength of relationships formed and the levels of trust created within them were essential to my research, and to living in Batticaloa more generally.

Being a part of the *Valkai* group brought me into contact with many different groups and individuals that I might not have ordinarily been able to so easily meet with. Alongside the groups of mothers whose children had been recruited, fathers who had been detained by the armed forces or were ex-militants, and children who had escaped from the LTTE, I also met with army officials, LTTE commanders, and members of the TMVP and other Tamil militant groups. Most often, in these encounters I was there as a background figure, observing and listening to what was being exchanged, although obviously the colour of my skin meant that whatever I did I stood out. However, my intention was that I did not meet one-on-one with any armed actors – my focus lay with those who were trying to work against violence and whose ability to do so relied on the very fragile relationships they held or negotiated in some way with armed state and non-state actors. When approached by any militants – LTTE, TMVP or government forces – I would play up my role as a 'tsunami volunteer' as this was largely seen as a role that was 'apolitical' (for foreigners, at least) in the first year after the tsunami. Given the number of foreigners who had flooded into Batticaloa to do tsunami work, it was mostly assumed that I was working on a tsunami project anyway (as the conversation with the old man demonstrated). In my everyday exchanges in shops, buses, and checkpoints, I would mostly draw on this volunteer identity; however, where possible, I preferred to emphasise my long-term commitment to the area and willingness to be with local people rather than the expatriate community exclusively. Whether this conscious selection of identities in the public sphere meant I was being dishonest with people constantly concerned me. However, it reflected a reality that in order to live and survive in the east, I needed to work with what was appropriate to different situations at different times, and to always try and minimise the risk to others and myself. This presented an ongoing dilemma: if I were fully committed to ethical considerations at all times, as some research guidelines suggest, it follows that I should inform all participants and people with whom I interacted of my research. I should also ask for informed consent. In reality, however, it was impossible to draw a clear line between those who were my participants and those with whom I participated in daily life. I would also be expecting people to be able to trust me in a climate of mistrust and suspicion, as well as take huge risks to talk to me.

Therefore, in trying to sensitively manage the situation, I decided that provided my interlocutors were aware of my research, and particularly that those close to me felt comfortable and secure in the knowledge of what I was doing, I was taking the most appropriate course of action in a confusing and constantly changing environment. I also needed to remain alert to the fact that, although at the onset of research, participants can be made fully aware of the researcher's role, they can also quickly forget and lose a sense of due guardedness. This is especially so in the case of long-term research that involves living in the context you are studying and being a part of everyday life. In light of this, I had to be careful in terms of what conversations and information I recorded and how the family might distinguish their private information from that to which I had access. The family themselves helped me in this process by stating which information was to 'go no further' because of personal and security implications (themselves being acutely aware of the risks of talking openly).

Ties that bind

On many levels, I was always working at social relations in Batticaloa and my awareness of my gender and colour, of being an unmarried white woman in a militarised-masculine, local (and therefore 'foreign') setting was heightened as I became more conscious of how and where I fitted in. This was influenced by the extent to which I felt secure within a given setting and the support and understanding I received from those around me. Yet, I also lacked control over the ways in which my femaleness and foreignness defined me and limited my subjectivity; they prevented certain social relationships from developing and creating meaning. Where my gender joined me to the women with whom I lived, for example, my identity as foreigner marked me out as separate. Meanwhile, my colour and outsider status aligned me with the INGO actors, while my place of residence and the local network within which I moved meant that I was outside of the expatriate scene, which was explicitly divided from the local way of life.[5]

The fact that I was embedded in a largely female world in Batticaloa and that most of my relationships were formed through their networks may have reduced my ability to move amongst male-dominated environments and to be accepted by men in their contexts. The perspectives of most of the women that I lived and worked with in the *Valkai* group were largely influenced by a critical feminist stance, which had been shaped by – and, in turn, shaped – their everyday life in Batticaloa and their understanding of the masculine nature of militarisation (see, for example, Connell 2002). Although I maintained friendships with a number of men, either through personal contact or through my research, the amount of attention I received, generally from the opposite sex, brought the focus back to my identity as a female, and, particularly, as a white female, in an unfamiliar and militarised setting. This meant that I had to be guarded and suspicious of gestures of friendship, and this made it much more difficult to trust men than women. It took the father of my local family to come out with me on our bicycles late one night to realise the extent of the attention and abuse I received from local boys. In the darkness of the small lanes and roads, he observed from behind, the groups of young males gathered on the street corners calling out, whooping, and cat-calling whilst making 'kissy kissy' noises to attract my attention. As mild as this heckling was, the fact that my gender and body transformed me into an object of scrutiny and optic appropriation was challenging and, at times, threatening.

A gendered gaze

In many situations, it was a sense of being objectified rather than being able to form subjective relationships based on more equal terms that held me back. While I had been advised to be friendly and cooperative at checkpoints, I worried that friendliness would be misinterpreted and give out the wrong signals. Often I would overhear vulgar comments being made by soldiers who did not know that I could understand a fair amount of Sinhalese, and, thanks to my teenage students in the south in 1998, I had a vast repertoire of the suggestive language often used by men. My reluctance to be friendly was also caused by the fact that at times I actually felt very angry and hostile towards the army. Spending most of my time with women whose lives were negatively affected by the militarisation of everyday life and knowing of the vast number of atrocities that had been committed by government forces and the IPKF especially, I struggled to put my feelings aside when face-to-face with soldiers. And, yet, I knew that it was important to do so, not only because hostility could often raise suspicion and cause the soldiers to prolong checking, but also because I needed to remain attentive to forming positive relationships in case I needed help from them in the future (see pages 79–80). How I presented myself, regardless of how I was perceived, was crucial for present and future negotiation of violent contexts.

Even though I usually dressed conservatively in shalwar kameez, I felt that I could not escape the sexual gaze of many of the uniformed men who stood about along the roads and at checkpoints.[6] This was more of a problem with government soldiers, whom I came into contact with more regularly (due to the overt presence on the roads at checkpoints and army camps) than the LTTE or other armed cadre. One of the tactics of the LTTE and TMVP in distinguishing itself from the government forces was to offer security and protection of women through linking moral purity in the broader ideology of the LTTE with Tamil culture. This was shown in stark contrast to the Sinhala army who became the 'source of cultural-moral corruption via sexual violence, liquor, pornography, and prostitution' (Tambiah 2005: 248). Within LTTE-controlled areas, the prohibition of rape and other forms of sexual violence, prostitution, pornography, domestic violence, and abuse of alcohol served to offer a 'partial sense of safety' (ICG 2011b: 6). Yet, it has also been pointed out that much of the LTTE's puritanical streak was for public consumption, and the lack of evidence and reports of abuses, including rape of women, does not mean that they were absent within LTTE-controlled areas (see Wood 2009).[7] Where the LTTE and the TMVP used the image of the promiscuous and immoral Western woman as an example and warning of corruption in their culture, many in the army seemed to thrive on the kind of ideas this type of woman represented.

One incident that powerfully captures my identity and vulnerability as a woman *vis-à-vis* men in a conflict environment involved a soldier deliberately masturbating while pointing his AK47 at me. This occurred when I was out on a visit with Anuloja and Krishna to meet a mother whose child had been forcibly taken by the LTTE. While Anuloja and Krishna were taking down details from the woman, tucked behind the door in the dingy shade of the hut, I was sitting in the opening making notes in my field diary. The hut was situated on an isolated strip of land, mostly overtaken by an army camp, which had encroached on the woman's land and hid her from the view of the main road. Clumsy bundles of razor wire trailed across the parched soil and a large well stood on the border between the woman's land and the army camp. As I was surveying my surroundings, a man emerged from behind the well. His camouflage trousers and heavy black boots told me he was in the army and most probably from the camp beside us. In the glare of the afternoon sun, the only visible bodies were my own and the soldier – mine in my blue shalwar and shawl, his stripped naked to the waist. Locking his eyes with mine, he quickly dropped his trousers and began to masturbate. All the while, his AK47 remained tucked under his left arm, the barrel along with his eyes framing me in its vision. The urgency and roughness of his actions did not seem pre-meditated and yet he knew that no one else could see him. He also knew that I was aware of this and that power was on his side; he was armed, I was not, and, moreover, he had not physically touched me. Therefore, I had nothing tangible with which to react and resist.

By the time I had alerted Anuloja and Krishna, who were locked in intense discussion with the mother, the soldier had disappeared. Trying to explain what had just taken place seemed futile, and knowing the extent of the abuse and violations local women faced I felt guilty for making an issue of an incident in which something and nothing had taken place. In fact, after writing about the incident in my field diary that night, I filed the experience away alongside many other uncomfortable memories of my time in Batticaloa and did not return to it until I was back in the UK. Yet, the reality was that this incident had disturbed and frightened me. It had sharpened my awareness of my femaleness and foreignness, which in light of the incident had translated into vulnerability and weakness. While I cannot know what was going through the soldier's mind at the time, what seemed clear was that he performed a deliberate act that took advantage of a vulnerable situation of power inequality. Furthermore, I can assume that a mixture of lust, frustration, and desire fuelled this encounter, capturing the intense and potentially explosive climate of power, dominance, sexual repression, perversion, and violence that can build up in situations of warfare and which defines the relationship between those who hold guns and those without. This type of relationship is reflective of warfare – powerful men, and powerless women (where power is defined here by the ability to commit violence); men as perpetrators, women as victims (Segal 1999). Yet, the ambiguous nature of this encounter, the interpretation and the anticipation of violence, which was caught in a context of potentiality emphasised the confusion which can invade certain spaces and the unclear boundaries which mark out everyday life.

My intention here is not to draw parallels between my experience with Sri Lankan women and the greater story of the many atrocities of abuse, rape, and murder committed against local women, particularly by the army and IPKF (as detailed throughout this book and particularly in Meena's story in Chapter 5). Yet, what I want to illustrate to a small degree is the powerlessness and fear felt when objectified by the male gaze in a conflict situation. This also highlights how in terms of my own identity, the window through which I was primarily framed differed to that of local woman on the basis of my colour and all that it implied. Furthermore, where previously I had encountered many of the problems that women, local and foreign, face in Sri Lanka in terms of male attention, what I confronted in Batticaloa felt much more specific to an environment of masculinised military power and my insider–outsider position.

Child's play

Another way in which I was able to form relationships and develop understanding of Batticaloa life was through the various family members that I lived with. In particular, living with a six-year-old boy provided a sense of family responsibility, which intensified through the months that I lived with Selvam. At first wary of, and at times angry towards the white woman who was welcomed into his home, Selvam and I grew very close over time. Being the youngest two in the household (despite nineteen years difference) there was a special bond between us, possibly because I was often looked after as one of the younger ones, and also because I worked flexible hours and so had more free time to spend playing with him. As such, Selvam grew to trust me and to rely on me in situations where previously he would have only turned to his parents or one of the other women in the house. I also found that the needs and demands of a child often diffused tense situations and created humour and fun where it may otherwise have been lacking. I first met Selvam just after the tsunami, and although he played and shouted around, it was clear that, like many other children in Sri Lanka, he had been deeply unsettled and shaken by the natural disaster. In the months following, Selvam was extremely anxious, and whatever he was doing, whether it was playing with other children or watching television, he would call out to his *amma* every five minutes. If she called back, he would carry on playing, but if she did not reply first time, he would run to find her. This seemed to be a reaction to the amount of fear the tsunami had created and especially to witnessing his parents being frightened, which for a child can have a powerful effect on their sense of security and levels of trust. Daya Somasundaram (2007: 27), a Sri Lankan psychiatrist who worked for many years as a lecturer and practitioner of psychiatry in Jaffna in the 1980s and 1990s, noted the submissive posture (for example, 'removal of hat, bent head and body, low and almost pleading tone of voice') adopted by parents when accosted by the security forces at checkpoints in Sri Lanka. He identified this as causing children to lose faith in their parents due to the fact that children see their parents as powerless rather than understanding that such acts are tactics learnt in order to protect their children. In a similar way, Selvam seemed to lose faith in his parents' ability to look after him in his everyday environment, which during the tsunami had been turned upside down. It took him a long time to learn to trust his parents again, as well as trust a new member of the family.

Being around a child, therefore, enabled me to see the ways in which youth, particularly young males, in Batticaloa react and deal with the violence around them. I was often particularly intrigued by Selvam's reactions to the militarisation that surrounded us. I would watch his face carefully as we passed checkpoints, armed cadres, and places of destruction. His mother told me that when he was a small child he had once noted, at a checkpoint, that the gun the soldier was carrying made him look as if he was playing a violin. Later on, however, a noticeable shift took place when he pointed out a statue to me in the cathedral grounds and claimed that the small object the saint was carrying was a grenade. Selvam was always full of questions – most were the regular why, what and how that any young child asks. Others, however, were more disturbing: 'What would happen if I put a rocket in your head and blew you up?' was a favourite, along with 'How many bits does a human body break into if hit by a shell?' More poignant was when he asked his father '*Appa*, why does everybody that we love die?' His father, who was cycling at the time with Selvam sitting in front of him over the handlebars, was taken aback and tried to give an answer that not everyone died and that it was to do with the tragedy of war. However, Selvam had twisted around to look into his father's eyes and said, 'In that case, I think everyone should be put together and shot now so that we don't lose people one by one.' While such comments highlight the influence of everyday violence on a child's perception and understanding, what interested me were Selvam's openness, and the sense of security he must have felt in asking me such questions and trusting me as a family member. This illustrates the extent to which we became connected and formed ties that bound us together in this context.

Permeable boundaries between self and other

The fact that I experienced first hand a number of significant events, such as the shelling campaign in 2007 and the tsunami, seemed to connect me to people in a way that conversations and interactions could not. The experiences of the tsunami waves, the peppering of fear in town, and the folding away of feelings that could not be immediately dealt with were strung out like thick threads, stitching us together through shared emotions. At the same time, by the nature of their unfamiliarity to me, many of these events also loosened that thread and separated me from others, especially where relationships were thin, and support, therefore, limited. Although my experiences were connected to, and shared with those around me, my physical and emotional reactions were individual, and often cast light upon the difference between others and myself. Tied in with my concerns about how I did my research, what the point of it was, and the weight of decision-making, my emotional world was at times difficult to manage. That I had a sense of the anxieties and fears of people in Batticaloa in one way meant I felt closer and more in tune with those around me. In another, it revealed the very different perceptions that non-locals may have of any given situation, which, therefore, enabled me to analyse reflexively the difference between those who live through violence on a long-term basis and those who step into that experience for a temporary period of time. Further, the temporariness of my experience, and the knowledge that I could leave at any time, often left me with feelings of relief, guilt, and shame.

Counting the loses

Although many experiences during my research were positive and enjoyable, a number were difficult and, occasionally, tragic, as might be expected in a place of conflict. In Vavuniya, in the early months of my fieldwork, one of the young women called Kaavya, working for the local NGO to which I was attached, committed suicide. Although I had not known her that long, Kaavya and I had been pushed together on the basis that we were a similar age, shared interests, and both wanted to improve our language skills in Tamil and English, respectively. Kaavya worked at a special needs school run by the NGO, and her brightness and enthusiasm had kept me motivated in the early days of my arrival. However, this exterior happiness clearly hid something darker underneath, for she filled her pockets with heavy rocks and jumped into the deep well on the farm where the NGO was based in early 2005. By the time her body was dragged up with a length of barbed wire, she had been dead for a number of hours.

Kaavua's death marked the beginning of a bitter dispute between the two heads of the NGO, which in its final stages saw the organisation split into two. Although I tried to stay neutral, and managed to do so mainly due to my move to the east, the death of my friend, and the arguments that followed affected me more than I was able to acknowledge at the time. The grief that everyone felt both separated and brought us closer together. A few weeks before her death, I had interviewed the Child Protection Officer (CPO) in Vavuniya who had talked me through the facts and figures for the suicide rates in the region. Most were among young people, and effected through drinking pesticides, ingesting yellow oleander seeds (*alari*), and jumping into wells.[8] At the time, these statistics were shocking but remained unreal. It was not until my friend died that they gained a reality beyond the pages of the CPO's notebook. Although I had encountered death both inside and outside of Sri Lanka, this situation still took me by surprise, especially as it started a series of tragedies and losses that I experienced in Sri Lanka. In January 2006, for example, another suicide happened. This time it was a friend of mine that I had spent time with in Sri Lanka over the summer of 2002. She died in the UK, but the news reached me quickly in Batticaloa because it transgressed that my local family knew her through her mother who was a fellow feminist activist. It was only through her death that I discovered this connection, and, as a result, we were able to support one another and make sense of this tragic experience in the light of shared understandings. Together we held a small memorial ceremony, lighting candles and sharing memories. In the days following her death, one of the women also started to open up to me, telling me about the suicide of her brother, and how she and her family had coped since. Therefore, unlike Kaavya's death in Vavuniya, this time I was able to talk through the experience, learn from my family, and also contextualise their links with activism, and personal experiences of loss.

Given the intense environment in which I was living, people both in Sri Lanka and outside with whom I had contact regularly suggested that I leave the east and return to the capital for a while. While I generally ignored such advice, I did try and keep options open for leaving if and when necessary. I also took occasional breaks in Colombo to escape the intensity of Batticaloa life. However, I noticed that the longer I stayed in the east, the harder I found it to extricate myself from the relationships and ties I felt there. In fact, some of my loneliest times during fieldwork were spent in Colombo and there were few moments, even when in the south, that I was able to disconnect and switch off from the violence. Decisions such as to whether to leave and the many others that I faced during fieldwork caused anxiety and aroused feelings of inadequacy and guilt, which stayed with me long after I left the field. Primo Levi (1988) speaks of the 'grey zone' in narrating the stories of concentration camp inmates who were often forced into mutual betrayal and complicity with the enemy in exchange for the smallest favours. While not intending to compare life in Batticaloa to survival in a concentration camp, the 'grey zone' of making decisions to protect oneself, sometimes at the expense of others, was very real. Therefore, I suggest that it is in the acknowledgement of feelings such as fear, the pain of loss and guilt, that knowledge and experience can be brought together to create a more intimate sense of life in the field.

Learning to know what not to know

Knowing whom I could talk to, how, and why were important issues that framed my research on a daily basis. Given that my intention was to listen to what people could tell me about their experiences of living through a conflict and how their lives had been shaped, this was something I could not escape and which I had to deal with sensitively and in relation to the shifting contexts around me. Early on in my research, Krishna, one of the women I lived with told me: 'People are scared of what will happen if they speak, but scared if they don't.' This in many ways encapsulated the dilemma I faced – I wanted people to talk to me because I had started to recognise the importance of documenting stories and giving people the space to talk, and, yet, in doing so, I could risk exacerbating people's fear and endangering lives. And I found that, at times, people would talk continuously, running over their words and leaving me to try and piece them together, whereas, at others, they would say nothing, their suffocating silences filling the room. Overall, however, I found that people wanted to talk to me. They wanted a chance to tell their story, and they wanted me to hear how it was from their perspective.

Silences, whispers, rumours, and gossip were all part of the social practices of living and enduring in Batticaloa in which bonds of intimacy and claims to knowledge were intertwined with risk and protecting the self. Although people told me that since the ceasefire they felt more able to talk and share information – and the stories shared with me certainly testified to this – at the same time, the increasing levels of violence and fear meant that conversations and activity were punctuated with gaps of silence and secrecy as the learned language of survival. Lawrence notes that in the 1990s people had to 'unlearn' normal reactions; for example, not responding to the cries from a neighbouring house for fear of surveillance. She states that Batticaloa has become a region of vulnerability to annihilation, where psychological effects of political oppression manifest in 'silencing' and sometimes denial, in learning not to speak and to know what not to know (Lawrence 1999: 198). Silences, therefore, were endemic in Batticaloa, and silence emerged both as a protective strategy, and, conversely, as a strategy by which suffering was intensified. The monitoring and silence around violence from all sides formed a tactic of, and a response to, violence, where the threat could be as powerful as the lived experience (see Galtung 1996). This was reflected also in the experiences of a woman I met in 2005, who was living deep within the border area. She described to me the night she had to sit in the dark behind a locked door as she listened to the cries of her husband and his friend who had been shot while guarding a storehouse nearby. Knowing the extent of the risks involved in going outside and being seen near her husband, she had to wait until morning before she could go to him. By that time, the friend was dead and her husband paralyzed. Enforced silence, therefore, separated her from her husband in a moment when he needed her the most and prevented her from acting on natural instincts and desires.

Strategic silence

In open spaces, and particularly public gatherings and meetings, very little could be said. When visiting a police station to try and ascertain information about the detention of four young men, I was warned by Anuloja to stay quiet and not talk back to the officer that we were dealing with. At the time I felt angry with Anuloja as the officer berated and taunted me by saying, 'Your country has terrorist problems so you should know what we have to deal with' and, 'Why do you British always feel sympathy for the Tamil terrorists?' Moreover, he tried to convince me that all local Tamils were members of the LTTE and, therefore, could not be trusted. During the time he talked I was waiting for Anuloja to put him straight, tell him that she had been working with the local communities for years, had dealt with hundreds of cases of unlawful detentions and especially torture, and, therefore, knew what the police were up to. However, much to my surprise, she remained silent, even deferential to the officer. Once we were outside the station and at a safe enough distance to talk, I asked Anuloja through a haze of frustration and sadness why she had not said anything. Her reply set me straight:

>(I)f I had talked back to him there would have been trouble. I might have got him angry and he would have been suspicious of you and me. You have to think about the future, Becky – we might need his help and if I had upset him, now that would never happen.

This was one of my earliest and most vital lessons in learning to self-censor and to remain silent in tense and volatile situations. Where the naive but impassioned defender of human rights in me had wanted to speak my mind, I had been forced to recognise the value of remaining silent and swallowing words in light of future possibilities. More significantly, I could also have put others at risk as well as endangering myself. This difficult experience revealed one of the many fragile paths that people have to negotiate in order to survive in Batticaloa.

Embodied silence

There was also much to be learnt from what people did not say and other forms of communication beyond even silences. For example, one man had agreed to talk with me about his experiences of being arrested and detained by the armed forces during the 1990s, yet for the whole hour that we sat together he barely said more than a few words. However, while we sat in awkward silence and he fidgeted in the heat, scratching at his arms and legs, he revealed a series of deep scars burrowed into the skin of his ankles and wrists. In our frozen exchange, therefore, his body told me far more than any words or even silence could.

On another occasion, I was waiting for a friend in Batticaloa hospital when a middle-aged woman was half carried, half dragged into the emergency room, and placed on a bed at the other end of the ward. Curtains were quickly drawn around her by a busying group of nurses, but this could not disguise her moans and cries. Through a gap in the curtains, I saw her body writhing on the bed. The skin looked like it had been badly burnt and was falling from her body. Outside the curtain, three young men lingered. A young nurse, drowned in an oversized but neat white uniform with white ankle socks and shoes was sitting at a large wooden desk by the door. In a notebook, she recorded the particulars of each of the patients in the room, detailing their injuries and treatment. I kept catching her eye as the woman behind the curtain wailed. As I had left the hospital, I paused by the desk and nodding towards the other side of the room asked the nurse if the woman would be alright. 'She has burns', was the simple reply. The following day I returned to the hospital with a friend to see if we could find out more about this woman, and, if possible, help. We went back to the emergency room where I had seen the woman the day before, and Krishna explained to the nurse on duty why we were there and that I wanted to check on how this woman was doing. The nurse checked the notebook and looked back at me, face blank. '*Illae*' (No), she stated, '*Inku ondrum illae*' (There is nothing here). The nurse I had seen the previous day was also in the room and I asked Krishna to explain to her why I had come back. Again we received a blank look, 'If it is not in the book she was not here', she told Krishna. The denial of the woman's body – its absence despite my having seen it behind the curtain, the lack of notes and recognition from the nurses – thus meant that she did not exist in certain terms. Going by what local sources told us, it is likely that the Karuna party had beaten the woman, and that the boys that I saw outside the curtain were TMVP cadres keeping watch. It is also likely that they insisted that no record be made of this woman and her injuries. Although much has been written about the difficulties of grieving and finding closure when bodies are absent and fates unknown (see Dorfman 1983; Perera 1995), it is hard to know how we approach the subject of living bodies that exist, yet are denied.[9] While this tells us something about the control of spaces and bodies, and how they are manipulated, it also leaves gaps where one feels the need for answers and action.

Comprehending everyday life

Stories such as the one above, which reveal the shifts, challenges, and, often, the confusion (of the self and other) in research, remind us of the kinds of questions that do not go away. Questions such as whether we should be there (as researchers in the field) in the first place, what our presence means to those around us, and, as asked by Krishna at the start of this chapter, what is the *point* of writing after an event has happened rather than trying 'to do something *at the time*'? As this chapter has illustrated, despite being able to anticipate a number of the practical difficulties I would face in the field, I could never have imagined the shape of some of the events that took place. Moreover, I certainly did not anticipate the centrality and importance of such challenges (and the opportunities they created in their wake) to the overall process and shape of my research and the insight gained. Having to face the tsunami and escalating violence, and engage with the practical and ethical questions that both engendered undoubtedly enriched my ability to better comprehend and question the everyday life that I had entered.

In the next chapter, I take notions of the everyday and the ordinary as the driving concepts to explore how ethnographic studies have tended to write people's lives into fixed dichotomies of victims and agents – those that succumb to the devastation of conflict and those that survive. Following on from an understanding of my own experiences *vis-a-vis* life in Batticaloa, I consider how the 'everyday life' of civilians might be interpreted and understood. I ask questions about the meaning of the concept of the everyday, and what the apparent disjuncture between theoretical meaning and 'lived realities' can tell us about experiences of daily life. Furthermore, I consider what is meant by an *ordinary life* in an area of conflict where violence is woven into the fabric of the everyday but also where the violence is not the *only* part of the everyday.

Notes

1 This is not to suggest that valuable work was not done. Many organisations such as Amnesty International and the International Crisis Group worked hard to corroborate information and publish reports that revealed the reality of life in the north and east.

However, very often the government (and previously the LTTE) has opted to ignore or deny the reports, thus burying valuable information and stories.

2 A criticism commonly levied against post-modernist ideas of anthropology (see Spencer 1989: 161).

3 In an earlier volume also co-edited by Nordstrom, the anthropologist is presented even more boldly as a researcher who is, by virtue of the ethnographic method, able to capture experience and reflect upon it through the use of theory in the writing process (Nordstrom and Martin 1992: 5).

4 The work of UTHR(J) came to a standstill after the murder of Rajani Thiranagama, and during the course of 1990 the others who identified openly with the UTHR(J) were forced to leave Jaffna; however, until very recently they continued to write reports on current issues relating to the conflict under the same name.

5 A particular social scene for expatriate workers had built up in the aftermath of the tsunami as more foreigners moved into the east. When I had first arrived in Batticaloa I had felt it necessary to decide which world to be a part of – the local world of everyday needs and interests or the INGO world of social activities and relationships. Given the common bad feeling and rumours that spread about expatriate workers, I was nervous about being judged and labelled as part of that world.

6 A shalwar kameez is a loose-fitting form of dress, consisting of a long tunic and loose trousers, which is comfortable and conceals the female shape.

7 In her research into why certain militant groups do not engage in widespread rape, Elizabeth Wood (2009) focuses specifically on the Tamil Tigers and the apparent rarity of sexual violence against civilians. Wood concludes that this can be explained by the strict code of conduct amongst Tigers within a hierarchical framework where draconian forms of punishment are meted out to those who deviate in behaviour. Wood's analysis, however, seems to be based upon the lack of reports of sexual violence in the mainstream and amongst human rights activists rather than taken from interaction with women living in LTTE-controlled areas themselves (which given the lack of access and widespread fear to speak against the Tigers is understandable).

8 The ingestion of yellow oleander seeds is a well-known cause of death, and, more recently, is reported to have become a popular method of self-harm in northern Sri Lanka. Research in 1995 found that there are thousands of cases each year, and a hospital in Anuradapura recorded that the majority of cases of oleander poisoning were amongst women and almost half amongst them were under twenty-one (Eddleson, M. *et al.* 1999: 266).

9 Ariel Dorfman's *Widows* (1983) is perhaps one of the most powerful stories of women's struggle to name and reclaim the bodies of their loved ones, taken away and never returned in an environment of political oppression and impunity.

4

Between violence and the everyday: questions of the ordinary

'Suyal nilamai' (the situation)

In the sweltering midday heat of a bright day in March 2007, my friend, Anuloja, and I sat outside a makeshift shelter talking with a family who had recently been displaced from their home. The family had set up their shelter on deserted scrubland, away from the main road, edging onto the barricaded borders of a sprawling government army camp. The area where the family were camped was littered with half-buried coils of razor wire. Scrawny flea-ridden dogs lazed in the shade of the trees raising themselves only to growl threateningly at approaching strangers. Washed sarongs and sheets had been hung across a rope suspended between a mango tree and one of the wooden poles holding up the shelter; clay pots sat outside drying in the sun. A few weeks earlier, fighting between the Sri Lankan forces and LTTE had significantly increased following a build up in tensions and hostility. The army had embarked on what they termed 'clearing' of the east, aiming to drive the LTTE out of their strongholds in the border areas, as described in the previous chapters. This campaign took the form of heavy shelling, which not only scattered the LTTE, but thousands of families too as they fled their homes and villages, fearing for their safety. Although displacement through conflict had become a frequent and familiar part of the lives of people in the north and east of Sri Lanka, this was the largest movement of people since the 1990s.

It was just after Anuloja and I had removed our sandals and settled down with the family on woven mats in the shade of a leafy mango tree that the shelling started. The first shell rocketed over our heads and others followed in quick succession. In those few seconds, the ground beneath us shook violently and the noise was deafening. It felt like time had stopped and space seemed to shut down as deep rumbling filled our ears. Without a moment's thought, Anuloja and I instinctively ducked, covering our heads with our arms and curling into ourselves. The shells were not directed at us, but we were in an open vulnerable space and they were very close. Although the previous weeks of outgoing shelling from the army's central camp in Batticaloa had familiarised us with the sound of multi-barrel rocket launchers (MBRLs), we had never experienced them in such close proximity as this. I had also spent the previous day in Batticaloa hospital visiting mainly women and children who had been injured by the shelling of IDP camps. Many of the women had been injured in the back and legs as they had thrown themselves over their children to protect them. One young girl was cut down the front of her face, slicing through her nose and into her lips. The same night, twelve people (including five children) had been killed in a nearby village when shells had landed on their homes. The main news that evening had reported that the shells had been fired by the LTTE, however, when we visited the village the morning after the incident, the families were adamant that the shells had come from the army camp just behind the village. When I visited with members of the *Valkai* group, people in the village were still in a state of severe shock. The bodies of the children had been removed but the blood splattered around a crater in the ground refused to let the evidence of violence be erased. Gesturing over in the direction of the army camp, people had shouted in disbelief, 'Let them kill us all now, they can finish us. They want to kill all the Tamils.' It was with awareness of this incident that my fear increased. I found myself feeling vulnerable and nervous, and I felt my heart pounding whilst my body tightened in anticipation of the next shell.

Only as I uncurled and looked up did I notice that the family had remained upright, the adults silent while the children continued to play in the sand around us. Seemingly relaxed, they had only glanced up in the direction of the noise. With a bemused smile on her face, an older woman, grandmother to the family group, gestured over in the direction of the army camp. '*Charrianna payam*' (very scared) was all I could understand from her fast Tamil, caught in the gummy softness of her red betel-stained mouth. It was not so much the difference between the responses of myself and the family that struck me about this incident, as what I was made to confront in that moment of experiential and potential danger and violence. I found myself wondering what this meant for people in and around Batticaloa where this was a daily reality. At first reading, the lack of obvious reaction suggested that the family, especially the children, were unaffected by the shelling. They knew that the shells were outgoing and not directed at them and they had experienced this before. Yet, in the way the grandmother spoke and from what the families told us later, it was clear they were frightened. The shelling had not only destroyed their home life and livelihoods, but also their normal patterns of daily routine. They were unable to sleep at night, and the mothers were anxious about their children playing outside for fear of a shell landing on them.

As we left the area that afternoon, I found myself puzzling further over what this all meant. How was the fusion of violence and daily experiences interpreted in terms of what formed 'the ordinary' and 'the everyday' for this family and others like them in the east? How did this experience fit with what had happened in the past, what was happening in the present, and what seemed likely to happen in the future? Moreover, how could an 'outsider' such as myself, who was both a part of this daily experience and yet found it unfamiliar and extraordinary, interpret and describe such incidents?

It was not only the experience of shelling that triggered these questions. As I described in Chapter 3, living in the east for many months meant I had witnessed the regular rise and fall of tension, and had learnt to recognise and respond to signs and indices of '*suyal nilamai*' (the situation). I had seen how people's lives were restricted, and how they worked around it. The narratives of many women that I had spoken with had provided an insight that showed how people's response to '*suyal nilamai*' went beyond the present and took in the years of violence and struggle that people had faced. Therefore, a greater understanding of what exactly constituted the meanings of daily life in this situation felt pressing. I wanted to know how people coped and moved through the 'everydayness' of conflict. Moreover, I felt that there was much more to explaining daily life in Batticaloa than the violence alone. It is this *everything else* of life that shifts and forms in and around the violence that sets the theme for this chapter, and, more generally, for the book as a whole.

Taking the notions of the everyday and the ordinary as the driving concepts, in this chapter I consider how the daily lives of civilians in Batticaloa might be interpreted and understood in the given context of protracted conflict. Opening with a brief exploration of the ways in which ethnographic studies have generally understood violence through the concept of the everyday, I consider how this has written people's lives into a fixed dichotomy of victims and agents, those that succumb to the devastation of conflict and those that survive. Looking at how the banal everyday has been pitted against the extraordinariness of violence, I suggest that we need a loosening of fixed and bounded ideas that may allow the everyday to move beyond what is mundane and routine, and concomitantly, open up alternative ways through which we might understand lives in conflict. This, I argue, might then allow us to look beyond violence as the determining concept through which the everyday of conflict is understood, to reveal not only how people suffer and survive, but also how the vitality of the everyday allows people to live around, through, and beyond violence. In the second half, so as to better understand how we might explore the meanings of everyday life, I suggest that we need to take the concept of the everyday back to its theoretical roots. Addressing the ways in which the everyday has been invoked within the broader reaches of social theory can reveal the everyday as a ubiquitously complex and problematic concept, but also as one that has been invested with power and politics. The connection between abstract theoretical models of the everyday and the reality of people's daily lives in Batticaloa may seem tenuous. After all, what comprises the dramas and details of life for people in violent contexts appears to lie far from the grounds of abstract theoretical debate, which probably tells us more about the ingrained attitudes and political attachments of a cohort of modern intellectuals than about the essence of daily life itself. However, what the theory can tell us is how the concept of the everyday has been shaped within social analysis, and how this may or may not fit with the ethnographic everydays explored in the reality of violent contexts. I argue that the apparent disjuncture between social theory and lived experience can illustrate the changes and shifts in everyday thinking. This takes us from regarding the everyday as an abstract fixed concept, devoid of experience, to a lived present, which can be fluid, unsettled, and an 'open-ended generative process; as practice' (Harrison 2000: 499). This draws upon both the narratives and ethnographic examples we have explored so far and sets the framework for the next chapter, which looks at the life story of a woman named Meena, and traces her everyday experiences through the conflict. Furthermore, this chapter also provides the platform for Chapter 6, which takes the idea of the integrity of the ordinary as the driving concept to consider the lives of a widowed mother and a group of fishermen in Batticaloa.

Violence, the everyday, and 'everyday violence'

The concept of the everyday is both complex, and, paradoxically, due to its ubiquity, often reduced to something that is straightforward and obvious. This ambiguity has played a part in making the everyday a central and highly diverse and problematic theme of modern philosophy and social theory (Crook 1998: 160). Ideas of what make up the everyday are notions of the familiar and reliable; the intimate interpersonal relationships, which are revealed through experiences of what is considered 'ordinary'. If we look back to grammatical interpretations, we can see that in both ancient and modern philosophy the everyday has been treated as habitual, static, and atemporal. This idea is also reflected in Bourdieu's (1977: 96) notion of 'habitus', in which, he suggests, 'certain things become unthinkable-extraordinary, whilst others become desirable and normal'. Sandywell (2004) notes that the word ordinary (from the Latin *ordinaries: ordodinis*, order, arrangement, system) implies a cluster of significations indexing the habitual, customary, regular, usual, or normal. Thus, 'what is ordinary is "real"' (ibid.: 162). He goes on to point out that like the dualism real/unreal, the ordinary contrasts with the exceptional and unusual.

As such, the extraordinary lies literally outside the usual order or normal course of things, and exceeds the limits and boundaries of ordinariness. With the ordinary connoting that which is timeless and commonplace, accordingly, the term *everyday* implies a life to be static, fixed, and, consequently, mundane. Anthropologists have often used the ordinary and its corollaries – the normal, the routine, and the everyday – as default analytical categories, which we determine by those things most-frequently done by the majority within keeping of local norms, structures, and events (Kelly 2008: 353). It can be argued that the limits of categories such as *normal* and *ordinary* are set by what is conceivable within our own realities and understanding, and as such, acts of violence, and the daily experiences through which they are generated, become both extraordinary and unimaginable for those of us whose everyday has not widened to encounter such experiences. However, measured in relation to other people's lives, conflict and violence are also constantly judged against the way things could or ought to be, which reminds us that an understanding and categorising of violence can be an extension of inherently personal lived experiences. Therefore, we might suggest that where violence is endemic, it does not necessarily become normalised so much as to challenge the boundaries of the analytical abstract categories of normal and ordinary. This, then, suggests that there are forms of everyday life in violent contexts, which cannot be understood through the juxtaposed categories of the ordinary and extraordinary. For example, where would the shelling described at the beginning of this paper be situated? Given that it is regular and unexceptional, in this particular context it might be seen as ordinary. Yet, at the same time, it appears to exceed the limits of 'ordinariness', and is not mundane or static in any way. So where everydayness has come to characterise experiences that appeared to be firmly embedded in the known rituals of practical life, we are left with events which are not seen as extraordinary in their context yet remain firmly outside accepted everyday routines.

Questioning the everyday

A common starting point for ethnographic studies of violence is often the profound incongruity of combining an indispensible and familiar, but un-momentous, idea of everyday with harsh disruptive violence. The fusion of such polarised notions reveals structures of violence which can be embedded in social institutions and cultural conceptions and reproduced locally. This, in turn, reveals the importance of exploring the quotidian through everyday experience as a way of understanding the resilience of agents and the brutality of social forces. In doing so, a particular hallmark of ethnographic writing on violence appears within which acts of creativity and extraordinary heroism are pitted against an oppressive everyday life of violence. Accordingly, the agency and action of those caught up in prolonged crisis is powerfully highlighted. Ring captures this dichotomy when she compares, 'the dull, rule-bound drudgery of quotidian existence and the dynamism of "genius"' (2006: 178), which echo through the pages of ethnographies. Green also states that in paying close attention to the quotidian in her context of Mayan women in Guatemala, 'one may discern not only the alienation and violence produced by modernity but also the possibilities for creativity that may emerge from these processes' (1999: 7). Similarly, Nordstrom (1997) takes an example of a nurse in Mozambique to demonstrate the creativity of resistance against the chaos of war. Resilience is also the focus of Scheper-Hughes work (1996, 2008) in Brazilian shanty towns and South African townships, where she shows how people make lives for themselves under conditions of extreme scarcity and adversity. Vigh argues that by recognising 'crisis as context' rather than 'crisis in context' (2008: 7–8), new terrains of action and meaning can be explored, in which people make sense of events inscribing 'the devastation in the everydayness of life' (Mbembe 1995: 331). As such, highlighting everyday activities, strategies of coping and resisting, and, crucially, hopes and desires for the future can reveal a social life within a state of ordered disorder (see Taussig 1992). This is the everyday experience of living in conflict areas, and is based upon negotiation, creativity, and endurance. It can be seen both as heroic and ordinary.

Victims and agents

The implicit ontology of suffering and agency – like the dichotomy of victim and perpetrator – tends to ignore the fluidity of boundaries and less-than-clear distinctions. Ethnographic writing about violence often separates out survival from subordination, and the ordinary everyday from extraordinary violence. This creates a fixed and determining sense of the everyday in a violent setting which prevents us from exploring the everyday as something more than mundane and looking beyond violence to the possibilities of new and different ideas. Ross (2003: 124) argues that when women in South Africa spoke about their agency and roles of resistance during apartheid, they seldom spoke in terms of the powerful tropes of 'heroes/martyrs' or 'victims and perpetrators'. However, their experiences were most often captured within the framework of violence, particularly sexual violence (ibid.). This indicates not only the categorising of experiences, but also the gendered framework through which women in conflict are often portrayed. Similarly, Meena's narrative in the following chapter provides less a sense of heroics and victimhood than it does a general feeling of negotiation and strategising to work with what is at hand, and to overcome barriers and hurdles. Therefore, positioned between and within the interconnected spaces of suffering and agency lies the endurance of everyday life – where people keep going, lose, win, hurt, survive, and cope with the patterns and rhythms of life that continue through violence yet are also profoundly affected. This is where I suggest writing about violence can find its own space – taking impetus from the everyday endurance and all that it might mean. In relation to the shelling incident, if the fear and suffering caused by the shelling are the only part of the experience described, even if it is as a daily reality, the unspoken everyday is lost. The washing that gets done, the cooking, relationships, and activities that are woven through the everyday experience of life with violence are unobtainable. Accordingly, with Meena and other widows across the east, if it is only the violence and deaths they witness and deal with which are conveyed, then the threads of endurance woven with finer details of conversations, dreams, impressions, and feelings are lost. In this, a sense of the future is also unobtainable, rendered hopeless by the tragedy and horror of suffering which is brought to the fore.

In an attempt to simultaneously bring the primary concerns of the 'everyday' theorists into anthropology, and to foreground moments in contemporary ethnography that might breach the Western-centeredness of everyday theory, Ries poses two questions. She asks, 'Where does the everyday fit into considering cultures, communities, families in *extremis*? And, reciprocally, how does pondering these events inflect our theorising of the everyday?' (2002: 735, emphasis my own). Ries uses these questions to highlight what she claims is an intimate link between the concerns of anthropologists who are increasingly working in sites of violence and destruction, and 'everyday' theorists concerned with commodification, alienation, and rationalisation of industrialised nations. Highlighting 'everyday atrocity and atrocity against the everyday' as a concomitant of globalising capitalism, Ries describes the everyday as 'the place where the most powerfully important things in life occur' (ibid.: 740).[1] The dichotomy of cultures in *extremis* (conflict/violence) as opposed to the non-violent and 'ordinary' presented by Ries mirrors a mode of writing used frequently in ethnographies of everyday violence. Although this may be a simplification by Ries, at the same time these ontological interpretations, regularly invoked by anthropologists and social theorists, fail to consider what may lie outside this dichotomy, and that situations may not fit neatly into such categories. Therefore, in addressing the apparent inability of traditional theories to explain the everydayness of situations of violence and instability, my aim is not to separate the everyday in *extremis* from an 'ordinary' everyday but to open up both ideas for investigation. As such, questions need to be asked regarding what such theories can tell us about the everyday, and how we might expand or divert from them to make sense of everyday life in conflict situations.

The everyday in social theory

An abstract concern regarding everyday life as a site of alienation was typical of much of twentieth-century European philosophy and sociology. While experiencing a resurgence of interest among social theorists from Habermas and Giddens to de Certeau and Maffesoli, it has remained a concept that has largely been considered within the parameters of Western modernity. Ries argues that this developed into something of a 'master narrative' around the everyday in which illustrations of everyday life were consistently set in familiarly Western locations. In doing so, it worked with a number of assumptions comparing premodern everyday life to everyday life in the West, which then played out in the kinds of ethnographic research that emerged. Marcus and Cushman (1982: 29) describe the idea of 'ethnographic realism' in which monographs conformed to a generic structure rooted in the structural-functional theoretical paradigm (and colonial interests).[2] Accordingly, the mundane household tool, the routine habit, the banal occurrence, and the items of daily production loomed large in anthropological perspectives of the everyday, which maintained a duality through implying a relegation of certain forms of knowing (and being) to the secondary position of the subjective. Therefore, anything that fell outside of what was regarded as the ordinary and everyday was assumed to be the substance of dreams and fantasies, and part of unverifiable and fleeting feelings accorded to the position of the 'native'.[3] However, the rise of structuralist, interpretive, postmodern, and postcolonial turns in the theory and representation in anthropology during the 1970s sought to shift the perspective to locating people within their own contexts (Marcus and Cushman 1982). Routine habits, everyday occurrences, and items of daily production, though of previous interest to the anthropologist, took on a new significance with these major shifts in theory. Studies started to emphasise and practice the importance of listening, engaging with, and reporting local knowledge in a way which allowed those being studied their own commentaries and theories of their possessions, practices and behaviours (Ries 2002), and challenged the power of anthropological theory to render adequately the lives of others.[4] Rather than diminish the importance of the everyday, this critique ironically seemed to bring it into sharper focus.

The development of such perspectives revealed a shift in focus to ally the terms 'feeling' and 'experience', where experience does not indicate the past tense, but rather modes of experiencing. Williams (1977: 131) describes this through the concept of a structure of feeling – as an attempt to grasp that which is 'actually being lived, and not only what is thought is being lived'. Perhaps most significantly, this way of thinking broadened out to show that in the everyday enactment of the world there is always immanent potential for new possibilities of life. In response to the limitations of earlier theories of the everyday, for example, the phenomenological theories of everyday approached everydayness as a topic of descriptive social science through which 'doing being ordinary' was mundanely, methodologically, and reflexively accomplished (Garfinkel 1952, 1967; Sachs 1992). Garfinkel, Latour, and others moved away from retrospective overviews, which explained what happened and pushed towards dwelling in the world 'as it happens'. The everyday then became considered as the grounds on which wider forces were played out and the grounds for enactment. This opened up new spaces of action, 'articulating a second poetic geography on top of the geography of the literal, forbidden or permitted meaning' (de Certeau 1984: 105).

The embodiment and the enactment of everyday life

Breaking with attempts to think of the social and cultural system as totalitarian and controlling, de Certeau's *The Practice of Everyday Life* (1984) associated the everyday less with the ensemble of scripted human activities than with unpredictability and creative potential. Influenced by reflexive anthropology, de Certeau explored the position of the subject in relation to the complex weave of everyday elements, and drawing from examples such as walking in the city, he illustrated experiences of embodiment and enactment. In particular, he emphasised the importance of looking beyond everyday patterns of behaviour and into what the 'cultural consumer' actually 'makes' or 'does' within this time (posited in the locus of hidden poetics).

Hidden tactics and daily strategies

Readdressing the top-down bias of Foucault's critique of the micro-technologies of power, de Certeau (1984: xiv) portrayed the everyday as a tactical resistance to the strategies of the powerful and drew attention to the 'inventiveness of the everyday', which challenged the idea of the consumer of the everyday as a victim. As such, de Certeau's notion of everyday, like Lefebvre and others, corresponds to a specifically 'human' and not merely technical or material content that designates the limits of the possible at a given moment (Schilling 2003: 38). This allows the everyday to be seen in terms of action and subjectivity, rather than merely confined by structure, and for an emergent ontology to be understood as 'fluid' and spontaneous (Deleuze 1993: 56).

Although tied to specific economic, political, and cultural systems, de Certeau's ideas of the everyday can also extend beyond the borders within which he worked. These notions introduce us to an everyday that contains possibilities for action and change. Encouraging a perspective that looks past the notion of the victim to how people resist and rebel against the system, de Certeau illustrates an embodied specific sensuous knowing (enacting) of the everyday. This is an everyday that is brought alive by intersignifications, such as actions, objects, relations, substance, texture, and shape. If we apply this approach of the everyday, in terms of potential and possibility for action, to situations of conflict and violence, we can consider how people find spaces and chinks in the structure of the everyday to act on their situations and move forward. In particular, de Certeau's 'hidden poetics', which powerfully emerge in the wake of human struggle, can provide a deeper reading of everyday violence because they speak of creativity and action which is not always obvious but knits a solid and resourceful path forward (see also Green 1994). Moving towards the unseen and indicating the edge of semantic availability, de Certeau's argument can enhance our understanding of how people live through difficult circumstances and make sense of conflict and violence by utilising the resources available to them. At the same time, while de Certeau's notion of everyday life may conjure up positive images of trickery and resistance, it also falls short of describing exactly how these take place and the extent to which this is done. The 'mobile infinity of tactics' (de Certeau 1984: 41) appear to be 'fleeting instants' within a homogenous social and cultural life which give us little reference to the extent of the actual 'intervention' taking place (Schilling 2003: 36). Such limitations are reflected in Ries's argument that traditional theories of the everyday offer little space for understanding the everyday in *extremis*. For although de Certeau offers us an insight into how people may push against a system and search for spaces and openings for change, the lack of lived examples beyond those of the Western city make it less applicable to alternative contexts and settings.

De Certeau (1984) portrays the everyday as a site of tactical resistance to the strategies of the powerful (see also Foucault 1977). However, we could also see daily activities themselves as tactics of negotiation, management, and, perhaps, even resistance to ensure continuity and survival. This does not mean that the everyday is eternally removed from what is considered ordinary but that in the everyday practical affairs and interactions are based on shifting and different contexts – which are being continually created and recreated. In this sense, in all its complexity, everyday life is lived in the world, or in what phenomenologists call the *lifeworld* – 'that domain of everyday immediate social existence and practical activity' (Jackson 1996: 7). Jackson's observations are useful here as he translates ideas of a lifeworld in terms of individual orientations to a social world, rather than a worldview statically reproduced. The lifeworld, therefore, is not a concrete unified domain in which social relations remain stable, but, rather, 'it is a scene of turmoil, ambiguity, resistance, dissimulation, and struggle' (ibid.: 27). This is illustrated most powerfully in the details of Meena's story in the next chapter in which her experiences of survival show the significance of tactics and strategies of the everyday, particularly amongst women, in creating close networks of consolation, cooperation, social tensions, and ambiguities. To Jackson's observations, therefore, we could add endurance as part of the everyday scene, through which accommodation of and resistance to the system emerge.

'For another first time'

This sense of endurance can be further explained through Garfinkel's (1967: 9) notion of 'for another first time'. Garfinkel uses this term to recognise the ways in which a familiar commonplace experience or activity is recognised as such. Accordingly, we make sense of events in terms of the differences they make to our lives, and how they are meaningful to us in terms of the wider web of experiences and life events. Thus, my walk is *my* walk, my daily work is *my* daily work; my kind of anger is *my* kind of anger, and my suffering is *my* suffering as opposed to *your* suffering. All of these are interpreted within a range of understandings consisting of a number of different situations, so that a rule or norm is always applied 'for another first time'. This suggests the way in which we re-orientate ourselves towards taking dialogically structured and relationally responsive events each time an experience takes place. In this way, the particular, unique understandings we arrive at in the different and particular contexts we have with each other depend on 'once-occurrent events of Being' as Bakhtin (1993: 13) calls them. Sudden, brief, unrepeatable, unique moments – rather than repetitions and regularities – become of fundamental importance to us. Although it is not necessary to go into the depth that a comprehensive enquiry into these notions would require, what is of importance here is that our understanding of events, and our body of knowledge are recognised as living, embodied, responsive relations to our surroundings rather than being based only on individual experiences. Although most examples of 'for another first time' draw upon social behaviours within a comprehensible rule-based society, we could also apply this view to an understanding of experiences in conflict situations in which people attempt to interpret and make sense of their daily actions and practices. For as Bakhtin suggests, what we perceive as facts – as simple basic happenings – are seen in relation to an unobtrusive, but nonetheless shaping and directive 'way of seeing'. It is in the contingency of everyday social transaction that the normative horizon is instantiated and rhetorically formulated, and thus, when in the midst of action, norms can be attached to behaviour and actions by means of discursive convections.

Therefore, for me, the concept of 'for another first time' captures this combined sense of accommodation and interpretation in a given situation, and if applied to situations of violence can tell us not only about actions for resistance and survival but also about what these actions mean. Take, for example, the everyday spaces in Batticaloa, such as borders, boundaries, checkpoints, and villages, which are subject to competing claims of ownership and control. So-called 'border villages', especially, comprise spaces which are not only marginalised, but also fracture internally, creating borders within borders.[5] One such border village between Batticaloa and Valaichchenai, which I visited regularly during 2005–06, presented a clear picture of this: located in a government-controlled area, it backed onto a large army camp where the two entry roads to the village passed small sentry posts. This meant that the security forces had the most visible control of the village. As with many other border villages, prior to the LTTE split in 2004, the LTTE had also staked a claim on the village, and took official control under the cover of darkness. This meant that families were susceptible to having their children forcibly recruited, and some of the locals were paid LTTE spies. After the split, however, the LTTE presence had all but disappeared at night and the TMVP had stepped up their operations in the area, during the daytime and the night.[6]

One of the most obvious consequences of this matrix of competing lines of control in everyday life in Batticaloa was a sense of confusion and insecurity. The checkpoint infrastructure contributed significantly to the militarisation of the landscape, but was more an institution and picture of domination than a serious hindrance to the militants. While civilians could expect to be stopped, checked, and scrutinised at checkpoints, the meaning that lay within these places could be ambiguous. The relationships between those upholding the boundaries, and those crossing them mapped onto an embedded and variable knowledge of people's backgrounds and allegiances. Thus, the fluid meanings they created, negotiated, and renegotiated could create a sense of anticipation and fear with every crossing and movement, each 'for another first time' (Montani 1999: 145–71).[7] Spaces are, therefore, not simply divided by violence and non-violence, but can be imbued with both simultaneously. The strategy of survival, therefore, becomes one of *listening* to spaces; of working out what is happening in the immediate moment based on the past and future, and shaping your actions accordingly (as described in relation to the work of the *Valkai* group in Chapter 2). Space can, in this way, embody a search for a referent, for something tangible or abstract upon which to develop a sense of the self and the world.

The strategies by which people re-orientate themselves to a particular moment points us towards a progressive and dynamic understanding of the type of everyday that is at stake in Batticaloa. Yet, at the same time, such arguments limit us to understanding the actions of an individual and fail to consider the social aspects of everyday action and meaning. Although meaning is created in relation to a wider perspective of experience, it also only makes sense of *my* suffering, for example, in relation to everyone else's. In Batticaloa, violent events have become an integral part of social memory and ongoing experiences, and can define events in individual life histories *and* collective memories. The propensity for violence at different levels of society, in shifting spaces and by changing actors, creates a web of shared experiences upon which groups of people as well as individuals must act. Therefore, when considering situations such as the family affected by the shelling, how they deal with the everyday in relation to themselves, each other, and the changing context must be examined.

The (un)remarkable ordinary

Understanding an everyday event 'for another first time' engages with the notion that events of being and lived experiences are the beginning of new dialogically structured 'inner social worlds' from which we make sense of our lives, and from within which our 'language-games' have their beginning. Language-games are crucial here, for as Wittgenstein suggests, 'The origin and the primitive form of the language game is a reaction; only from this can more complicated forms develop' (1980: 31). Like Garfinkel and Bakhtin, Wittgenstein suggests that in human affairs – everyday experiences – there can be some 'first time'; a new way of seeing, hearing, feeling, judging, and of talking and acting. The importance of these new beginnings lies in the enactment and embodiment of an experience as a new way of bodily responding to our surroundings. Ideas of embodiment are important because they consider forms of interplay in which language may not be used. Wittgenstein (1953: 228) describes this as interplay of the 'imponderable' kind – in that we are incapable of describing it – but the fact is that as soon as we do, in fact, become engaged with an activity or with another being, we can have an almost immediate sense of that person in relation to us.

On the edge of life: A descent into the ordinary

For Das (2007), Wittgenstein's ideas of forms of life, in which he takes language to be the mark of human sociality, answers her questions about how, after experiencing extreme violence, the subjectivity of a person can survive: 'What is it to inhabit a world?' and 'What is it to lose one's world?'. Noting that violence can push people to the edge or limit of what can be recognised as human – 'a vertical sense of life' – it is in the anticipated end of the form of social life that the significance of the everyday takes shape (2007: 1–4). Das argues that a form of 'shared language' has to be developed, since 'a possible vicissitude of moments of violence and trauma is that one can become voiceless – in the sense that words become frozen and lifeless' (ibid.: 8). Speech, suggests Das, could be 'without voice'; that is the real voice is muted by the violent event, leaving empty and absent words in which the violence endured always seemed to be 'on the edge of the conversation' (ibid.: 8–10). Accordingly, words carry fear and pain from the past into the present, woven through everyday events and experiences. As such, 'descending' into the ordinary and paying repeated attention to the most mundane events and objects is what is needed to recover social relationships and connections (Das 2007; Martin 2007: 9). Furthermore, it is through the body that grief and mourning are enacted, allowing the performance of daily activities to interpose and mediate past experiences of violence. Exploring the fragile flow of life between the past and the present and between violence and mundane living, Das suggests that the self is made not in the shadows of a ghostly past, but in the process of making the everyday inhabitable. She looks specifically to what can be recovered after violent experiences, and demonstrates how violence and tragedy are woven into the texture of individual lives. As such, the importance of the small and routine activities are revealed, demonstrating that what might initially appear insignificant can actually hold the key to re-affirming the possibility of life within and outside the genres that people make available in the descent into the ordinary and everyday.

The present in the present

Moving away from the simplistic dichotomies of victim and agent, survival and resistance, Das does not look for the specific role of the subject but to *how* their subjectivity lives on through violence, and how this is conveyed to us through everyday existence. Using the example of the story of Asha, a fifty-five-year-old woman, widowed in her twenties in 1941 following the partition violence of India and Pakistan, Das shows the past is constantly interposed and mediated by the manner in which the world is inhabited in the present (see Das 2007: 71). However, when considering life in Batticaloa the emphasis lies on the ways in which the present is explored *in* the present rather than the past in the present. This is partly because the conflict in Sri Lanka is protracted, and, therefore, ensnares the present as much as the past. However, more significantly, it is because amongst the people with whom I engaged and the lives I observed, the emphasis was on the present, on what was possible now. While people talked about their pasts and relayed their experiences as crucial tracks upon which their current lives travelled, the essence of their everyday living, and current needs and concerns were powerfully demonstrated in that particular moment.

Through a focus on the present, it is possible to see where and how the past has seeped through and violence continued. Furthermore, it also becomes clear that there is also much more to life than violence, which was not always so visible or specifically marked out from other areas of everyday life. Although people in Batticaloa learnt to live with past experiences of violence, they must do so in continuously threatening and unsettled environments where continuation of violence seems inevitable. This is not just violence, which emerges from the fear created by fractured relationships and loss of trust, but the violence that is very much present in a conflict environment. It is also important to underline the fact that given the context of protracted violence, people in Batticaloa cannot repair and remake their lives through a return to the ordinary but rather must remake their lives as an *ongoing process* in and around violence. For many families displaced by the wave of fighting in 2007, for example, it was not the first time they had been displaced, nor was it likely to be the last. They lived through years and, thus, layers of violence, which affected them at different times in different ways. Also, as the previous chapters have shown, violence can emerge in multifarious forms as socially and culturally constructed manifestations of everyday life in Sri Lanka. Where the tsunami took only a few minutes to violently destroy landscapes and homes, the tendrils of conflict spread out through years and decades of everyday lives. As a woman in an IDP camp told me, '[T]he tsunami was just one big wave and it was gone. The fighting keeps coming and coming. One day it will take us all and then there will be nothing left.'

(Un)remarkable actions

The notion of a descent into ordinary life and carrying out mundane activity offers a dynamic and creative approach, which helps to shift focus from victims and agents to everyday living. The notion enables an understanding of how people live on in spaces of destruction. It also allows us to consider and incorporate alternative stories, which not only tell of the violent realties but also allow living and endurance rather than death and passivity to come through. However, focusing on a descent into the ordinary offers less space, perhaps, for a deeper questioning of the everyday and ordinary, and of how boundaries may stretch and reshape to encompass possibilities for (un)remarkable action in the present. Therefore, in recognising violence and the everyday as neither fixed nor static, we should consider the categories of living through violence and the meaning of the everyday as equally blurred. In this way, by addressing the everyday as more complex, we can render an understanding of it as more effective.

This brings us back to the initial problem of how we can understand an everyday in Batticaloa, which is both framed and shaped by conflict, but also tells us much more than just the violence. Having looked briefly at other ways in which the everyday is invoked, I have shown that, as a concept, the everyday is not as straightforward as it seems. While debate about the concept of the everyday explores the basis of human life, of relationships, and, of systems, language, thought, belief, and imagination, it also evades precise understanding. In Batticaloa, the fact that the violence continued as an everyday lived reality also challenges any clear understanding, especially where the tactics of terror and fear blur relations of space and time. The local dynamics of violence created surges in the intensity of violence and spatial shifts in its occurrence. It was the blurring of these boundaries of violence and non-violence, of restraint and routine, of paralyzing fear and constant movement, and of now and then that seemed to defy any ontological framework of the passive and active in war, and of the lines dividing ordinary from extraordinary. The slippage between categories of violence and of the categories of those who lived through it simultaneously spoke of that which worked through and around violence, that which endured and ultimately sought to find a balance in life. Where theory of survival and resistance may go some way in helping us interpret people's actions and intentions, it does not fully capture the complexity of the everyday realities.

Through challenging the very framework within which the everyday is considered and by questioning its purpose and meaning in relation to contexts of conflict and violence, it has become clear that any explanation must acknowledge that violence does not consume the everyday. Nor does the everyday become *only* about violence. Instead, just as patterns of violence rise and fall, punctuate and flow, expand and contract so can the meanings of the everyday and the ordinary.

The most effective way to explore and question the shape of everyday life in Batticaloa and its meaning is to return to the narratives of those at the centre. Therefore, in the next chapter I explore the history and lived reality of the conflict in eastern Sri Lanka though the experiences of one woman, Meena. Moving between the past and the present, and the experiences of things now, tying in with how they were then, Meena's story offers a comparative version of life which allows us to see some of the connections and disjuncture's as they have developed through time in the east and through Meena's life. Reflecting on lives that have come and gone, her narrative is the story of a woman striving to negotiate the everyday spaces that are variously closed, and opened up around her as she finds her way forward.

Notes

1 Ries discusses the role of consumer capitalist society as a 'terror machine' in its own right that targets the ordinary through the everyday. She states 'Terror – so well hidden from the view of end consumers – clears the way for and maintains the possibility of oil exploration, mining, the gobbling up of forest, riverine, ocean, and labour resources across the planet, the replacement of localized production and consumption systems with multinational ones' (2002: 740).
2 See Ortner (1984); Marcus and Fischer (1986).
3 Such a path of questioning is now well known. See Deleuze and Guattari (1994); Taussig (1992).
4 Abu-Lughod's *Writing Women's Worlds* (1993) is an eloquent and strong example of how the subject, in this case the Bedouin women of north-western Egypt, are themselves the primary voices in the book. Through their stories, songs, poetry, and essays, Abu-Lughod conveys in greater depth the richness and complexity of the Bedouin women's lives.
5 Spencer (2011) notes that 'border villages', far from being peripheral to the operations of the postcolonial state, are actually politically and economically central – being both a product of and dependent on state support (see also Das and Pool 2004).
6 Given the close relationship between the TMVP and the government forces, it was easy for TMVP cadres to gain access to government-controlled villages. In this area, most of the TMVP camps and offices were located next to or close to the security force camps. Young teenage boys with arms, identified as TMVP cadre in their unofficial uniform of checked shirts and plain trousers, were often seen on patrol alongside the security forces.
7 For a discussion of checkpoints as markers of identity, see Jeganathan (2004).

5

Meena's story

Weaving stories

When I first asked Meena if she would be willing to tell me her life story, she happily agreed, eager it seemed to have some time and space where she could sit and converse, away from the demands of her daily life. She was a good friend of Anuloja and Krishna, the women I lived with, and worked in the centre of Batticaloa town as a trainer with a local NGO that supported children affected by the conflict. We arranged to meet one afternoon a week in the out-building of a local women's organisation along with Krishna who was going to translate for us. This allowed us some space and privacy where we could talk with little interruption.

The building was bare except for a few dated and fading posters pinned to the wooden frames between the wire-mesh windows. One poster was for Women's Independence Day 2001 and another stated the right to live in a violence-free world.

We sat on mats on the floor facing one another. Meena would always wear a sari neatly folded and pinned at her shoulder, the blouse sleeves tightly pressing into the flesh of her upper arms. The trail of her sari would pool around her and as she talked she would play with it, coiling it around her hands and into tight balls. She did not require me to say much before she started talking about her life; beginning from the very day she was born. Hardly pausing for breath, and often talking over Krishna's translation, her memories, feelings, and thoughts spilled out on to the pages of my notebook in my indecipherable scrawl as I tried to keep up with her pace. Meena followed the central thread of her life, which she framed mainly within a domestic setting and structured by the societal conventions, which cast her as a daughter, wife, and mother. Starting with her birth, through childhood, adolescence, womanhood, and to the present, the edges of Meena's world would expand to include her wider family and kin, her community and the population, and then retract to enclose her within her home and on her own isolated journey. Weaving stories together, Meena revealed a rich tapestry of daily life, which reflected not only her own but many other women's lives in the east.

Meena's story felt important, not just because she told it in such detail, but because it brought into sharper focus the significance of personal experiences and stories as ways of understanding the history of a particular place and people. Furthermore, her narrative highlighted two main issues, which are significant for both this chapter and for the book as a whole. The first is in the emergence of the everyday – both as a means of addressing tasks at hand and pushing forward, and as a method of dealing with the many levels of loss and violence that Meena and those around her experienced. The threads of small routine mundane activities – feeding the children, finding ways of earning money, sending the children to school – stitch together a fabric of endurance that composes everyday life. The second issue, which is intrinsic to the first, is the way in which the story is told and how Meena positions herself within the spaces of everyday survival. The way in which Meena tells her story from the very day she was born suggested to me that she had either told her story before (which would not have been surprising given the number of researchers, anthropologists, and journalists that have worked in Batticaloa), or that she had in mind the kind of narrative that I was looking for. It could easily have been both. While her story moves in a general linear direction – through childhood to adolescence to motherhood and widowhood – what is perhaps more important are the less visible flows between the past, present, and future, which emerged as shaping both the experience of the story and its telling. People infuse meaning into their lives, into the events they have experienced, and into the choices they have made through the stories they tell about themselves. As such, the life story told by Meena was not only a way of telling herself (and others) about her life but was also the means by which her identity took shape in relation to Krishna and me. The strength and importance of Meena's story lie not in its construction of reality, her identity, or her claim to the truth, but in what it tells us about the nature of life and encounters in a particular time and space. Given as a variation on, but also framed within the master narrative of the east's history, Meena's story made visible the basis for contextualisation and interpretation, and the dynamic tension between voice, memory, and lived experiences.[1]

As it is a long and richly detailed text, I have divided Meena's story into three parts. The first is from Meena's birth in 1960 up until the end of 1984. The second is from 1986 and the arrival of the IPKF until the late 1990s, and the final part takes us from the late 1990s when Meena began training with an NGO to try and support her family through to when Meena and I completed our interviews in 2006. I have broken the narrative into sections with sub-headings, which represent various significant times in Meena's life. Where necessary, the transcript of Meena's narrative is accompanied by explanatory notes, which clarify or expand on some of the issues and events referred to by Meena. I have done this, not to detract from the significance of Meena's words, which are powerful enough on their own but to ensure the reader does not encounter Meena's story stranded without being moored to a wider frame of reference. As such, Meena's words and mine work together to present Meena's experiences of the past as her version of the truth and interpretation of meaning.

Finally, it must be noted here that all of the transcript marked as Meena's narrative is written as verbatim, the explanations I offer are based on my choice of texts and information, and, while intended to be as unbiased as possible, inevitably reflect my own understanding and the meaning created in the space of dialogue between Meena and myself. In order to protect Meena's identity, I have removed some of the specific names and references to places and people, and used pseudonyms where necessary. X, Y, and Z are used at various points to replace specific locations, names, and other details

Growing up in Kokkadichcholai

'A special baby'

I was born in 1960 in a taxi on the way to my mother's hometown of Munaikadu, Kokkadichcholai. My mother had got the pains at Kattankudy and so she never got home. My father used to say that I was a special baby because I was born to a Sri Lankan Tamil mother and Indian Tamil father in an auto driven by a Sinhalese person in a Muslim area. My father said that the auto driver had put a ten rupee note into my hand and said, 'this one will be a person that will work with the whole community'.

I started school during the 1970s after the British had left, at the time when the government asked us all to study Sinhala. At that time, the school gave us a small letter asking if we wanted to. I studied close to O' Level. I remember they [Meena did not clarify who she was referring to here] shot the teacher. When I was twelve they gave out coupons at school. Sri Lankan people got yellow and Indians got green. People started to say '*kalatanoi*' [Indian] to me. I fought some of them and got into trouble. The manager (head teacher) was known to my father, and he called my father. Then my father beat me. So I asked him [my father] why he came to Sri Lanka and married my mother. He was angry and replied, 'OK – you go and ask the government why'. This was in 1972.

My mother had married in 1966 and then married again. I don't know what really happened but she took all the children to another man. My father took four and I was one of them. We had many difficulties. My father worked in the paper factory but we had no permanent home. Many people made comments. My father left his job and then he became a *pōtiyār* [landowner]. We used to join up his sacks in the house – this was his work. People knew he was a speaker on behalf of a local MP and a landowner. So my mother's relatives were happy because they thought he was looking after us well with his jobs. Meanwhile they [the relatives] were angry with my mother, so they stopped her coming [to visit].

Then my mother's sister's husband died, leaving two children. Relatives thought it was better that they [her aunt and father] married. My father did not want to but for the children he did it. Then we really had an experience. '*Siththti*' means aunty but it can also mean cruelty. Violence. She was with us for three years. Siththi had two children with my father. Then Siththi's son got married – but his wife died in the tsunami. He was in Saudi at the time and people said not to inform him of her death. But he heard the message. He later died in an accident in Saudi – the body came back – he was involved in one of the militant groups.

Meena frames her entry into the world through the prism of the ethnic mix of people in the east by pointing out that those involved in her birth represented all four communities inhabiting the east at that time including: Sri Lankan Tamil, Tamil-speaking Muslim, Sinhalese, and Indian Tamil. Meena's birthplace, Kokkadichcholai, a home to some important temples (*kovils*), holds historical and cultural significance for the Tamils of the east (McGilvray 2008). Kokkadichcholai is also an area that, like many others in the east, has been continuously fought over by the LTTE and government forces, falling into the hands of one then the other, rendering civilians vulnerable and facing continual violence in the process. For example, Kokkadichcholai was occupied first by the army, recaptured by the LTTE in 1989, and then in 1991 government forces took the area again. They then abandoned it in 1995 when the state starting moving additional troops to the north, and this meant that the LTTE were able to coopt it as a strong hold (see UTHR 2007). The experiences of civilians in Kokkadichcholai reveal how, under the control of either government forces or the LTTE, no one was safe. In January 1987, for example, the STF carried out a horrific massacre of civilians in what has became known as 'the prawn farm massacre'. Furthermore, under the LTTE, civilians faced conscription of their children, a crippling taxation system, and the daily fear of being targeted by the government forces for living in an LTTE-controlled area.

Meena does not offer an explanation as to how her father arrived in the east and became a landowner. Given that Meena was born in 1960 and was attending school by the early 1970s, it seems that her father must have arrived earlier than the groups of Indian Tamils who fled the famine and the 1972 violence in the hill country (as noted in Chapter 2, pages: 33–4). This could possibly have been after the 1958 riots, which also included violence in the hill country (Vittachi 1958). However, the anger that Meena's father harboured towards the government can be explained by the history of South Indian Tamils (see Chapter 2 in which I highlight the transportation of Tamils from Tamil Nadu by the British in the 1860s to work on coffee, tea, and rubber estates in the hill country of Sri Lanka, then called Ceylon). Meena emphasises the use of the word, '*Kalatonai*' (Indian), which she told me refers to 'someone who has stolen over on a boat', by other children to mark her out as different and 'other'.[2] This fits with the observation that many Sri Lankan Tamils treated Indian Tamils as belonging to one low-ranking caste (Kearney 1987: 576).

For Meena's father to have married a Sri Lankan Tamil woman is also a point of interest given the violence and isolation of northern Tamils at that time which would have reduced the opportunity for Sri Lankan and Indian Tamils to interact. The marriage could have been due to Meena's mother being destitute at the time, Meena's father being an itinerant trader (who could, therefore, have visited his wife's family home), or he may have been a reasonably established trader.

Facing poverty

We faced many problems with Siththi. My father was out at work and would only be back once a week. He sent money but she never gave us meals. Siththi took all my mother's things when she died but she never was with my mother. There was not enough food. She gave us one tiny size bit of rice and left. We went with no meal to school. I did lots in the school; I was good in acting and many things. But back home I had no one to share my feelings with. There was nobody at home. In the meantime, my sister was sent by Siththi to do domestic work. My father was always encouraging me – he brought me presents and used to call me 'doctor' to make me feel proud.

We lived in a mud house and there was a place where there was lots of soil against the fence. So I wrote things in the soil about my situation. Then one day my father saw this – he did not say anything but he gave the money to Siththi, said he was not coming for seven days and then left. Siththi took the money and went. My father came back early and she was gone. He opened all the cupboards and there was nothing there. All the coupons had been pawned and my earrings sold. Then my father filed a case for divorce and the courts gave the divorce.

Siththi is still alive. She has children, two with my father, and two from before. Two boys have died, one in Saudi and the other while fighting in the LTTE. We were then in X [an uncleared area] and we used to see Siththi. Siththi's daughter's husband died in the 1990s. He was fishing. That was the time of the Muslim/Tamil situation – Muslim people killed him. After that, my father did not marry. Meantime Siththi sent my sister for domestic work in a teacher's house. My younger sister was also sent. Father did not know. She got the money. In the night, if my father asked where they were, she said they were in Kokkadichcholai. I got all the beatings from her. One day she hit me and so I pushed her. She then left for five days and did not come back. People knew what was happening but they were frightened to say. When Siththi is number one in the house, then people had to support her. She was a good liar.

The 'Tamil-Muslim situation' referred to by Meena is a theme that runs throughout her narrative, which also underlies many of the important junctures in the history of the east as noted in Chapter 2. The situation that Meena describes, of Siththi's son-in-law working in Saudi Arabia, is quite common, and as Fuglerud (1998) states, the historical importance of migration in the Tamil areas stems from it being one of the few, and, therefore, major forms of increasing capitalism. It is worth nothing that there has always been considerable migration, and from their heartland on the Jaffna Peninsula, the Sri Lankan Tamils made routes of migration, from the earliest times, to other parts of the island (see McDowell 1996: 69). The entire Northern Province had a dense concentration of Tamil populations, and from there they moved to the Eastern Province, especially towns with a rural hinterland such as Trincomalee and Batticaloa (Wilson 2000). A large number also made their way to Colombo in search of jobs, and to Kandy, the second largest city. Daniel and Thangarajah (1995) have described migration in terms of three phases. Phase one comprises mainly upper- and middle-class Tamils leaving Sri Lanka after Independence in 1948, and phase two is mainly students who, in reaction to restricted and discriminatory educational opportunities, sought the chance to study and work outside Sri Lanka. Phase three describes mostly 'refugees' – leaving after the 1979 Prevention of Terrorism Act (POTA), the 1983 ethnic riots, and the continually worsening situation in Sri Lanka. However, while this model gives us an idea of the types of migration that have taken place, based on the Tamil population's reaction to changes in Sri Lanka, it also simplifies a complex and multli-dimensional picture of diverse experiences and understandings which include multiple displacements, as Meena's narrative goes on to describe. Furthermore, it fails to account for the thousands of economic migrants to the Middle East, such as Siththi's son-in-law, driven by poverty and lack of job opportunities to seek work as labourers and domestic workers in countries such as Kuwait, Lebanon, Saudi Arabia, and the United Arab Emirates. While the vast majority of these migrants are Sinhalese from poor rural regions in the south, a number are also from the north and east, including Muslims displaced from the north in 1990. Although this does not fall under the category of forced migration, the fact that these migrants have sought work abroad as a result of poor economic opportunities, mainly due to uneven development, is intricately tied to the effects of violence and conflict.

1976–83: Marriage and adulthood

Then in 1976 there was this boy who had seen me in a drama at school. He was my stepfather's cousin's friend and came to my house saying he wanted to marry me. By now, my elder sister was grown up. The boy talked to my sister and they decided that since the family have nothing, we should marry. I was fifteen years. At that time, I had no proper clothes as my stepmother drank all our money. But my sister said I should get married. That time though I did not even have a bra or vest and my panties were made from old cloth. The boy started visiting more and when I explained to him our family situation he said he would stay with us. But his mother was not happy with that, as we owned nothing. He fought with his mother. One day my stepmother took us to the police station. It was 1976, March 18. She made an entry of marriage in front of the police. Police advised my husband that I was good and to let me study well. But my father did not know about this and was upset at first. But he was then OK. Me and my husband, my younger and elder sister all lived in X [an uncleared area]. My husband was good and supportive and used to let me just play. We did not know what to do ... [indicating that she meant sexual intercourse] and so we would eat then just sleep.

April 1976. New Year. My husband's father came and asked us to come to the house. That day my mother-in-law put a white cloth on a mat and talked to her son. That was the first night we slept together. We did not really know what to do or what happened. I thought my time (period) had come, so I washed the cloth. Then the mother checked the cloth. I was sixteen and in June I found I was pregnant. We made a small hut in his family land and stayed there. But my mother-in-law was a problem and only gave me minimum food. I was young and I would cry. After my marriage, I stopped visiting people. The culture meant I should stay with my husband – but I did not know what to do. I used to play with my husband's younger sisters like a child. When I was six months pregnant,

> my husband stopped being with me. He would go away for one week for work and come back on the Sunday. (This was) the same life as I had with my father. At this time, my husband's father would cause trouble for me and he even tried to abuse me but I got away. I was scared to be near him.

What is interesting about this part of Meena's story is that she describes the lived realities of kinship practices and marriages in the east whereby the everyday experiences of poverty and marginalisation were often defining factors in deciding on partnerships and family structures. This, of course, stands in stark comparison to the desired structure described by many anthropologists and scholars (see Chapter 2, page 32). For Meena, marriage at such a young age was driven by a lack of options stemming from extreme deprivation. She describes, for example, her marriage (which was simply an entry in police records) alongside the details of her lack of clothing and undergarments, and not being able to pay a dowry. Furthermore, the way that Meena describes 'playing' with her husband's sisters and her ignorance to sexual intercourse and pregnancy reveals the reality of Meena's youth and desperate situation.

Ruwanpura (2006: 98) has also noted that while the matrilineal customs, with the emphasis being on the provision of adequate dowries for daughters, should ideally place eastern Tamil women in a strong negotiating position in intra-household relations, this is dependent upon the financial situation of the family. In Meena's case, it appears that she did not have a dowry, and, thus, her husband's family were unhappy about the union since they would not gain materially. Ruwanpura (2006: 98) also points out that in spite of the existence of matrilineal practices, men are traditionally the visible agents of the social community in eastern Sri Lanka, and, thus, intra-household relations are shaped by 'the coexistence of patriarchal institutions and matrilineal structures'. The details of Meena's experiences mirror this assertion, particularly her reference to her vulnerability as a young woman around her father-in-law. While this is the first reference Meena makes to the prevalence of sexual abuse and her vulnerability as a woman, it is not the last, and, in fact, is a theme and tragic reality that runs throughout the everyday experiences in her narrative.

Life, death, and the rise of the LTTE

> My baby was born in 1977 on March 8 – he was a month early. A boy was born and my father was happy, as it was all girls in my family. We called him Prabharkaran. But after sixteen days, he died. I had leaked milk at five months and people had said there was something wrong. When the child died, I sent a message to my husband but he did not come. My mother-in-law came and told people that my child was not her son's but my father-in-laws. Someone tried to hit me at the funeral.
>
> I lived with my father and he [Meena's husband] lived with his mother after that. But after one year my husband fought with his mother and so came back to me. He started to bring money and life was better. I became pregnant again but at six months I miscarried. After two-three months, I was pregnant again and I had a daughter in 1979. I moved to X [a cleared area], took government land and

built a hut. I used to visit my father, and my elder sister, who was now married. I also got a job with Sarvodaya [an NGO] as a nursery teacher. I had fifteen days of training.[3] My mother-in-law looked after my child and then the child started nursery school.

In 1980 July 22, my father died from cancer – at that time two of my sisters were not married – and this made me feel sad about his death because he had expectations of us all being married. I think he knew he had cancer. He had always advised me and I really felt the loss of him. I used to talk about politics with my father and so I knew all of the political history. I knew about what the British people did – separating the country and being in charge.[4] My father said that they had done some good things, and that if I could learn English it would be good for me. But I had no chance to do this. He had given me a name that meant 'God's child' – he always looked for meaning. After he died, whatever experience or struggle I was facing, father always came in my dream. Then after his death, my last sister married – so now all the girls were married. In 1981, my son was born. He was the fourth child but only the second to survive.

In 1982, the problems really started. We knew that a TELO leader was in Kalmunai prison, being tortured. It was a new experience for all the people, and the village people all got together to discuss the incidents. We did not know very much about the situation at that time. In 1983, the Sarvodaya president came to Batticaloa and then went back to Colombo. We tried to listen to his visit on the radio, but we only got sad songs. That's when we knew of the 1983 riots. People came back from Colombo and we heard. We were confused and very tense. Army were on the main road. We had heard about PLOTE and TELO then because my father had told me about the groups. But it was only at this time that the other movements became known. I had read a book about the movements. We heard that PLOTE had separated into two – into the LTTE and PLOTE over a girl. There had been a shoot out because this girl loved the PLOTE leader, and then they did something against the LTTE. So then there was a fight between the two and the girl got shot.

The LTTE was not in public at this time. There was one guy; he was around the village and trying to do a fishing business and other business for the LTTE. But in the village people never knew that he was from the LTTE. He moved with the people. The LTTE members never introduced themselves as LTTE. But the LTTE did have support in the village. At that time, it was made up of a lot of people from Jaffna. We heard about Kittu appa who was killed by the Indian army. He got caught by the IPKF at sea, and in prison there was seven members – all top LTTE. While in prison, the LTTE put cyanide in their food and they all died. IPKF said it was not them but the LTTE denied it too.

Meena's comment about the LTTE being 'made up of a lot of people from Jaffna' reflects the issues discussed in Chapter 2 in terms of the eastern Tamil youth being initially unsure of the northern dominance of the LTTE. Despite this reticence, following the violence against Tamils in 1983 and subsequent mass displacement of Tamil people, as well as the establishment of the ruthless rule of the STF, support from the east coast dramatically increased. The two stories involving the LTTE are variations of particular incidents which took place between the late 1970s and 1993, and appear to have either taken on new form and meaning as they have filtered down through the village or have been merged together through Meena's recollection of what took place.⁵ Although Meena's account varies from other reports in terms of specific detail and chronology, she signposts a number of significant shifts in the structure of the LTTE, which are generally known to have been highly influential in affecting the shape of the conflict. Moreover, the way Meena tells these details suggests how stories and rumours must have circulated in communities at this time as people tried to understand the actions of the LTTE.

Anti-Tamil riots

> At that time of the riots, lots of Sinhalese people started moving to Colombo. We had lots of sayings about them and we would say that the Sinhalese pull the sarong differently because they are cruel people. So we would say this is *our* country. There were lots of Sinhalese people in Batticaloa, and though we talked about them [the Sinhalese] as killers in Colombo, we did care about the Batticaloa ones. We advised them to leave. There were Sinhala schools in areas between Kayankerny, Eravur, and Batticaloa. The Sinhalese did fishing and coconut cultivation. They were good business people and we had a good working relationship. But when we heard the stories of all the cutting in Colombo though the Tamils told the Sinhalese people to go, don't stay here. Mostly those who left did not come back. But still, their farms are here.
>
> After the LTTE entered the village then the caste problem was reduced. They told people that there should be no caste system. Before this, there were a lot of caste discriminations. The barbers were the low caste and the laundry castes [*dhobis*] were a bit up and then there were higher castes. The barbers could not come into other areas and there was no intermarriage. Now there is intermarriage and the washing caste is less. The high caste, the *Kalinga* [*Kāliñkā*], which I am, went abroad and many sold their land to other castes.⁶ So then, the washer caste became more united and the *Kalinga* more divided. An example of how the LTTE operated – the barber caste found a *pilliayar* statue and they took it to their land and said they wanted to build a temple.⁷ But that meant that then the washing people could not wash there. It became a fight. Someone went to the LTTE and the LTTE called all the castes. People said that whatever they say we will accept. So the LTTE said to put the statue in the Sarvodaya nursery land. So the land where the *dhobis* wash is still there but now they are not doing it. They wash at home.

Meena's comments about the Sinhalese in Batticaloa in 1983 are particularly important here given that the most common version of events in the 1983 riots tends to focus on the growing hostility and tension between Sinhalese and Tamils in the south. Very little consideration has been given to what was happening in the east where communities were living tightly interspersed (see Chapter 2, pages 35–6). While direct violence did not break out in the east during the 1983 riots, relations were not purely harmonious. There is evidence, for example, of violence between Sinhalese and Tamils in the east in the 1958 anti-Tamil unrest, which led to an anti-Sinhala response in Batticaloa (Vittachi 1958), although this does not seem to have permanently disrupted communal relationships in the area.

Meena notes that one of the ways in which the LTTE gained support was

Meena's story

through appealing to and mobilising traditionally degraded and peripheral social groups within the Tamil formation, such as women, 'low castes', and peasants. Some suggest that the intention of the LTTE was to 'balance out' a hierarchical and oppressive society by breaking the rigidity of the class system and gender divisions (Bose 1994).[8] Many local stories describe various incidents such as the one Meena mentions in which the LTTE intervened in village disputes caused by caste. However, an argument more in accordance with the LTTE ideologies of a homogenised Tamil community, which is hinted at in the context of Meena's story, is that they did not fight caste because it was injustice but because it divided the Tamil community, which they needed to be unified (Hoole *et al.* 1988). The claim to the dissolution of caste in Tamil areas in Sri Lanka is also not one that can be tested given the extensive erosion of the social structure and networks in villages and neighbourhoods during war-time.

1984–6 The Special Task Force (STF)

During that period, the movements were very active. Whatever house you visit at that time, at least one person will be a member of one group. At that time, the LTTE did not feel so special – each one was the same. In 1984, the army started to check ID cards more. People felt this change, they were scared, and because of the fears many young formed with the movement for protection. Then they started doing round-ups in the night. When they came to your house, they would ask '*thampi irukaa*?' ['Is your younger brother here?'].[9] Because of this, many joined the movement. They put up a sentry point too. There were two big officers there. The village people named one 'axe man' and the other one 'jasmine bud'. The second one was called that because of a pendant he had on a chain. When 'axe man' came out at least twenty boys would be taken … and finished. During the time that the LTTE moved amongst the people in the east and controlled them, the oppression through the caste system was minimal.

In 1984, the STF came to Batticaloa. I had another son on November 17. When I was in hospital with the new baby for the first time in my life I saw the STF. This was because someone was injured – a famous person was injured – and the STF brought him to hospital. STF at that time were so frightening and we were scared of them. They would immediately take action. I was with my baby and very frightened. I knew of the army but not the STF. My husband was arrested in 1984. I was seven months pregnant. He was in Karadiyanaru camp. The women used to go to the camp to look for their husbands. One STF had a palmyrah stick and he used to beat the women calling them '*Puli amma*' [Tiger mothers].[10] I was pregnant at that time and I had to move from the line so that he wouldn't hit my stomach. One STF picked up a stone and said, '*Kuti Puliya*' [Little Tiger] and he threatened to throw the stone at my stomach. I was separated from the other women at that point as they were in the other side. However, one other army man observed me and called me over. He asked why I was there. I explained and he asked my husband's name. He then went to check. He came back and said that he was in there and I could take him. My husband was beaten so badly that he could not walk straight. I put him on the bus and told the bus driver not to take money from him. My husband said to me, 'If I did not have you or child I would join them' [meaning the LTTE]. He told me that they beat him with an S-Lon pipe and then burnt plastic shopping bags and put them on their bodies.[11] It happened in the night. It would be the lower-level people who would do this, he said. He told me all the torture; they would rub chilli powder into the wounds. There was one officer asking questions and a boy was screaming because the officer had a pen in his ear and he kept slamming it. They would also hit people on their heels. They would tie their hands and hang them up. They did not take women at that time but most women were at the camps looking for their husbands and they got beaten.

One day I was teaching when the army came and took a man. He had a fourteen-day-old child. His wife was behind the army begging them to leave him. The next day they shot him. Another time there was a boy who had been in PLOTE and left. They caught him in the village, and took a stick and with his underwear they hung him from the stick. This was our experience during this time. It was our life.

The army and the STF had assumptions that the movement boys won't drink alcohol, won't marry, won't drink soda, smoke, or take betel. So then at this time all of our young boys started to do these things so that they would not look like the movement. Then my family moved to an LTTE area. At this time, PLOTE and TELO joined with the army and so they were with them. Before this, they had all lived in the same areas, so they knew each other. So when the people joined with the army, they were able to point out the LTTE families. There was one experience in my village – when the army was coming on a round-up, everyone would ask the boys to hide. One *amma* told her son to run – but the army caught him. They kept him in one place and then went to this *amma* and asked for her boy. She said I have no son. So then they brought the son in front of her and said, 'So he's not your son?', and they shot him. From 1985, there was at least one body every day.

The experiences that Meena faced during this time with extreme threat and violence from the STF and the many different Tamil militant groups in the east are difficult to fully comprehend. Yet, it is important to try and understand just how desperate and violent life was during this period. Meena's stories reveal the sheer vulnerability of women – young and old – who had no choice but to go to army camps to search for their husbands, brothers, and fathers; once there they faced intimidation, beatings, and worse from the armed forces. Tamil men, of all ages also found themselves caught in the webs of violence between the SLA and the Tamil militant groups. This was also the time when the LTTE were fighting to assert themselves as the sole representatives of the Tamil population by targeting previously fraternal Tamil militant groups (as noted in Chapter 2, page 37). Meena's comment about the young Tamil boys joining PLOTE and TELO shows how the youth, who were strategically pitted against one another, sought the 'protection' of one group or another. Tamil men, whether they were a part of an armed group of not, faced heightened risks – risks to be out in public, to travel around, to interact with the armed forces and militants (when it is virtually impossible not to), and to leave their wives and children at home. Against such risks, women were forced further into the public sphere to take on greater responsibilities and burdens, and deal with everyday experiences of violence that demanded strategising, negotiation, and endurance. The description of the wife chasing after her husband taken by the army and the young boy killed by the army in front of his mother who had tried to protect him reveal the intimacy of the everyday realities of life and death for families in the east at that particular time.

Around this time, the Batticaloa Peace Committee, initially composed of elder citizens in Batticaloa, was formed (see UTHR 1991). The committee originally formed to deal with the number of Tamils displaced from the south in the 1983 riots; however, as violence and killings increased they started to keep records of the incidents, and made regular representations with regard to missing persons. This included a massacre in Kokkadichcholai when 120 civilians, men, women, and children were killed, a number of women were also raped and beaten, and many people injured (Trawick 2007; UTHR 1991). In August 1990, the Peace Committee sent letters to the military authorities in Batticaloa, one with a list of over 400 missing persons in the Batticaloa area. In her letter to the Commission concerning the Sathurukandon massacre (as noted in Chapter 2, page 39), Lawrence detailed the difficulties faced by the Peace Committee and other human rights groups in the area as they tried to gather forensic evidence of the killings.[12]

Widowhood and survival: the occupation of the east

The Special Task Force (STF)

In 1986, I had my third child, a girl. My husband was always frightened and he told me that he should take everyone to the jungle. He said don't send the children to school. I fought with him. He wouldn't go for work and wanted to sell the land. At that time there was no income from Sarvodaya but I had been getting Rs 100 a month. I did not have enough food when pregnant and no clothes. I only had an underskirt and sarong. So when they [the STF] did a round-up, I had to cover myself with a towel. The army felt sorry for me – so in the next round-up, they said not to come but they took my husband. They said that they won't hurt my husband but I had to go the next day to get him. The others in the village had to go and they came back angry with me. I had no sari and I had to borrow one from my neighbour. The next day, they released him. But every time they [the STF] came, they took him; there was always a problem with my husband. There was no food, and my husband started drinking. He had all this body pain and so he drank. Most men drank alcohol at night. I had a nutrition problem and I lost my teeth. The doctor advised me that I did not have enough calcium. I tried to pull one tooth out myself. At thirty-two I had all my teeth pulled [out].

I wanted to go early to the hospital to have my baby. I was frightened because of the situation, and the children were scared, so I thought it was better to go one month early to hospital. We would be able to get food then too. This was 1986 in November. In the meantime, in the village my husband's mother pawned the land to others and bought food items, and took her son [Meena's husband] and my children and went to the LTTE jungle area. They had no ID cards.

My baby was born. Some other lady from the village was in the hospital, so I joined her and went home. No one was there. I went to my stepmother's house but no one was there. Because of the problems I had with my stepfather, I did not want to stay there. During that time, there was no food for me, only bread and manioc. But there was a family planning place, and if you went for the meeting you got Rs 20 – so I went and with the money bought some milk for my baby, as I had no breast milk. But then there was no more programmes like that and so nothing. I managed to pass a message to my husband about the baby and asked him to come. But he asked me to go to that area. I managed to look after the child alone for five months but then for two days the child had no food and died. Just before the baby died, one of the EROS member, working in the area, asked me to give him some tuition. When the child died, he gave me Rs 600 to bury the child.

Then I started to make *vadai* [a fried chickpea snack] to sell in the village. I went back to my land, made a small hut and was living alone. My land hadn't been sold but pawned, so I took it back [Meena later expanded on this by saying she managed to borrow the money to buy it back]. My mother-in-law had said that my last child was not her son's and that is why she died.

During this period, we lost two sister's husbands. They were missing. When the first husband went missing he had gone for work but he did not come back. He had two children. After three months, the second sister's husband was taken. He was twenty years old. He was taken by the police and kept in Boosa for six months.[13] Then he was released, he started work as a carpenter. Then again one day he went for work and disappeared. That was what happened – you got taken once, then that meant they would probably take you again and you never knew if you would come out.

By this time, my husband had returned with my children. They all had caught scabies. I told him, 'leave me and my children and go', as I did not want him, only the children. At that time, I had a Sarvodaya placement. My husband told them at work that I did not want him, and they all spoke to me and finally persuaded me to take him back. In the meantime, my stepfather, my mother's new husband, was not giving any food even to his own children. They all came to me and complained. One day, the stepfather got angry because they came to me, and he came to my house and hit my son. Then my son took a stone ready to throw it at the stepfather.

Violence, in terms of fighting and killings between the occupying STF and the LTTE, is routinely noted as framing life in the east during the late 1980s and early 1990s. However, what is often ignored is the reality of daily existence for people, especially for women, as they fought to care for their families and to keep going. The many descriptions in Meena's narrative of extreme levels of poverty – lack of food, lack of clothing, lack of healthcare, hygiene, etc., highlight the struggle faced. The death of her baby due to starvation, and her own lack of nutrition and good health was not uncommon for that time, and for Meena this tragedy sat alongside the many other threads of everyday hardship and violence including isolation, fear, lack of access to safe and secure spaces, and lack of support. The many small everyday coping mechanisms are also revealed in Meena's story, alongside the many losses. She describes how families moved around, often

Meena's story

shifting to LTTE-controlled areas to escape the threat of the SLA while many men turned to drink to numb the pain of the violence and fear they faced. Meanwhile, women like Meena had to make strategic decisions and tactically manoeuvre across obstacles in order to survive. Meena, for example, made and sold *vadai* to be able to feed herself and her children, and gave tuition to a young man, who in return was able to help her pay to bury her baby; demonstrating the kinds of supportive inter-relationships that could emerge between community members, neighbours, and even on occasion, the members of the armed forces.

The Indian Peace Keeping Force (IPKF)

Then I decided to move back to X [an uncleared area]. Me, my husband and three children, stepfather and his four boys and two girls (five children from his first marriage). We moved and my husband's attitude changed. He would give food and everything because in the landlord's house they would check the money and everything. I knew the landlady [from Jaffna] and trusted her. So everything was OK. I felt close to her – and particularly because one day I had a dream that the landlord was hit in the paddy field and injured ... three days later that happened.

My two sisters were widows. One was without children, so she went off for domestic work in Kalmunai. The other had two children, so she stayed with our older sister. One of those children died in the prawn farm massacre in Kokkadichcholai. That is why I never go back to Kokkadichcholai. But my older sister's husband was bad to her and hit her. She complained to me, so I said to come and stay with us. So then I had my other sister with us too. This was still the IPKF time, so it was good that we were together as women were scared to stay alone at that time. The IPKF had a bad reputation. They would rape women. We called them the Indian People Killing Force.

One day an IPKF soldier came to my home and was waiting at the gate. I went outside and was hiding from him because I was so scared. But he came looking for me but I was hiding behind a wall of the house. He came around the outside and I crept around behind him. We went around in a circle seven times but he did not catch me! What I did not know was that on a small study table in the house he had written me a letter in English. I did not know but my husband saw it. He took the letter to the *Mudalali* [merchant] who said that it was saying that I was beautiful and that he would come for me next time. I was five months pregnant at that time and so scared.

At that time I used to help a lot of people. For example, if the army came to their [her neighbour's] homes, then they would come to my house. People had many bad experiences. I don't think the men planned rape but they came to the house and then did it. One young girl was raped twice. It was in an isolated place in the jungle. Luckily, her husband understood the situation and did not blame her. If we heard the food lorry coming for the army, then we won't stay in the village. We would leave for about one day. If the men are not at home, then at least five or six families can sleep together. The LTTE was a problem because the army was scared of the LTTE – so then the army had more men guarding and patrolling. In the village, all the women were very frightened. If the LTTE threw a grenade, then [the] IPKF came after you. They would ask for '*thannir*' [water] and then follow you into the house.

> So many problems: if it is the Sri Lankan Army, then the women send their husbands away; if it is the IPKF, then even the women cannot stay. This is how we were trapped. The boys in the village – the ones who were without a moustache – they [the IPKF] would take them too and keep them separately and rape them too. They used Manresa [a building located beside the lagoon close to Batticaloa] – it was a Catholic seminary that was captured by the army and used as a prison. First in 1988. That was the first place that women were raped. Then, later at Thanamunai, which was six kilometres from Batticaloa. It would be reasons like – the IPKF vehicle got caught in a landmine then they would get angry and rape many women. They never distinguished between the women; married or not, young or old.
>
> The IPKF opened a dispensary, so people used to go for medicine. It was a way of forming relationships with people. At one point, I got a headache and had to get medicine from them. During this IPKF time, the women started joining the LTTE. There was my stepfather's eldest daughter. My stepfather used to say she looked like a widow woman even though she was only twenty years old. He said that because of this he could not give a dowry, so then he said he would propose her to a disabled man. She told me and said she was afraid. So then she joined the LTTE. She stayed with them ten years. Now she is back with us and after two years of leaving she got married but after six months he left her. My stepfather's two sons also joined the LTTE because of how their father was. After two years, the family wrote to the LTTE, and they came back and got married.

As Meena points out, the Indian soldiers who arrived in the north and east of Sri Lanka under the Indo-Sri Lanka Accord (ISLA) are largely remembered, particularly amongst women, for their reign of terror. Initially, given the atrocities being carried out by both the Sri Lankan forces and the LTTE in the east, the eastern Tamils had been welcoming of the IPKF. However, the IPKF simply added to the number of armed players causing suffering and loss for civilians as they carried campaigns of killings and rape of local girls and women (see UTHR 1989, 1990a; Alison 2003). Lawrence (1997: 269) has highlighted the fact that Tamil people living under military occupation on the east coast consider rape the ultimate form of violation, and that victims of rape are considered 'irredeemable and utterly ruined'.[14] This is explained by the strong ideological values placed on virginity (*Kannimai*), which is expected of a Tamil bride, and chastity (*Karpu*) understood to be a part of the symbolism of the marriage *tali*, tied around the neck of a woman upon marriage (see Reynolds 1980: 46). The stigma attached to rape has led to many families concealing attacks that have taken place and has also caused a number of women to escape the 'shame' by committing suicide, or joining the LTTE.[15] Although women had been part of the LTTE since 1983, and despite claims that the role of female Tigers offered 'liberation' for Tamil women, the experience of Meena's stepfather's eldest daughter, like many of the other stories I heard, reveal that many women joined as a way of escaping difficult situations at home, including poverty, abuse, and unhappy relationships. This is also supported by evidence that the period around 1989 in which women suffered high levels of rape and violence correlates with the highest recruitment rates for the LTTE (de Silva 1994; Alison 2003; Trawick 2007). Although many women's groups and feminist campaigns have rejected the Tamil term for rape, *karpalippu* meaning 'destruction of chastity' and have sought to re-shape local concepts of rape, the shame and silencing has continued (Maunaguru 1995: 166).

Early 1990s: displacement and disappearances

My last son was born on 17 March 1989, and in the 1990s big problems started in Sri Lanka. The government forces were trying to clear areas and so some families were camped at the Eastern University campus, others [went] to Vinayagapuram [a paddy area] and so I went to that area. My sister and her family came with us – so we were all together. One sister did not come with us, she went with another group.

There was a gradual build up. My elder sister's husband went for work. The *mudalali* [merchant] was Muslim and OK with him. But there was another man who was upset with the *mudalali*, so he told the army that he was keeping LTTE. So they cut him [killed him]. He was my mother's brother's son. So then they all moved to our area. During that time in our area we were not used to the plane bombings. One plane did a round and then we saw these things falling from the plane. The children said they were birds. But then we saw the fire and realised that we could be killed by the things from this plane. And then there would be the helicopters in the sky. They would see people on the street and come low behind them and shoot. We used to hide under a tree. It was a very muddy area and there was lots of water. People could not see the tree from the sky. However, it wasn't a good area as there was lots of crocodiles and snakes, etc. We did not know what to do though. Until the helicopter left the area, we would all be hiding in the tree.

One day though, a person was trying to move from there and he was seen by the helicopter. They shot him and he got very injured. In the 1990s, so much happened. The EROS office was destroyed by the army. We were in the jungle area. The Muslim community would do business with us as they were working in their area. We had to work with food exchange, as we had no money. We gave paddy. But then one day the LTTE killed one hundred people in Eravur, and after that the Muslims stopped coming to that area. At that time, some Tamil people did not know about the incident in Eravur, so they still went to their side and then they got killed.

Meena associates the arrival of 'big problems' in the east with the incursion of the armed forces into the east, and the use of planes and helicopters to bomb and fire onto LTTE areas. She also outlines the fragile communal relations in the east which had the capacity to implode at any time if communities were threatened, felt betrayed, or sought retaliation and revenge as a result of grievances. While interactions and working exchanges took place between Tamils and Muslims, as Meena's example of Muslims trading with displaced Tamils demonstrates, risk and violence simmered at the edges and were easily fuelled by those in power. For example, the communal violence that broke out in 1990 when the LTTE murdered hundreds of surrendered Muslim policemen triggered Muslims to violently target Tamils in response. As in 1985, the anti-Tamil violence was

The Eastern University tragedy

> There were nearly 45,000 people in the Eastern University. They had nothing. Those families would try to get to their area to take food but then the Muslims would kill them. So they had started to take whatever they could, even furniture, etc. The army found out, so took it to their side. Then, in 1990 on September 5, the SLA did a huge round-up in the University. They took 156 men and they all went missing. This included government officers, bankers, the GS [*Grama Sevaka* – government official], school children. All of them gone, unaccounted for ... this is what they managed to do and nobody could stop them.

As Meena notes during the 1990s the Eastern University became a refugee camp for families from surrounding villages in the east who felt unsafe and were fleeing fighting between the army and LTTE. As families arrived at the camp numbers swelled from 10,000 to 46,000. Although the government expressed concern over the numbers of people in the camp, they did not have the resources to support the IDPs, and so allowed the camp to continue. Meanwhile the LTTE, irritated by the loss of civilian cover in adjacent villages, attempted acts of sabotage by planting a mine outside the entrance of the university and blowing up transformers supplying electricity to the university campus (UTHR 1990a). In accordance with Meena's version of events, the UTHR report (ibid.) states that 158 detainees were forcibly taken from the Eastern University refugee camp to the Valaichchenai Army camp, and from there they were 'disappeared'. Many locals also recounted the story to me describing how everyone in the camp had been ordered to line up and prepare for a routine check of ID cards. However, once they were outside the men and women were separated, and then the men forced to line up. At the front of the line a row of men with hoods over their faces were made to 'identify' whether the men were militants or not. They would nod or shake their heads, and those identified were put in the group that was taken to the camp.[16] While many other such large-scale incidents took place, in which large numbers of Tamil-speaking men, women, and children were taken away and disappeared, the events at the Eastern University seem to have remained lodged in people's memories. This could perhaps be seen as a reaction to the state's attempts to erase such memories by refusing to investigate, and even to acknowledge what took place at that time. With the reality of the event being denied, people have held more tightly onto the obvious absences and painful loses endured at that time.

1991–2: Survival against the odds

> In our area [Viyaganapuram], we were safe. There was sometimes bombings and shootings but we managed. In cleared areas, they had the problems. One day we heard the army moving close and we all got scared and started to run. My husband took three children, my sister's husband had one, I had one, and my sister had one ... we were all running. Then the helicopter started firing. I could

see them, my hair was flying, and I could feel it behind me. I crouched down at the side and was trying to hide the children under me, trying to keep them covered. Then my son started shouting – three children were with my husband and they were still running. The helicopter was going from side to side and bullets were spraying everywhere – into the palmyrah trees that were around us. I am still terrified of the noise of the helicopter. My daughter is also scared. I used to get really bad headaches.

We spent one year in the jungle. In 1991, we all started to come back to the village slowly. Sometimes people left again because they were scared and then they waited and then they came back. We were always going and coming, going and coming. At that time many women lost husbands through the shooting. When people think about war, they only think of that kind of widow, yet many husbands also died from snakebites and illness too.

I was working as a midwife at the time. I delivered six babies [one girl and five boys]. I had no training but I just learnt. One child was born at 2 a.m., and then the next day we waited for the placenta but it did not come out for hours. The mother was just 16 and that was the first child for her. At that time there was lots of incidents inside houses with the army – you would come and find blood and bras. If you had paddy sacks then the army would take it for their sentry points. From X [cleared area], I moved to another place. I was frightened to stay in the house and so stayed in my mother's house. My stepfather had married a second time. My elder sister had gone back to Kayankerny. Amma was in X with children and she put a small shop. I went to Y [an uncleared area] and I got some land and built a house. It was 1991. In November, with my family we went to that house. Through the back of the house there was a TELO camp with the army. They were pointing people out. They would kill them and leave a note.

Meena's train of descriptions of survival strategies here all highlight the levels of 'structural violence' (Galtung 1996) embedded in daily life in the east. Violence, that is, of the quotidian kind, the physical and the psychological violence of poverty, the violence of hunger and disease and of not being able to protect one's children, the violence of blocked access to jobs and futures, and exclusion from the means to a better life. These were all forms of violence and vulnerabilities that surrounded Meena throughout her adolescence and adulthood. The way in which Meena retells these experiences also suggests that they existed in some way on a continuum – physical violence, environmental violence, emotional violence, sexual violence, all ran into and overlapped with one another as people sought ways of surviving and coping. Meena's description of working as a midwife without training also reflects the severe shortages of medical support and equipment in the east in the 1990s as well as restricted access to hospitals. HRW (1992) documents the restrictions placed by the Sri Lankan government on the import of essential supplies into LTTE-controlled areas, which put heavy burdens on medical staff and the civilian populations. Food was also reported to be in dangerously short supply in the uncleared areas of north and east. This problem was compounded by government restrictions on the amount of food people were allowed to transport into these areas, reportedly to be only what is sufficient for one person for three days in the case of the northern Batticaloa district (ibid.).

Tragedy

July 1992. My husband was killed. He went for work and was killed. During 1992 there was so much control and you could not take much into uncleared areas, no batteries, etc. Army limited everything so that you could not give them to the LTTE. So my husband went and said that for ten days he would not come back. He went with a team for paddy work. I had a dream that night and a tense feeling in my body. I predicted a negative effect to my family. Before he died, my husband visited all of his sisters and even said to one of them that maybe there would be some problem for our land – but that he knew I wouldn't allow that.

He left in the morning around 7 a.m. I was teaching. I came home and lit the lamp. I was trying to make a cup of tea for my son using palmyrah leaves. Then I heard shooting. I thought someone was running towards our house, so I shouted to the children to get a knife. But no one came. That night no one slept. The next day I felt that someone was telling me to tie the door shut. Without knowing why I felt I had to take some kind of responsibility. The next day I heard people talking and heard that someone had been shot and it was very near us near the bridge.

The second morning people were talking about it again. I advised people not to go and find out, and I went back to school. Then the GS arrived at the school. I thought he was arriving for work. But he asked me to come and then took me to the camp. He said that there was one body there. I asked why they would kill my husband, as he has no connection. We went to the body. I identified him only from a photograph he had in his pocket. His face was so badly damaged that I could not tell. Even my sister's husband could not tell who it was. My friend had been to India and bought back a temple thread. I had tied that to my husband's wrist, and so when we went into the camp and I saw the body I could see that the thread was there. But his body was so damaged – everything was coming out of his head – he had only one eye looking at me. But the thread was there.

Just before this incident there had been a landmine set for the Valaichchenai train. When the train had stopped and people had got out then they had been shot dead. When I was in the camp after finding my husband's body a lorry arrived with the Muslim bodies from the train. I tried to jump into the lorry, as I wanted to die. But the lady behind me held onto me tightly. The day before my husband had left, someone had seen the army talking to my husband. This person had wanted to tell me but he had met someone on the road and got chatting. It had then got late, so he had decided to tell me the next day. If I had known that night then I could have gone to the camp and saved him.

While I was still in the camp, a person came along with a palmyrah cap. I jumped on him and grabbed his shirt saying that he killed my husband. He was a TELO man. Then they brought a van and took the body with the army escort to the hospital. The police asked me questions and asked me to sign for the body. I refused. What world is this? They killed my husband and I have to sign to get him back dead? But a Muslim man persuaded me. I asked for the body. We went to the mortuary. There were sixteen army bodies there too. They did not clean the body and I could not see which one he was because of the sheets.

Then we took the body home. We were stopped at the Eravur border and the army were around us. A group of Muslims were looking for Tamils to kill because of the train incident. They stopped us and asked us to open the van and show the body. If the army had not been there, then me, my brother's wife, and others who were with us, all would be finished. We took the body home and had a ceremony. We could not keep the body there for long as it was badly injured, so we buried it. The villagers helped. We had just put a new cemetery in the village, and he was the seventh person to go. I had to go there on the thirtieth day. My sister was with me. We were really worried that the army were around the area because they had been saying that my husband was an LTTE supporter. It wasn't true but they [the army] had said that so that people wouldn't come to my house.

Meena stopped talking at this point in the interview, and it was clear that all three of us in the room were visibly upset by what she had just described. Prior to the interviews, I had been aware that Meena had been widowed but I did not know the circumstances or any of the details of how she lost her husband. At first, I was surprised by how she described her husband's horrific death in the same way that she had described other details in her story, and as if it simply flowed as a part of the many other losses she and others experienced at that time. However, the more I reflected on this and on Meena's story, I realised that, for Meena, this was the only way to narrate, and, perhaps, to make sense of what had happened – that each loss added to the thread of other losses – although this did not mean that it was not felt more heavily or painfully. Meena's husbands' death, like the deaths of so many other men in the north and east in Sri Lanka, was saturated with pain, brutality, and the sheer inhumanity dealt by the armed forces at that time. Yet, because these deaths did not happen just once but happened over and over again – each time the thickness of violence ripping apart a family – they could not be seen as an isolated incident. That Meena dwells on the fact that she had to sign to get back the body of her husband after he had been tortured and killed illustrated to her the absurdity of the context and of the world in which she was living. Nothing about it was 'normal', and, yet, she had to take control of the situation, reorder in that moment, to be able to collect her husband's body, to tell her children what had happened, to organise a burial, and to provide single-handedly for her family thereafter as a matter of course of life at that time.

Making ends meet

1992–4: Widows and NGOs

At that time I was still working with Sarvodaya as a volunteer. With no pay we had no food. One day my son, who was three, vomited something a white colour because he had had no food. I talked to the next-door people and told them my problem. The lady shouted, 'Why did you not tell me?' She gave me rice and sugar for the children. I was frightened by that experience and felt that I needed to earn some money. It was not long after the funeral and I had four children in the house. They were always crying and were very frightened. So was I. I bought some paddy seeds, and made rice by boiling and breaking it. I wanted to sell that. But I did not know the exact boiling time, so that got spoilt and I had to give it to the children instead. At that time you got a food stamp, and if you gave one *sindu* [tin] then you would get coconut and chilli. So I pawned my food stamp and got the money. I bought the ingredients to make *vadai* and for the first two days that went well. But after that it did not. Then I talked to the shop man about making *kadalai* [boiled chickpeas]. I started making this and made Rs 90. This was 1992. That time the situation had slightly reduced. There was less round-ups.

My children missed their father. My daughter was always crying and seemed to miss him. My son was always asking questions. His body had been in the sun at the camp for so long that his skin was coming off. My child thought someone had pulled it off. People had also said that he had been chopped in the head. One day when I went out my second son made a doll and hung it from the tree. He would play killing with his friends. My elder son would wake up at night and run, thinking his father was there. One day we were all sitting outside and we all fell asleep. Early the next morning we woke up with a dog barking. We woke up and saw the army around us staring. The army asked us where's the husband. When I said he was dead they said we did not need to come for the round-up. They took others, and even beat the women.

November 1992. We made a widows society. In that group, some of the women used to meet with the AGA [Additional Government Administrator] Section. Within that section was the RDO [Rural Development Officer] whom we used to ask for help. But that man used to shout at the widows. One woman cried because he shouted so much. So I went and met him, and shouted back at him. Then after that he kept quiet ... and then said that he would help me. He directed me to ERO [Eastern Rehabilitation Organization) and I came to Batticaloa to meet them. There I met a person in ERO. He thought that I had just brought the other woman with me, and did not realise that I was also a widow. But then when he found out that I too was a widow he told me that there was a group coming from Colombo to meet with widows to run a workshop at Manresa. I really wanted to do this, so I went home and pawned my food stamps (at that time with the food stamps you got Rs 240 every month for six months).[17] Then, if you pawn it people will give you Rs 120 and you can buy the food yourself. So I pawned three stamps and got Rs 360 to buy all of the food for my children and my sister's children. I had to buy for all of them. And I sent my children to my sister's place. Training was good. I was selected as the second-best person in the training, and so then selected as a field officer. I got Rs 500 per month for six months. I had to work in my village and then come to Batticaloa once a month. My work was mostly getting documents such as ID cards, birth certificates [of the deceased] with the widows. During the training, someone from the *Kachcheri* [district administrative headquarters] had come down and advised us on how to get the information. This was a very difficult thing for the widows to get.

Meena's descriptions here of dealing with the aftermath of her husband's horrific death are told here mostly through the needs and the suffering of her children. Given the situation for them at that time, space for grieving were filled with the rawness of loss exacerbated by the inability to meet the family's basic needs. Her children, it is clear, were profoundly affected by the loss of their father, and the vulnerability and isolation of being alone with only their mother. Meena, meanwhile, had to negotiate ways of dealing with their extreme poverty – finding items that she could cook and sell to make money, and pawning her food stamps.

It is clear that Meena situation was relieved somewhat when she was able to access training through various women-based organisations. This reflects some of the work that was being done to provide support to widows in eastern Sri Lanka during the 1990s. However, as Meena demonstrates, despite this specific support, the majority of widowed heads of households continued to face a constant battle for economic stability, privacy, and physical safety. Ruwanpura (2006: 212) has identified the significance of 'non-economic' networks amongst female kin in eastern Sri Lanka, with a movement from support from men to support from women. In particular, the experiences of dislocation and displacement faced by some female-heads have shown how women have given support by meeting each other's practical needs. Furthermore, Ruwanpura notes 'in rare instances some women show a feminist consciousness that can be used to meet strategic gender needs' (ibid.).[18] Based on what I heard and observed while visiting widows and mothers with the *Valkai* group, I would suggest that this was more than 'rare' in the border villages, and that a number of informal networks of various shapes and forms existed between women across communities. Meena and other women like her, for example, were well aware of their positions in society as well as the kinds of restrictions and problems they faced as women in Sri Lanka. This awareness, though not always explicitly articulated, helped bring women together to strategically work in various spaces to support one another, and to challenge their everyday experiences.

Gendered vulnerabilities

While I was in training, my three daughters became big girls [began menstruation for the first time] but I did not know.[19] When I had finished the workshop I was travelling home and had to stop at the checkpoint. I was in the queue, and the woman behind me was pulling at my sari and crying. I got scared about what might have happened. But after checking, she told me that my daughter had got big.[20] The Rs 500 I was earning was not enough for me, so I made *kadalai* in the night and from that made another Rs 500. In that way, I could manage my family.

I worked in Kalmunai and Ampara [on the east coast] but that meant that I had to leave my family. I stayed with a widow who I knew because, although the organisation gave me my travelling fees, they did not give me any accommodation. I put my daughters in a hostel. And then the three boys – they were sometimes with others and sometimes alone. They would cook and eat on their own. One day when I had come home, I was looking for my coconut spoon to do some cooking. I started shouting that people had taken it but then my son said that they had used it for firewood! Then I was looking for a teacup, and they had broken it and buried it. I came home every 2–3 days. I feel that in that period my son, who was twelve-years-old, changed a lot. There was a lot of responsibility on him like cooking after school, etc. Within our area there were a lot of children without a father or whose mother was abroad. They would all get together at my house and eat. They wasted a lot of things.

During that period I had lots of opportunity for training. So I was mostly out of the home with training. But then, my younger brother went missing [he was the tenth child]. Before him, the army had taken another brother, who was also in the movement. The army had brought him in front of my mother and beaten my mother.[21] They kept him in prison for two years and eventually a friend got him out. I had another brother in the movement too. He had been working to mend a bridge, and the army had come and beaten them, so then he ran to the movement. He did not come back to Batticaloa but went to Jaffna. So I had two sisters and two brothers in the movement. One sister had joined after her husband had died as she felt she had no protection for the family. My stepfather had abused another sister, so because of that she joined. I felt at one time that with so many family members in the movement, maybe this could be a reason for my husband's death.

One time I had to go to Ampara for a programme. I had sent all of my family together to one place and I got a bus to Batticaloa. But two days earlier there had been an incident at a checkpoint – the army had killed everyone by cutting them with a knife. I did not know this and so I was travelling in the bus and then the bus had stopped at this point. The driver then told me what had happened. The army made everyone get down. I stayed on with one lady with a child and an old woman. One STF guy got on the bus and was staring at me. He asked me why I could not get down. I told him that I could not walk. He asked for my ID card. I had three ID cards at that time. The STF then asked the other lady why she hadn't got down. He then turned to me and asked me if I was working. I had an SLRC [Sri Lanka Red Cross] ID card. That made the man nervous. I told him that I was a committee member because I knew that the bodies from their killing would have been collected by the SLRC. Then everyone was allowed back on the bus. The driver said, 'Because of this lady, you have all been saved'.

I used to be involved in a programme for released prisoners. I formed a group and went to Colombo. But then they said that there was no money for our group because it had been given to the south. So we were all upset as we had lots of expectations. Then another day when I went for the meeting they said that there were clothes I could take for Batticaloa people. But they did not open the door and show me what clothes were there. Yet, when people from the south came, they opened the door so that they would get first choice. Another time Z [an NGO] had got sponsorship for twelve children. In a meeting, they decided on six children from the south, four Tamil children and two Muslim children. I got up in the meeting, and asked why they had such discrimination and why could it not be four from each? But from that time onwards people made it tough for me, and were always making jokes and trying to get me out.

There was a director there who seemed to care about people who travelled from the east. But the others questioned him. This man resigned, and we all got upset and decided not to work for Z anymore. We were angry with the director because before he left he had organised training in Batticaloa but never did it. After he left it was decided I should work with an NGO coordinator in Batticaloa. I had to start a vocational training programme. I suggested starting it right away and he said yes. But then I got a letter from Colombo saying, 'Who told you to start?'. I had a letter proving that I should start immediately, so I sent that and they gave me the money. But all of these issues forced me to leave the NGO.

One day a Colombo team came to Batticaloa for an evaluation of the work. I had to stay in Kalmunai, so I asked the Kalmunai team whether they can take care of me. They said No. So then I had to go to Kalmunai and stay in the office. I prepared everything, and then kept my files by my bed as I planned to get up early in the morning and finish my work. However, there was one accountant from another organisation in the same building, and at 10 p.m. he opened the door and asked what I was doing. I said sleeping and he went away. Around 1 a.m. I woke to feel someone touching me, and I shouted, '*Sir Niingalaa?*' [Is it you?]. He said don't worry I am just coming to sleep with you. I grabbed the key and ran to the watcher. The watcher asked me what had happened, and I told him that there was a ghost but actually the watcher knew because this man had abused many women.

That man was angry with me when I warned other people, and said I was spreading rumours. He was so angry that he even tried to push other men onto me. You know it is a point because now people are writing about the abuse of NGO people after the tsunami but people know that from the 1990s that women were getting abused in NGOs. After this I resigned from Z and on 1 June 1996 I joined another local organisation working with children affected by trauma from the violence. For me, this was like heaven from hell. There was a big difference with this kind of work with children. But still there were administrative issues, which disappointed and saddened me as I had expected more of a difference.

Again, Meena's narrative reminds us of the stark reality of life for women, and particularly widows, in the east. She highlights the extent of sexual violence that women suffered in the 1990s, and the lack of reporting on and action against it by contrasting it with the attention given to the post-tsunami controversy around women working for local and international NGOs in the Eastern Province in 2006. This stemmed from a scandal in which it was alleged that local women working for national and international agencies had been forced into appearing in pornographic 'blue' films, followed by the distribution of informal leaflets in April 2006 calling for women to cease working in NGOs to protect their culture and purity (Women and Media Committee [WMC] 2006).[22] The contrast in the way that the latter controversy was dealt with in comparison to the frequent and systematic sexual violence that Meena describes is most likely due to the fact that the former is by men from the same culture and community of their victims, and, therefore, is tied into many layers of secrecy, fear, and denial. Abuse by 'outsiders' (both Sinhalese and foreigners), however, is less problematic and the apparent perpetrators can easily be condemned. This brings us back yet again to the intersections at which different forms of vulnerability and violence play into one another and trap women in eastern Sri Lanka within a web of complex and destructive forces. For example, the intended sexual violence by the NGO accountant who tried to attack Meena in the night was made possible by the context of relative isolation and vulnerability of women created through the wider context of political violence.

Another layer of abuse and discrimination described by Meena is found in the ways she was treated by NGOs. Orjuela (2005: 213–23) states that the divides in Sri Lankan society between the north-east and south were reflected in civil society organisations and particularly peace movements (see Chapter 2, pages 40–1). Echoing Meena's experiences, Orjuela notes that most large peace organisations had their base in Colombo, and many were perceived to be Sinhala-dominated. Moreover, many Sinhala peace activists did not speak Tamil and a lack of interaction across boundaries and geographical distances also led to a lack of understanding of Tamil perspectives (ibid.). The elite nature of the best-established and most-prominent civil society organisations also serves to explain the lack of emphasis placed on socio-economic rights and class inequality in preference for the 'middle class orientated' Human Rights agenda (Keenan 2003; Orjuela 2005: 222). Goodhand and Hulme (1999: 27) have shown that locals in eastern Sri Lanka were critical of NGOs, which they saw as unreliable, serving their own agendas, and favouring the wealthy over the poorest such as widows, the elderly, and the landless.[23]

Factional politics, fractured lives

In October 1996, my son, who was fifteen years old, with a school friend joined the LTTE. He joined because my brother had been violent with him, and he was angry and revengeful and wanting to get his own back on his uncle. I asked the LTTE to release them but they wouldn't. But in 2000 he came home – at that time the LTTE used to send boys home, which they said was for the family but it was really for them to gather intelligence. My son did not want to go back and so he stayed with me. I had to keep him at home. He had no ID documents. But on 12 January they came for him. About ten of them came and took him away in the night. I went behind them but they wouldn't give him back. Then the LTTE sent me a letter to meet them at Illuppudichenai, so I went. He [Meena's son] was in punishment, and they said that after three years of punishment they would release him. So 12 January was the last time I saw my eldest son. Those who were with him or in the LTTE told me that they had sent him to the Vanni in the north.

Sridevi, my eldest daughter who was born in 1979, was upset about her brother leaving. She had not completed her O' levels and was at home. She was quite close to him. She joined Manresa [a Catholic seminary and training centre] for one and a half years, on a sewing and hairdressing course, after which I took her home in 2001. On the 4 February 2001, she got registered [married]. In 2001, she started working with World Vision [an INGO] as a social mobiliser. In 2002, she gave birth to a daughter and then on 10 September 2004, the LTTE took her husband away. This was just after the LTTE split. The LTTE said that her husband was supporting Karuna. That was not true. Karuna and the LTTE were the same – they both came from the same thing. My daughter went to the

LTTE several times but they just said that he was a traitor. For two years, my daughter was unable to see him. She went to the LTTE continuously, and finally they told her in 2006 that he had been sent to the Vanni. They said that as long as Karuna was here they would not show him in Batticaloa.

Like many of the other mothers noted in this book, Meena did everything possible to try and get her son back from the LTTE. Although she states that her son initially 'joined' the LTTE, she also notes that he was fleeing violence at home, and, therefore, joined as an escape route, and for revenge. Revenge, poverty, deprivation (particularly in the border areas), abuses, and suffering under the SLA, alongside a sophisticated LTTE propaganda machine, are factors that many parents have identified as being behind child-recruitment (HRW 2004; interviews with families in the east). Once recruited, most children were not allowed contact with their families. The LTTE would subject them to rigorous, and, sometimes, brutal, training, and used public punishment of those who tried to run away to discourage other children from trying. One of the biggest problems for parents in the east whose children were taken was that many were moved to the north for training and fighting, and, therefore, parents had no way of contacting them or knowing their fate. This was particularly the case in 1997–9, the time when Meena's son had been recruited, when the army fought a large-scale offensive to recapture the Vanni. It is reported that the LTTE only managed to survive through the influx of hundreds of cadres from the east, which ironically was organised by the LTTE eastern commander at that time, Colonel Karuna.

The story that Meena tells here of her daughter's husband being taken by the LTTE and sent to the Vanni shows how these kind of loses were repeated for women from generation to generation. Like her mother before her, Sridevi had to repeatedly visit the LTTE asking for news of her loved one, and find ways of negotiating around the everyday risks and violence. However, as became common during and after the time of the LTTE split in 2004, people became trapped by the shifting contexts and boundaries of control. From mid-2004, there was a major surge in political killings, not just in the north and east but also in Colombo where Karuna's group engaged in the kidnapping of wealthy Tamil businessmen. In the east, as noted throughout this book, people and families became trapped by the 'shadow war' between the LTTE's two factions, and hundreds of civilians, such as Meena's son-in-law, found themselves victim to escalating tit-for-tat arrests and killings.

A disaster of a different kind

On 26 December 2004, there was the tsunami. This did not directly affect my family but there is not a person who is not affected here in the east. So many people died and it was such a big trauma for so many.

At my work with the children – many children lost their parents or brothers and sisters. It was so sad as many would be crying, crying and X [who runs the project] would be trying to comfort them but what can you say? If it is the war then others know this pain and we know why even if it is not right but with the tsunami, it was so unexpected and no reasons why. And the tsunami brought in so many people to do more NGO work. Too many people were here, and they had all this money – but you can't bring people back with money. That is not the answer. It made people angry and it started these problems with local people and foreign people too.

As I have already noted in Chapters 1 and 2, the tsunami brought more strain to a region already faced with multiple displacements and losses from the conflict. In her comments about the children at her work who were struggling to cope with the loss of their family members in the tsunami, Meena highlights the differences between the kinds of violence and loss engendered by the conflict and tsunami. Where people had developed strategies and tactics for dealing with the violence of the conflict, the tsunami created an unfamiliar situation for communities. In the following chapter, I look at the use of space by local communities and particular the *Valkai* group to suggest that the chaos and confusion caused by the tsunami inadvertently allowed people to do things and connect in ways they had not been able to before. However, running through this context is also the reality that the tragedy of the tsunami also brought more and new suffering and pain to communities that had already lost in so many ways. As Meena notes, unlike the conflict, people were not prepared for this loss in anyway, and had no previous experience through which to comprehend and filter what had happened. While no loss during the conflict can be seen as 'normal', at the same time the high levels of threat, risk, and violence meant that people were aware of and feared disappearances and deaths. However, when the sea suddenly receded and then crashed down onto homes, schools, churches, and temples, people were completely taken by surprise, and their everyday sensibilities and ability to navigate risks momentarily ruptured.

2006: Family burdens

Then my daughter had a problem in her workplace and she gave the job up in June 2006. After leaving she met this new man who was a widower with three children. I was unaware that she was secretly married to this man and I only got to find out through my niece. I was very upset by this. At this time we were celebrating the tenth anniversary at my workplace. My family was together. There was my sister's children, my daughter and her husband and one-year-old son. We all cooked together. We had everything together and were managing. But then my sister died in an accident with fire – it was 22 July 2005 – so her two daughters came to me. Then, Deepan, my third child got married, and was pregnant living with me too. It was an unimaginable burden on me.

Deepan's child was born on the 9 September 2006. When her husband went to visit her in hospital ... I went too to see the child ... at that time the husband was coming out to get hot water and was delayed in coming back. I started looking for him. When he did not come back at 2 p.m. I came out looking for him and was thinking what could have happened to him. Then I overheard the hospital security saying, 'See – that boy who went to get hot water was taken away.' The moment I heard this I pounced on the security guard and asked him what had happened. I went to the TMVP office and they told me that he would

Meena's story

come out. He did come out and he was really frightened. It was apparently a case of mistaken identity – they had handcuffed him and tied him up – and then only started to find out who he was. He is now a little settled after that fright and has put a small shop next to the house. He also does many odd jobs – masonry, wiring, and carpentry. Many men try to get by like this – they are always so scared of being taken – and there are so many groups to take them – so they never know what they can do and what they can say.

As Meena explained what had happened to her son-in-law, I observed how her voice had dropped lower, and she had seemed less at ease. It also seemed that the closer we got to the present the more fractured and stilted Meena's narrative became. This could be attributed to the fact that Meena had been telling me her story in great detail for long stretch of time and, therefore, was tired and emotionally drained. Moreover, we were arriving at events that were recent and, thus, more raw. At the same time, however, it also seemed to reflect a fragility of the present moment. Something about the current complexity of the situation, the shifting lines of control, the shadow violence, and the threats and fear that ensnared and darted between the past, present, and future seemed to be captured in Meena's telling. Whereas the past had somewhat consolidated in shape and experience as time had passed, the very recent past and the present remained fluid, raw, and dangerous.

'This is what it is'

On 19 January 2007, another of my sons, Theesan, was taken by the TMVP. They took him from home. He had completed his O' levels and was following a course in plumbing. From 21 January, I went repeatedly to the TMVP, and with others continued asking for him until they released him.

Back to Sridevi – she came to stay with me and with her husband gave birth to a baby boy on 10 July 2007. Then we came to X as I sold my house in Y. I sold it because of the problems I had with my sister's husband, who I heard had told the TMVP about my eldest son being at home at that time. But then my sister's husband died of electric shock. It was exactly one year after he had betrayed my son to the TMVP. Since then I have been trying to get by. My niece, whose mother died in the fire, has been trying to complete her studies at Jaffna University. However, she had to come back after the split problems because she was scared, and she hasn't been able to get back since. She wants to study but what can she do? We can't move about as we want and if she goes there [to Jaffna] will she ever get back to us? I am still trying to get land. I am going this afternoon to talk about the deeds but the problem is that you make an agreement, you exchange money, but even then you might lose out.

I don't want to leave my area now; we are all together there. But my son is scared of being taken again and I don't want to lose any more. This is what it is.

It was a hot and sticky afternoon when Meena and I completed our series of interviews. We had moved from the office to the house where I was living with Anuloja and others at that time. By the time I had finished scribbling down the last part of her story, Meena was lying on her side across the mat, her head cushioned in the crook of her arm and her eyes following the movements of the slow steady fan above us. The room felt thick with sadness, anger, and anticipation; the words that had formed Meena's narrative edged around us on the cusp of tears, a scream, or some noise that would break that heavy quiet. Yet, besides the whir of the fan and the faint chatter from the road outside, there was no other noise and silence remained in the room. Thinking back now to those hours with Meena, at times during the interviews, there appeared to be solipsism to her narrative. This stemmed not from self-obsession or vanity but from her perception of herself as the fixed point in all of the chaos and discordance. It seemed to me that Meena was always looking for her own edge, exploring how far things could go, and amidst all of the pain and loss she experienced, where she could find solid ground to put her feet. Despite the many fragments and disruptions to her life, Meena's narrative moved smoothly between the *now* of the present and *then* of her past. Although she would distinguish between the two, they were also 'narratively co-present' (Gilsenan 1996: 96); they existed together in the same moment, shaping each other back and forth. While there were obviously details and moments that got lost in the process of translation, the simple act of being there – sharing in the experiences of Meena's life – allowed her past as an active ingredient in her present and future to come alive. These were all parts of her life story that Meena remained in the midst of, and with which she continued to grapple; unlike conventional stories, for Meena the story's outcome was far from given.

In conflict, violence creates many traps, blocks, and situations of powerlessness. Yet, in the face of this inequity, strategies of endurance and survival also emerge. It is the various spaces in which these factors play out that Meena's narrative represents a reality of the past that means she does not get labelled as a victim or widow. Instead, her reality troubles the boundaries of fixed categories, and pushes us in the direction of narrative histories that acknowledge the positioning of the author and the subject, and do not privilege one interpretation over another. Meena's narrative also emphasises the necessity of recognising moments in history, of noticing where and how people are located within space and time, both literally and metaphorically, and how this, in turn, shapes the telling and remembering of stories. It is from this platform of the significance of competing narratives and multiple versions of reality and truth that all of the narratives and experiences in this book speak out.

In the next chapter, the experiences of a widowed woman grieving for her son and a group of fisherman returning to the sea after the tsunami are explored to understand further the importance of recognising the everyday and ordinary as open and fluid contexts, which allow for multiple meanings and changing frames of reference. Using the stories of Rani and Sivam, I challenge what has come to be seen as 'ordinary' in contexts of violence by showing that 'normalcy' in violence-prone areas does not always directly link to peace and productivity.

Notes

1 The difficulties of tracing a country's past lie in the competing claims made about the 'truth' of the past and the blurred lines between fact and fiction. These claims are versions of the past, which are attributed status and recognition as the history of a place or people. Events, which are commonly recognised as significant by the wider public, are often located on a timeline of the past, mapped in an arc from cause to consequence. Moreover, they can be used as a powerful tool to lay claim to a particular place as home, often enlisting ideological, religious, or mythical idioms as explanation and legitimation.
2 Daniel (1996) cites another word '*vatakkatayan*' (northerner) which was used as a derogatory term by Jaffna Tamils towards those from the hill country.
3 The Sarvodaya Shramadana Movement is one of the largest NGOs in Sri Lanka in terms of the scale and territorial reach of its activities as well as in terms of its public profile. It was formed out of the socialist ideology of working to empower marginalised groups across ethnic lines (see Orjuela 2004).
4 This refers to the way in which prior to colonisation Sri Lanka had existed as a series of regional kingdoms, ruled by affluent kings. The maritime districts including the Tamil areas of the north and east were occupied first by the Portuguese who arrived in 1505, and from the late 1660s by the Dutch. The Portuguese and Dutch administered the Tamil areas as a separate entity to other areas and kingdoms on the island. When the British arrived, however, they pushed for a centralised approach to power, which brought all of the kingdoms under one central rule (Wilson 2000). It is argued that by doing so, the British cemented previously unacknowledged fault lines by creating three administrative systems, a Sri Lankan Tamil region in the north, and two Sinhalese (upper and lower) in the centre and Southern coastal areas (ibid.).
5 The incident involving the LTTE and PLOTE leader is most commonly reported as a quarrel between Uma Maheswaran (alias Muhundan), who was the regional commander of the Vanni (northern region) and Prabakaran (leader of the LTTE) over a female LTTE cadre called Urmila (Swarmy 1994). The quarrel eventually led to Muhundan leaving the LTTE to form PLOTE in 1980 (ibid.). The second incident appears to refer to an event in October 1987 when a number of LTTE cadres travelling in a boat, off the coast of Point Pedro in the north, were apprehended by the Sri Lankan navy and arrested. As they were about to board a flight to Colombo, all the cadres swallowed cyanide capsules. This particular incident, however, did not include Sathasivam Krishnakumar, alias 'Kittu appa', the Jaffna regional commander for the LTTE, who died in a separate incident at sea in January 1993, when the Indian navy intercepted their vessel on the Indian ocean (Swarmy 1994).
6 Although Meena uses the term 'Kalinga' (*Kāliñkā*) to describe her caste, I have only been able to find references to it as a clan or *kuti* name. According to McGilvray, this term refers to one of the '*Mukkuvar Kutis*'. '*Kāliñkā*', writes McGilvray 'was a medieval kingdom in Orissa and also a famous name in Sri Lankan dynastic history' (2008: 173–5).
7 Pillaiyar, also known Ganesh, is one of the best-known and most widely worshipped deities in the Hindu pantheon.
8 While hierarchical ranking is an important element of caste, McGilvray (2008) points out that the precise ranking of castes within clusters of roughly similar status is ambiguous, and, to some extent, variable over time and place. Moreover, in eastern Sri Lanka, as previously noted, caste and matrilineality influence one another, and are,

therefore, not static and unchanging concepts. The ranking of the castes has its reflection in ritual roles and responsibilities relating to Hindu and Buddhist temples; to some extent, ideas of purity and pollution play a role here, but local (and colonial) political dynamics are equally important (McGilvray 1982c, 2008; Whitaker 1999; Dirks 2008).
9 The term '*thambi*' (younger brother) refers to younger males – not only immediate family but also in a more general term for younger male compatriots. Hughes (forthcoming) has noted the similarities with the conduct of state forces entering homes.
10 The *Palmyrah* palm is often described as the single most useful plant in the northern and eastern region of Sri Lanka. It is easily cultivated and also found to grow wild. Cultivation requires little labour in planting the nuts and protecting them from cattle till they grow above reach. The tragic irony here is that the *palmyrah* was 'useful' as an instrument of violence against the Tamil people.
11 S-Lon pipes are plastic construction pipes that the STF filled with sand and used as an instrument of torture; the heavy pipes were used for beatings because the body would suffer multiple internal injuries but the skin would not break, and, therefore, there would be little visible evidence of the brutality (see Daniel 1996).
12 While there has not yet been a specific documentation of the Batticaloa Peace Committee, discussions of their work and influence can be found in many of the UTHR reports. One prominent member of the Batticaloa Peace Committee was Father Eugene Herbert, an American Jesuit Priest, who disappeared along with his Tamil driver, Bertram Francis, in August 1990. Another Jesuit Priest, Father Harry Miller, has worked tirelessly, to this day, to publicise the culture of impunity in the east (see Miller's (2011) poignant article 'We Remember: After 21 Years').
13 One of the largest army camps in the South of Sri Lanka is located in Boosa, on the outskirts of Galle. Many men and women who were arrested and detained were taken to Boosa, which became notorious for the torture of prisoners. It was very difficult for family members to find out what had happened to their loved ones since travel to the south was difficult, and getting information from the army even harder. Many who were taken to Boosa never came out (UTHR 1992a).
14 See also Thiranagama's 'No More Tears Sister: The Experiences of Women' (1988: 305–25).
15 One woman, who I met in an IDP camp outside Batticaloa in 2007, made this clear to me. Drawing my attention to the rumours that women in Vaharai were being raped as the SLA took control, she firmly told me, 'Only I am saving the kerosene oil to burn myself if that should happen.'
16 This form of 'hooded-informant' has also been used as a counter-insurgency tactic in a very prolific way during the JVP violence (*the Bheeshanaya*) with the informant largely referred to as '*Goni Billa*' (see Hughes forthcoming).
17 In 1992, Rs 240 would have been approximately £3.07 (£1 equal to Rs 78.66), www.lankanewspapers.com/news/2007/11/21660_space.html.
18 See also De Alwis 2002; Ruwanpura and Humphries 2004.
19 Meena refers to her sister's daughters as her own here.
20 This refers to the time when girls begin menstruation, and is seen as an auspicious and special time marked by puberty rituals and celebrations to mark the 'coming of age' (see McGilvray 1998a; and of Tamil women and puberty rites in Southern India see Good 1991; Kapadia 1995).
21 The beating and torturing of siblings and parents in front of one another to gain information was a common counter-insurgency tactic, also used widely both in the JVP 1971 repression and in the 1987–91 repression.

23 The leaflets followed a speech by a TNA politician in April 2006, which claimed that there was a high rate of abortions in the Eastern Province, and cited the employment of young women in NGOs after the tsunami as being responsible for extra-marital sexual relationships, pornography, and the spread of disease. Although the source of the leaflet was unconfirmed, it was generally assumed to be groups linked to Muslim extremists and the TMVP (ibid.).

23 See also Walton's (2010) discussion of role of civil society in relation to the 2002–08 peace process.

6

'Kutti annar maram' (my older brother's tree)

Encountering the everyday: Rani's story

Often when I asked people in Batticaloa about how they coped with the violence in their everyday lives, they would answer something like 'this is our life' accompanied with a shrug of resignation or a bemused smile. This did not imply that they accepted the way things were, or that there was no hope for change, but it instead reflected the general recognition of daily life in Batticaloa as one of violence and fear. Many, if not all, I spoke with felt and expressed some sense of powerlessness and despair; where the fragility of the everyday was revealed, so was the fragility of the capacity to cope and to continue. This struggle was captured particularly in the stories of two women I met after the tsunami. One woman had lost both parents and her two-year-old daughter (whom she had waited five years to conceive) in the tsunami. Her husband, who had been working in the Middle East (having left Sri Lanka for security reasons), had returned for their daughter's funeral just days after the tsunami. Two days after his arrival in Batticaloa he was shot dead. The first time we met, this woman told me, 'I don't want to think. I am waiting to die. If the gods are kind, I will die very soon.' The other woman I spoke with had also lost members of her family in the tsunami, along with her home and all her belongings. She had been staying in a camp for the displaced with her husband when he was gunned down as he rode his bicycle in Batticaloa town.

These are not unfamiliar tales of tragedy from Batticaloa as the stories in this book have testified so far. Moreover, it was certainly not unusual to find women alone, having to manage without their husbands and any wider support. As Meena's story in the preceding chapter powerfully highlighted, while men often joined an armed group, or were forced into hiding from the security forces or LTTE/TMVP, women took on the challenge of survival. Caring for their families, they had to find ways alone to provide for them financially, and to deal with the everyday realities of displacement, risk, and fear; as a Catholic priest pointed out to me, '(I)f you want to know what is happening in the east you have to speak to the women as the men have all gone.' However, what is less familiar and less reflected on is that daily life still carries on, even after such tragic experiences. This is not simply the daily life of coping with pain and loss, but the more 'unremarkable' agency of women to endure violence and displacement. Dealing with the present, and moving into the future, all within the quotidian sphere of daily life, reveals how violence is not the only reality in the everyday world. Furthermore, to look for more depth in the everyday – and to question its meaning – is not to deny that pain and hopelessness exist, or that violence is woven through everyday tasks, but to emphasise the richness of present narratives that can capture the different layers of integrated feeling and experiences. In Batticaloa, in the encounters sustained, whether people felt like they were holding on tightly or giving up, in some way the everyday moved on.

Therefore, when meeting with families and individuals in Batticaloa, it was often not so much what they told me about their lives, but what was revealed through their actions, interactions, and their bodily movements. For example, when I visited mothers in their homes, many found it difficult to talk openly, yet all the while they would perform their daily household chores: sifting rice, washing vegetables, and preparing fires. While their sense of everyday could not necessarily be accessed or articulated, it was simultaneously embodied and enacted in front of me. Everyday life, then, became the process of *doing* and performing, which was revealed in the embodied encounter between the informant and me. Jackson writes that storytelling events are '*lived through* as a physical, sensual, and vital interaction between the body of the storyteller and bodies of the listeners, in which people reach out toward one another' (2002: 28, italics in original). In Batticaloa, this embodiment was also revealed through everyday routines and rituals; acts that were carried out regularly over time to compose a familiar and expected sense of the everyday, but which also challenged life as it was, and asked questions for the future. Through the two stories that follow, following on from the discussion of the meaning of the everyday and the ordinary in Chapter 4, and from the details of Meena's narrative in Chapter 5, I illustrate ways in which everyday endurance plays out. That is, that violence is not just dealt with but through endurance is pushed, shaped, and, crucially, questioned for all that it might mean. Moreover, through the experiences of a woman, Rani, learning to deal with the loss of her son, and of a group of fishermen returning to the sea after the tsunami, they show that certain moments can provide space and opportunity and be grasped as times at which change may be effected, or at least imagined.

The life of forty-year-old Rani illustrates many of the hardships and suffering experienced by women living in the east of Sri Lanka. Like Meena's narrative in the previous chapter, Rani's story weaves through landscapes of loss and endurance, creating conversations between what has come to pass and what might be. There are many similarities between the stories of Rani and Meena: both are widows, both have struggled to bring up children while facing the risk of child-recruitment by the LTTE and TMVP, and both have had to deal with the cleavages of fear and threat driven through everyday life by the state forces. However, where Meena set out to tell me her experiences of the past and to create a 'lived' sense of growing up in the east as an alternative form of history, Rani's engagement and the conversations spun a different focus and understanding.

Rani's story

I met with Rani on numerous occasions over two years. As well as an informant, Rani was also a friend. I attended her daughter's 'big girl' party (which marked the start of menstruation), and Rani and her husband came to many of the *Valkai* group meetings and took part in one of the tree-planting ceremonies. In 2004, Rani's eighteen-year-old son had been killed. He had joined the LTTE in 2002, and although he had since escaped it, he was thought to have been killed by members of the rival TMVP. At the time of his death, her husband, Gumesh had been in LTTE detention, and did not learn of his son's death until he was released weeks later. Rani was, therefore, alone, looking after her other children and having to deal with the loss of her eldest son. Following his death, Rani had sent one of her other sons to work in a garage in the town in order to protect him from LTTE recruitment but kept the youngest two (a boy and a girl) at home with her since they were still at school.

I first met Rani in 2005 when I was out on family visits with the *Valkai* group. Rani had initiated contact with the *Valkai* group after she had been denied access to her son's body after he was shot, and so she had sought the help of an INGO who had connected her with members of the *Valkai* group. They had tried but been unsuccessful in helping her to get her son's body back. My first visit to Rani's house was with Krishna – she had told me a bit about Rani's situation, and wanted to visit her to see how Rani and her husband were managing after the loss of their son. Below is a description of that first visit.

9 February 2005

As we arrived at the gate of Rani's compound, Rani was behind the house washing pots. We called out to her as we stepped around the potholes in the road, which had been filled with last night's heavy rain. Rani appeared from around the side of the house (which was more of a hut), smoothing down flyaway hair with haste, and wiping her hands on an old piece of cloth wrapped over her skirt. She apologised because she was in the middle of preparing lunch. Krishna assured her that we were happy to chat with her as she finished her cooking. So we sat down on mats placed just outside the door to her hut. Rani squatted down on her haunches just beside us, and sifted through rice grains as she talked. Knowing the turmoil that had recently gone on in Rani's life, the compound was a wonder of normality, calm, and neat. On one side was the small hut made out of woven palm and plastic sheeting that constituted the house that Rani and her family lived in, and, on the other, the foundations of a new brick structure. They had started building the new house a few years ago but had run out of money and so the building was never completed. The compound was framed with a woven palm fence pushed deep into the sand. Along the bottom in certain places, the fence finished a couple of inches above the ground where the dogs had burrowed underneath. There, through the gaps, you could see the disembodied feet and ankles of the people next door moving about. Cracked and dusty heels slapped against the soles of old slippers; the anklets of a young child jangled as the child ran around.

At one point, Rani turned to us and dropping her voice to a hushed whisper said, 'I don't feel safe. I am very alone in this area because people talk and say things about my son being killed ... they [nodding to next door] are being paid by them [the LTTE] to keep an eye on us. That's why I don't talk much.' Krishna whispered something back and Rani answered, 'they pay them every month. Other people do that too. Nobody trusts anyone' Rani began to wash the rice in the big steel pot, and as she swirled and squeezed the grains in the water, she commented on how her son had not had a proper meal on the morning that he was killed. She remains troubled about this, she said, because at his death he would not have been in a good state since he was not full.

'Getting on'

Each time we visited Rani, we would sit and talk with her while she carried on with her cooking and cleaning, or occasionally she would take a break with us to drink tea. Often the two children would come home from school, tired and hungry. If they sat down with us, then Rani would always change the subject. She never talked about her fears for her family in front of the children. But whatever she was doing, the very essence of Rani's everyday, and how she coped with violence was silently and unconsciously demonstrated. The swirling and squeezing of grains, fast but methodical, in the preparation of lunch powerfully revealed a sense of her 'getting on' with chores of her daily life within the parameters of normality, while also not hiding the pain and sadness that saturated her body and actions. The need for routine seemed to imply some sense of control over external events. Although it might be argued that Rani had no choice in doing this, I suggest that such actions both embodied and revealed her determination, endurance, and imagination of the everyday. Where violence lies 'on the edge of conversation' (Das 2007: 49), attending to the ordinary can affirm the possibility of life by removing it from the circulation of words. Examining how we can conceptualise an understanding of violence in the weave of everyday life, Das suggests that we begin to think of pain in terms of acknowledgement and recognition rather than as a challenge to our own or others' reality and experiences. 'In the register of the imaginary, the pain of the other not only asks for a home in language, but also seeks a home in the body' (Das 2007: 57). The importance of this idea lies in the emphasis on the role of the imagination to challenge and transform unspeakable experiences of pain into actions, and the ability of the body to enact or perform in a world where violence lives on (ibid.). This does not have to be through a broken or damaged body, but through one that keeps going. Therefore, for Rani, the performative force of routine, and her reflection on its meaning and purpose, allowed her to inhabit a fractured present, while also creating space to look towards the future.

In 2006, Rani's husband, Gumesh, was killed. Months before his death, Rani had told me that she feared for his life. Having been detained by the LTTE, Gumesh had been under threat from the security forces and the TMVP, who were likely to brand him as an LTTE supporter. Rani spoke of her worry about him and the loss of her son in terms of the disruption to her daily routine:

> When my son was killed, it was like I was in dark smoke and could not face anything. I always had this headache – at the top of my head – and I still have that. After my son's death, I could not get back into a regular routine; could not get the cooking done on time and get the house organised – nothing felt like normal. Only last month did I start to get back to normal but I'm not sure – we're not even safe with my husband released. He may be taken again. We need him to work on the land so that we have some money – the only reason is for income – it's not safe there. I lost my son in that area and my husband has to go there now. I remain tense until he returns back to me. I may have my children and my husband now but I don't feel safe.
>
> I can't think of any place where we can be safe – where can I go? Then I put my son in the garage – I felt he would be safe there. Sometimes people said not to sleep at home – but I said my husband is not here, my son is dead – this is where I live – if they want to come and kill us, then let them finish it off.

On one visit, it had started to rain heavily. Sitting inside Rani's cadjan house with small trickles of rain running through holes in the roof, Rani commented, 'when my son was killed it was raining heavily. My mother-in-law gave me 100 cadjan to fix the roof.' Similarly, when I had attended a party for Rani's daughter's attaining age (starting menstruation), I asked Rani how she was feeling. She had replied, 'I can't say happy because there is something missing.' The absence was her son. In this way, Rani always seemed to come back to the death of her son through her daily activities. Cooking the lunch reminded her of the meal her son missed on the day that he was killed; the rain coming through the roof reminded her that on the day her son had died it was also raining; and the celebrations for her daughter attaining age reminded her of her son's absence from the family party. Thus, the everyday – and the routines, rituals, and patterns it prescribed – was both a reminder of the past and symbolic of moving on through the present and into future too.

'Kuti annar maram'

In early 2006, Rani's husband, Gumesh, had attended one of the tree-planting ceremonies organised by the *Valkai* group. As described in chapter 2, these ceremonies were for families who had recently lost loved ones in the conflict. Rani had also been due to attend, but this was the time when her daughter attained age, and so she was busy at home with the preparations for the party. The ceremony was held in Batticaloa town at the home of one of the *Valkai* group members with eight different families attending: there was a woman whose sister had been beaten and killed by the army; a man whose brother had been 'disappeared' by the LTTE; a father, with his daughter and granddaughter, whose son had been shot by the SLA as he tried to help a friend injured in a grenade attack (as described in Chapter 2, page 51). There were also a number of mothers present whose sons had been taken by the SLA or one of the Tamil militant groups.

Tree-planting ceremony

Throughout the ceremony, Gumesh had sat quietly on the cool cement floor, leaning back against a wall with his legs crossed out in front of him. To his chest, he clutched a plastic bag, which held a framed photograph of his eldest son. The photograph was taken not long before his son had died. In the picture, standing to attention in a neatly ironed shirt and trousers, his son held the gaze of the camera, his tall figure incongruous against the mock background of a luminous flower garden. During the ceremony, the photograph had been placed in the middle of the room with the other pictures of men and women whose lives had been taken (see Chapter 2 for a description of the tree-planting ceremonies). Gumesh was silent throughout the ceremony. When his son's name was read out and a new candle lit, he had begun to sob. His tears had splashed silently onto the back of his hands as his chest heaved painfully, and his body gave way to grief. After the ceremony, a few of us went with Gumesh back to his house to help him and Rani plant the coconut tree in their compound. They had placed chairs in a semi-circle in the compound, and as we sat they passed around cups of a fizzy orange drink and sweet sponge cake.

On every subsequent visit to their house, Rani had pointed out the tree and commented on how it was growing. On one particular visit, she told us:

> That's how his name (her deceased son) is still here. We are always calling out his name and the tree has become a place that we use to talk about things – 'That side – near *kuti annar*' (older brother). My daughter will ask me for something and I will say, '*Toni maram*' (coconut tree). She will then ask, '*enne toni maram?*' (which coconut tree?) ... I answer, '*Kuti annar maram*' (older brother's tree).

For Rani, the symbolism of the coconut tree lay not only in its relationship to her son but in the way that it seemed to open up a space for conversation and shared meaning which may not have existed before. Through its personification as '*kuti annar*', the tree allowed Rani and her family to keep their son and brother in mind, both as remembrance and as a marker of present and future activity and movement. For example, part of Rani's daily routine involved watering the tree, and, therefore, she incorporated her memories with purposeful quotidian activity. Furthermore, Rani had told me that if they were ever to leave their house, then she would want to take the tree with her; her uncertainty of the future being marked by a concrete need and activity.

Rani's engagement with daily life, demonstrated by the physical continuance of her household chores, raises the question of what was happening to her sense of the 'ordinary'. We could argue that such attendance to the details of everyday life makes the everyday inhabitable and tolerable, and, yet simultaneously, they also make the everyday something more than a simple form of *ordinary*. While Rani's chores and tasks were part of a routine of necessity and normality, at the same time they were not outside of the severe disruption caused by the loss of her son and disappearance of her husband (taken for questioning by the LTTE days before her son was killed). In this way, Rani's everyday was not only to do with simply 'getting on' in a difficult situation, but also revealed how the everyday was altered and questioned to encompass and negotiate new meanings. While Rani's sense of ordinary continued (through her completion of tasks), at the same time it took on new meanings from situations of loss and suffering. These were not familiar and normal meanings but were ratified and understood by an appeal to the wider context of violence and the everyday as 'for another first time' (Garfinkel 1967: 9). The needs, fears, questions, and desires all held within the 'ordinary' act of planting and nurturing a tree were a powerful example of this.

A fragile everyday

The importance of the tree also introduces us to another kind of everyday, which moves through the banal and mundane but recognises the fragility of daily life. Where Rani's everyday life had been fragmented and shattered by violence, embracing new and different meanings allowed Rani to continue to live an 'ordinary' life – where ordinary meant many things. Where the household symbolised the basic needs, the coconut tree offered a space for escape from all that was real in the immediate present. The tree and the space it demarcated symbolised an everyday that offered the possibility of imagination and hope. In de Certeau's understanding of the everyday (as discussed in Chapter 3), we might recognise this as the 'hidden poetics' – as Rani's creative attempts to find chinks of opportunity in the repressive structure, and to use whatever resources were at hand to sustain her life and push for change. Rani's actions revealed the ways in which the loss and pain in her life had folded into the recesses of the ordinary as a particular way of inhabiting the world after violence. However, this everyday and ordinary also held more depth and reflection; Rani recognised what she could and could not do; that some actions were for moving forward, others were for keeping still; some were for remembrance and mourning, others for hope and desire. This is a different type of everyday and ordinary that symbolises a need for aspirations and hope for change while working with what is at hand, and knowing what can be lost. The emphasis is not only upon the function, reproduction, and progress of the everyday but introduces an idea of potentiality and small politics based upon what is possible in the present (see also Spencer 2007). Where Rani sought to negotiate a path forward through her loss, she also projected a sense of possibility, which in itself impinged upon her experiences of loss.

In August 2006, Rani's husband was killed. When I returned to see Rani in April 2007 after I had been back in the UK, she grasped my hand and holding it tight said, 'Now we need another tree.'

An ordinary beyond routine

Looking at the importance of rituals in the everyday highlights the juxtaposition of different areas of life, which, either taken together or separately, can hold different meanings. The propensity for different kinds of violence in shifting spaces and by different actors creates a web of shared but diverse experiences upon which people must act. In a context of restriction, control, suspicion, and distrust created by the militarisation of the east, some spheres of people's lives reflect endurance and necessity, whereas others are marked off as spaces for escape from the mundane. Where some spaces and rituals might be about making steady progress forward, others might be less tied to a specific outcome and, while part of the routine framework of the everyday, they also hold meanings which challenge the normal distinctions of day-to-day routine. The activities of a group of fishermen led by their *mudalali* (chief), a forty-five-year-old man called Sivam, illustrate the contrast between everyday routines that have a visible purpose, and those that do not seem to work in a conventional way. Sivam's personal experiences of growing up in a frightening and risky environment highlight the contrast between different kinds of violence, and the influence they hold over the meaning of the everyday.

Sivam and the fishermen

Sivam has been a fisherman for most of his life, taking over the job from his father, who had always lived and worked in the same area. The area is situated beyond the main bridge out of Batticaloa, and is built around intimate pathways and small hamlets of houses which lead up from the beach, the pathways dragging the sand and smell of the sea with them. Creating what many might see as a picturesque seaside village, it also meant that on 26 December 2004, when Sri Lanka's shorelines were hit by the tsunami, this area was extremely vulnerable and thus one of the worst affected. In the island's eastern region, over 10,000 people were killed, and thousands of homes and livelihoods destroyed (WB 2005a). The fishing industry was one of the most badly affected. Of the country's 29,700 fishing boats, about two-thirds were destroyed or significantly damaged, along with outboard motors, ice storage units, fishing gear, and nets. Entire fishing communities were dependent on these fleets (see ADB, JICA, WB 2005). Sivam and his group of twenty fishermen lost all of their fishing boats, nets, and other equipment. Two men in the group were killed, and all the other fisherman lost at least one family member. One of the fishermen, Kanthan, lost his wife, three young sons all under the age of eight, his parents, his sister, her husband, and their three children. Two days after the tsunami, after searching for his family members and realising they had all died, Kanthan tried to commit suicide by drinking poison. He survived, however, and when I met him, he was staying with Sivam and his family, and being cared for by the fishing group.[1]

Having lost their homes, the fishermen faced many problems due to the government's proposed regulations for reconstruction post-tsunami, which included a ban on construction of dwellings within one hundred metres of the beach (Athukorala and Resosindarma 2005).[2] Most of the fishermen, therefore, had to find other land to build on (having refused to stay in the IDP camps which were miles from the beach), and ended up building on and sharing smaller areas of land owned by Sivam. The devastation caused by the tsunami also added to the many problems the fishermen had faced throughout their lives due to the conflict and violence in the area. Working outdoors and depending upon a natural resource for their living rendered the fishermen and their livelihoods vulnerable with uncertainty stemming not only from the physical elements but also from the social environment in which human livelihoods and human securities were constantly fought over. Focusing on how people cope with risky environments, in terms of the ability to dynamically adapt to shifting risks while constantly seeking to minimise danger and maximise opportunity to secure livelihoods, Bohle describes vulnerability as embedded in social and environmental arenas, where human security, freedoms and human rights are 'struggled for, negotiated, lost and won' (2007: 9). For Sivam and his group, the dynamics of local violence created many risks, which shifted with the fluctuating levels of tension and boundaries of control. Given the context of fear and threat in Batticaloa, young men were particularly at risk of being abducted by the LTTE, TMVP, and SLAF. For the fishermen, this risk was heightened by their visibility as strong active men working out on the beach. At least two of the men in the group had spent time during the 1990s in Tamil militant groups, and many of them had been questioned and detained by the army (echoing what Meena notes about men being trapped by the conflict in the 1990s).[3]

When I first met Sivam in 2005, amidst the devastation of the tsunami, he told me that after the 2002 ceasefire the situation with the army and LTTE had greatly improved, allowing them to go out to sea regularly, and build up a good, productive, and profitable fishing business. The team had increased the number of boats they owned at this time, and had built extra tubs and containers in which they stored fish, ferrying them to and from town on bicycles. The sea and lagoon in Batticaloa provided a livelihood and source of income for many, but also became a focal point of contests for power and control. From the 1990s, the security forces attempted to maintain a tight reign over the eastern shorelines of the sea and lagoon along with the most fertile (for paddy, coconut, and vegetables), densely populated, and urbanised coastal strips with its access to open sea fishing. The LTTE, meanwhile, controlled vast areas of the inaccessible jungle regions of the interior countryside. Sivam noted that despite the overt fighting having abated since the ceasefire, the factional split in the LTTE in 2004 had meant that control over land and people had become even more contested. He noted:

> The incidents that happen – shootings and people being taken – mean we are still not comfortable. The LTTE and army come to this area... and other groups. You never know what will happen. I advise my group either all sleep in [your] homes or together in the *varddiya* (fishing hut).

The contested control over the shorelines and the areas of land around Batticaloa meant that the fishermen had to adapt their work to the regular nuanced shifts in the situation, and work with what felt possible and relatively safe at that time. Although, since 2002 the army were rarely a visible presence on the beach during the day, they were still known to carry out checks at night, and the fishermen told me that some of the soldiers would drink and get violent, often taking it out on the fishermen. On occasions when I found myself staying late at the homes of the fishermen and their families, I witnessed soldiers patrolling the beach and inspecting the huts and tents where the fishermen would take turns sleeping in order to watch their boats and equipment.

A closer look at the network of fishermen under Sivam revealed stratification in terms of ownership of boats and equipment, and access to resources, which meant that Sivam was less affected by vulnerabilities than the men in his team. Prior to the tsunami, Sivam owned all four of the handmade timber boats while the rest of the team shared the responsibilities for their upkeep. Of a team of fishermen in Palameenmadu (an east-coast Tamil village), Bohle (2007) notes that for boat owners, their asset structures, their participation in social networks, and their access to political power holders made them less economically vulnerable, and equally so in terms of recovery after violent impacts. Bohle describes that boat owners received more financial credit for the reconstruction of their houses, received new boats and nets from NGOs through the Fishermen's Cooperative Society (FCO), and could afford to send relatives to more secure areas. They also received better health care, and had more chance of getting family members released if the police or army arrested them. Therefore, according to Bohle, the abilities of boat owners to respond actively to risks and uncertainties were higher than that of fish labourers and petty fish traders. For Sivam and his team, some of these factors were relevant; Sivam did have greater access to resources, social networks and more influential contacts; however, with the post-tsunami frantic distribution of fibreglass boats by many INGOs working on the east coast, most (if not all) fishermen owned at least one boat (as did many who were not fishermen). Sivam also lived further away from the sea in a better and stronger house on land that he owned, whereas the other fishermen lived in densely populated settlements mostly in low-lying areas of the beach. The tsunami, however, had shifted resource and power balances by leaving all fishermen vulnerable, and then distributing to all, regardless of previous structures and relationships.[4] Despite the competition introduced in the post-tsunami response, Sivam's team remained together and sought to replace the four timber boats they had previously owned, which, as noted, once again belonged to Sivam but were cared for by the group. They rejected the NGO boats, which they claimed were not sea worthy due to being noisy and heavy in the water, thus frightening away the fish as they approached.

Violent environments

The notion of 'violent environments' developed by Peluso and Watts (2001: 25) is useful here in highlighting the relations between the environment and violence from the perspective of political ecology. The environment is viewed as an arena of contested entitlements in which conflict and claims over property, assets, labour, and the politics of recognition are played out. In Batticaloa, the tsunami had created another dimension, and, despite being a natural disaster, in its aftermath it became highly politicised, both in terms of the ongoing violence and new conflicts generated by disputes over aid and reconstruction (as discussed in Chapters 1 and 2). Bohle and Fünfgeld (2007), for example, point out that the total clearing of the mangroves along the shoreline of the lagoon and sea in Batticaloa by the armed forces in the years preceding the tsunami was disastrous for the coastal ecosystem. This became most apparent when the tsunami hit the eastern shores, as the villages bordering the exposed fringe of the lagoon were no longer protected by mangrove belts, making them fully exposed to the tsunami waves. Environmentalists have since found clear evidence that thousands of lives could have been saved if the right action had been taken at the right time to enforce regulations to preserve the coastlines. Damage from the tsunami was much greater in areas where the incidence of violation of environmental regulations was greater (Clarke 2005). For example, the death toll on the island of Simeulue in Indonesia was relatively low partly because of the mangrove forests that surrounded the island; in contrast, however, the uprooting or snapping off at mid-trunk of mangroves caused extensive property damage in Thailand (Athukarala and Resonsindarma 2005). In Batticaloa, there was very little to protect the coastal buildings from destruction, and many locals living along the sandbank between the sea and the lagoon found that they had nothing to grab onto as they tried to escape the waves, and were, therefore, washed into the lagoon.

The cross-cutting effects of the conflict and the tsunami on the lives of the fishermen is, therefore, revealed most sharply in the context of vulnerability through which physical factors map onto a social landscape of differentiation and inequalities. Access to and control over 'livelihood assets', for example, becomes a matter of shifting power relations. While, on the one hand, there is the physical destruction of assets; on the other, there is the transfer of assets from the powerless to the more powerful actors (Le Billon 2000: 4). Bohle and Fünfgeld (2007) suggest that a sense of the 'political ecology of violence' can help explain the ways in which components of livelihood systems are subjugated to and determined by the logics and dynamics of violence. Although their research is restricted to lagoon fishermen in Batticaloa, and, therefore, does not consider those who work at sea, their exploration of fishermen from two separate coastal villages in eastern Sri Lanka provides a starting point through which the violent struggles over environmental entitlements and the politicisation of resource-based livelihoods can be explored.

Sivam's story

Out of all the men in the fishing crew, I knew Sivam the best. This was partly because as the *mudalali* he was in charge of all activities and so, rather than being at sea, tended to be on the beach or in his home where I could sit and talk with him. Sivam could also speak good Sinhalese and a little English (whereas the other fishermen knew only Tamil), so moving between the two languages he and I could hold a decent conversation. He was also very keen that I get to know his family, and I spent many afternoons playing with his two young daughters and being fed fish curry by his wife. Sivam described himself as a businessman, and claimed that he needed to not only expand his fishing business but also find other ways to bring in more money for his family. As well as his immediate family, he had many other relatives who were dependent upon him, including his wife's family, who came from an LTTE-controlled area towards Vakari and had very little income and access to support. Sivam had already brought one of the young girls (his niece) from this area to live with him and his family so that she could be schooled with his daughters in Batticaloa. Sivam's talk was always of improving his work and helping the group, as he put it to 'come up'. He distinguished himself from the other fishermen because he had been educated up to A' Level and also worked for some time in the Batticaloa paper factory. He was the only member of his family to continue with the fishing business, and whereas all the other fishermen in his team had small homes on the beach, close to the sea (and, therefore, all destroyed by the tsunami), his house was large and well-built, standing on a road named after his father. He had high expectations for his eldest daughter, whom he hoped would eventually become a doctor. As the eldest of nine siblings, Sivam felt he carried many responsibilities, although apart from a widowed sister, he was the only sibling to remain in Sri Lanka. The rest had gone abroad to France, Holland, and the UK, where they had settled with their families, returning every few years to visit if at all. This reflects the discussion in Chapter 5 about the out-migration of Tamils from the north and east.

I saw Sivam most days during my time in Batticaloa, and in addition to the regular conversations, carried out a number of informal interviews with him. However, I struggled to find out many details about his past life, and, in particular, his childhood. It was not that he was unwilling to talk to me about his past, but rather that every conversation, wherever it began, returned to his fishing business and his work with the group. For Sivam, it seemed the past had been difficult and, at times, painful. When he did allow his mind to revisit the past, he told me about the many times he had been taken by the security forces and hassled by the LTTE. On one particular occasion in 1990, he had been taken in a cordon-and-search operation (the army had told him it was because he looked like Prabharkaran, the leader of the LTTE) and detained by the security forces for fifteen days. Sivam described that time to me as the worst in his life:

> That was a time of torture for all. That was how the army related – no talk, only beating. Some (men) they put on rubber tyres and burnt. I was burnt all over and I thought – this is my story finished. But then, the day I was released I

wanted to hug everybody and cry. It was like a rebirth. This is death and birth for me.

I had followed this by asking Sivam whether he had talked to others including his family and friends about his experience in detention.

No, I did not share much. Only 10 per cent – I did not share deeply. I told my mother but not about the beatings. She would have been too upset. I did not tell my friends because when, they see the army they will get more scared. I want the fishermen to feel OK and be OK with me. If they are scared, we cannot do this. Some of the men are not good fishermen but I keep them with me as they depend on me. I make them do other work on the beach.

Sivam's answer revealed the means by which he coped in relation to his wider social network, and mirrored the strategies of silence to protect others – which I have discussed previously in the book – and maintain his perceived position of responsibility and authority (see Chapter 2). This also reflected the profoundly personal nature of such embodied violent experiences, which Sivam had felt should not, or could not, be shared (see also Daniel 1994; Das 1995, 1997). It also signified the connection and flow between his past and his present and what emerged as most significant in his everyday concerns. The importance lay with balancing the past and present with the productivity of everyday as a means of getting on. This, for Sivam, was not a denial of the past or suspension of the future, but focusing on the richness of the present moment, which held the many meanings of the everyday within it.

Returning to sea without a catch

Like Rani, Sivam and his team's experience of the everyday was revealed through their daily performance of activities and tasks. The strong sturdy bodies of all the fishermen, darkened by the sun, reflected the amount of time and energy that was put into their fishing; the dragging in of huge water-saturated heavy nets, mending of boats, and the regular travel to and from town on bicycles, balancing huge crates of fish to be sold. The other group members did not talk to me much, and this seemed more to do with my age and gender than the language barrier, although of course language also played a crucial part. If my Tamil had been better, I believe we would have spent more time chatting. Every day, this group of men, in checked sarongs wrapped and tucked tightly around their waists or old knee-length shorts, would haul the nets dancing with fish out of the water. Some of the group would dive beneath the waves to help ease the nets gently off the sea bed (which was covered in tsunami debris), while others staggered ashore, quickly spreading the slippery catch out to dry in the sun. Many of the local children would join me to gawp at the dying fish quivering and gasping for their last breaths on the wet sand. There was something almost hypnotic about watching those last moments of life drain away in the hot morning sun as the seagulls ducked and dived over our heads, loud and boisterous, waiting to see what might be left behind for their breakfast. Each member of the team played a role, and, often, when the catches were large, the wives and children would hurry down towards the sea to assist in pulling in the nets; theirs was an everyday of constant activity, movement, and routine.

The activities of Sivam and the other fishermen presented an interesting contrast to the daily lives and experiences of Anuloja, Meena, Rani, and many of the other women and mothers in the border villages with whom I spent time. Amongst these women, I noticed that there was always talk of what more could be done, what the risks and threats were, what boundaries could be pushed against, and what spaces could be kept open. This was perhaps something to do with the fact that many of them were based at home, and, therefore, constantly faced with the absence of their loved ones, or the problems that the everyday violence around them brought. Therefore, thinking about pushing forward and looking for new avenues was not only important, but also natural in their situation. The narrative told in discussion on the mother's meetings in Chapter 2, for example, where the mother fought for her child in the LTTE camp and threatened to kill herself if they did not release him, demonstrated her constant active attempts to keep pushing; a stoic determination to beat down the obstacles that blocked her. Meena's narrative in Chapter 5 also revealed her everyday experiences of working around restrictions and limitations in order to find better paths forward.

In contrast, the 'getting on' of the fishermen seemed to be more about passively working with what was available within the given boundaries and restrictions, to keep going out to sea, and keep up a routine so that they could earn money for their families and keep the business alive. Yet, this was not a form of the 'ordinary' that was any less invested with hope and change for the future than those who worked in ways that were more active. Sivam's constant return to the present everyday in his narratives reflected this. Although their activities were less about pushing for new spaces and more about keeping present spaces open, the fishermen seemed to question and challenge the everyday as much as anyone else. Their focus on 'getting on' did not seek immediate change but rather presented a kind of action that worked with what was available, familiar, and safe. The routine of fishing marked a step-by-step approach to daily life, which simultaneously reflected mundane repetition, and, also powerfully, revealed a reflexive approach to the meaning of these rituals.

A clear example of this was when the fishermen went out to sea when there was no catch. For many weeks after the tsunami, the fishermen took out a small fibreglass boat, borrowed from a girls orphanage in Batticaloa town. Pushing the boat out onto the waves and guiding it round in a semi-circle, they dropped what was left of the expansive nets into the sea and waited. The fishermen all knew that there were very few fish in the sea at this time, the tsunami having disrupted the balance of the seabed and filled the sea with debris. Furthermore, people were generally refusing to eat fish as rumours had spread soon after the disaster that fish were feeding on the bodies of those washed out to sea. The fishermen were also scared of another tsunami, and the constant panic amongst locals whenever the sea seemed to be rough or change in some way did not help. Yet, the fishermen still returned to the sea. As Sivam told me:

We wanted to show them [the locals] that we could go back out there. So many people said we shouldn't. My wife was scared and my family even rang from abroad to tell me not to go back to the sea and that they would support me to do something different. At that time [of the tsunami], I thought I should leave this work and go abroad. I can't come up from this now. No chance for me. But after one week, I got confidence. After one week, the fishermen and I went to the beach and looked around and shared our experiences. I was thinking and the others said my thoughts, 'We will start!' Then I talked to a friend and we got our old nets and a boat. We were all scared but we knew we had to do it. We knew there was no fish. That day we took the boat ... it was about two weeks after the tsunami. It was not the right kind of boat – we lost all of ours in the tsunami – but we went in it anyway. The sea was very disturbed and rough. There were no fish. We went to sea and we showed them. I told the other fishermen, 'We can take the boat out and die at sea – but at least we can say we did it'.

This idea of keeping up routine without the active pursuit of outcome unsettles the accepted ideas of the everyday, which speak of purposeful and obvious activity. We might say that, on one level, this is a pattern of the 'meaningless ordinary everyday' that one descends into in order to survive and cope with loss (of lives and of income). Reports of the dramatically changed status and loss of role for men in the aftermath of the tsunami support this idea. Findings show that a disproportionate number of those killed by the tsunami were women and young girls, and, therefore, men have found themselves experiencing serious difficulties and having to take on unfamiliar tasks.[5] This relates to a wider argument about the gendered effects of violence discussed in the previous chapters in relation to vulnerability and widowhood. It suggests that in comparison to men, women are more able to cope with loss due to their domestic responsibilities, having to care for their offspring, and the new demands placed on them by the loss of their male counterparts. As I noted in Chapter 1, in Sri Lanka's conflict areas women have had to take on new roles as principal income generators and heads of household throughout the war (Rajasingham-Senanayake 1998). However, I have also pointed out that, as much as we cannot assume that this is a straightforward case of 'empowerment' for women (as the rhetoric of victim and agent may imply), we cannot assume either that returning to sea was a meaningless form of coping. Rather, I suggest that this is an everyday and ordinary that goes far beyond routine and acceptance, for it is imbued with an investment in possibility, and making use of what is at hand.

Maintaining an ordinary everyday

Like Rani, the fishermen were reflexively aware of the nature of what they were doing; creating an ongoing dialogue with themselves as they pursued their activities; they remained aware of daily needs, and the fragility and preciousness of each day. For the fishermen, it also meant that when they returned to sea, they were establishing and remaking their meaning and identity as well as doing something *ordinary* to keep going. Furthermore, far from being an individual and isolating task of re-engaging with the world, this held collective and relational meaning, which connected the men through threads of meaning, both within and outside the performance of the everyday. In this way, the everyday emerges not just as a matter of reproducing the same thing over and over again, but is also a reaction that can step away from the mundane by challenging the accepted and asking questions of the ordinary. This can be rooted in the significance of finding a balance in daily life as revealed in Rani's experiences here. The awareness of restrictions and boundaries means that people struggle to create something manageable in balance with the greater scheme of things – persons, relatives, ancestors, histories, and religion.[6] Finding a balance also highlights the fact that the everyday is not static but rather generates a cycle of awareness; finding balance – dealing with fracture – finding balance. In this way, the *ordinary* of yesterday is not necessarily the *ordinary* of today.

Balancing the everyday

This existential search for balance also challenges the ontological forms of ethnographic writing which place the ordinary of conflict against the extraordinary tactics of survival. This does not imply a denial of the horrors that daily living in a violent setting can bring, or even an acceptance and normalisation of them. Instead, it focuses on imagination and possibility, which take on the reality of life and work through it. This also illustrates the importance of recognising the different ways in which people can respond to different forms of violence, and the ways in which they simultaneously work in and around everyday lives. Where Rani's daily chores and tree-planting, for example, were instrumental to carving out a space for the future, they remained restrained and silenced by threat and fear of the kind of violence, which rendered public expressions of grief and open resistance impossible. As testimony to the climate of threat and fear in the border villages of Batticaloa, this is made more visible by the contrast of the tsunami, which did not discriminate against its victims and provided a reason, however tragic, for death and destruction, as described in the previous chapter. Although the effects of the tsunami very quickly became politicised, the initial tragedy, emerging from physical and environmental destructive forces, was seen as apolitical and, therefore, allowed some kind of closure, and new space for the public expression of grief to be found.

The everyday lives described in this chapter and previous chapters demonstrate the different kinds of actions that take place within an environment where movements always have to be measured and controlled, and decisions evaluated against risk. I have argued that from these narratives, everyday endurance emerges, and reveals how people deal with their pasts, present, and futures. Life is not simply explained through alterations to the ordinary but demands further questions about how the ordinary is understood; whether it could hold different meanings and how a frame of reference may stretch according to what type of everyday sets the context. The physical bodily reactions to violence compel us to consider the significance of the body's role in taking on the everyday and moving

Plate 6.1 Returning to the sea, Kallady (Batticaloa) (2005)

forward. Rather than looking for what is said, the focus is about where you are in the world and how this is revealed through everyday actions such as daily chores, or fishing without fish. In this way, looking beyond the acceptance of the everyday and of a banal and mundane ordinary, we are required to explore the possibility of new contexts for daily life. Therefore, the everyday is not only a matter of reproducing routine and doing the same thing time and time again, but can be about imagination and investment in hope. Finally, for the individuals in this chapter and for the *Valkai* group, embracing the everyday, personally and collectively, meant questioning life through the politics of small gestures, of working with what is available, and always trying to do more. As part of this quest, the ways in which people are tied to one another and their networks of connectivity must also be considered as a part of writing people out of victimhood and as part of the endurance of life.

Notes

1 The day I met Kanthan he was particularly distraught as a photograph of his wife and sons had washed up on the Batticaloa side of the lagoon and had been returned to him. This was the only item that was ever found from Kanthan's home. Now, in his new house built by the fishermen, Kanthan has the photograph enlarged and framed on the living room wall.
2 The buffer zone proposal became a major stumbling block for the government's resettlement programme. Prior to the disaster, a 300-metre buffer zone had existed but had been ignored and openly flouted by most (see Klein 2007: 385–405).
3 It was indicated to me that many in the group had previous involvement and connections with armed militants, which is not surprising. However, I did not pursue questioning the men on issues of this nature, given the prevailing climate of fear and threat.

4 Although the government had promised to restore lost livelihoods for fisher-folk, the lack of capacity within the state bureaucracy to cope with these claims resulted in serious delays over compensation and the opening of a space for local and International NGOs to step in. However, as previously stated in Chapter 4, this created an extremely competitive environment, and the *ad hoc* distribution of boats compromised sustainable livelihoods (see Stirrat 2006; Klein 2007).

5 A survey on the impact of the tsunami carried out by the Suriya Women's Development Centre in Batticaloa found that 64 per cent of children and 91 per cent of adults who died were female. One of the main reasons given was that the time the tsunami struck coincided with women taking their morning bath in the sea or close by, and, therefore, taking on the full impact of the wave crashing over them (Emmanuel 2005).

6 Another example can be found in Finnström's (2008) description of the Acholi people in Northern Uganda, and how they create 'good surroundings' (*piny maber*) where conditions are frequently described as 'bad surroundings' (*piny marac*). He writes, 'The young Acholi did not passively wait for future solutions; rather in everyday life they built for a future despite displacement and social unrest ... and good surroundings were about living under endurable conditions where future could be imagined and planned' (Finnström 2008: 14).

7

In light of new beginnings

Searching for an ending

In early August 2005, the body of a young woman was discovered in a schoolyard in the centre of Batticaloa town. The identity of the young woman was not known and neither were her killers. Her body, which showed signs of rape and torture and was badly bruised and battered, was taken to Batticaloa Teaching Hospital where it was kept in hope of a family member coming forward to identify her. News of the discovery spread quickly, but as usual in Batticaloa, when rumours start to flow and stories abound, silences also crept in and froze information at the edges. For weeks, no one came forward to identify or claim the body. Eventually, a hospital porter buried the woman in an unmarked grave close to the hospital. A local women's organisation had followed the case, and arranged for a group of women to come together and hold a small vigil at the unmarked grave. Candles were lit and a small notice was erected at the head of the grave, with the words 'sister' written on it.

A few weeks later, a widow, whom I shall call Duwatha, approached the woman's organisation. She was looking for her daughter who had gone missing after being called by the LTTE for an enquiry. Although the LTTE claimed that they had let her go the same day, she had not returned home. Duwatha had been searching for her daughter ever since, visiting LTTE camps, police stations, and hospitals on a daily basis. Even though she had heard about the body in the playground, and had in fact been in the hospital the very day the young woman's body was found and brought in, Duwatha had been too frightened to enquire whether it was her daughter, and so had just kept looking. The women's organisation by then had a photograph of the deceased young woman from the police, and so when Duwatha produced a picture of her daughter they knew straight away that this was the young woman's mother.

Despite finally knowing the fate of her daughter, Duwatha was too frightened to share her discovery with anyone, even the rest of her family, and, therefore, she continued to maintain the pretence that she was still searching for her daughter. She also refused to make a police report, stating that it would only bring her more trouble since her family were a martyrs family and so were regularly hassled by the army and police anyway.[1]

One of the members of the woman's organisation was Kamla who was also a member of the *Valkai* group. Kamla arranged for Duwatha to meet with Anuloja, Krishna, and other *Valkai* members, and also for her to participate in one of the tree-planting ceremonies. Duwatha's participation in the tree-planting ceremonies was significant because until that point she had not spoken to anyone other than Anuloja and Kamla about the loss of her daughter. In the ceremony, however, Duwatha found a space to momentarily let those feelings out. As previously described in Chapters 2 and 6, the shape of the ceremonies allowed those who wanted to speak the space to do so while those who preferred to stay silent were also respected. It was only after other individuals had spoken of losing their loved ones that Duwatha started to weep in twisted painful cries. She talked a little about her daughter – her involvement in sports at school, her ambitions, her love for her brother who had died in the LTTE, and the many days that she (Duwatha) had been searching for her daughter – swallowing back tears as the words poured out.

After the ceremony, Anuloja had pointed out that even when Duwatha was finally able to let the tears flow, she had remained guarded and fearful – aware that the ties that currently held her in a space and network of support remained tense and fragile. She had refused a lift home from one of the members of the *Valkai* group who drove an NGO vehicle, saying that it draw would much attention to her and too many questions would then be asked. Instead, Duwatha took some money for the bus and went home alone to carry on pretending to search for her daughter while quietly grieving inside. Later on, recalling Duwatha's experiences, Anuloja had commented on the fact that Duwatha had been forced to find a way to grieve without ever being able to actually see her daughter's body or actually knowing what had happened to her. Like cases of disappearances where a body is never found, much of this story was left unanswered. While she had been able to surreptitiously visit the grave, and look from a distance (since the risk of being seen at the graveside was too great), Duwatha had to trust the women from the *Valkai* group that this was her daughter's grave without being able to ask anymore. Therefore, for Duwatha, it was only ever those with whom she came to share an intimate open space that she could acknowledge and grieve for her daughter not as the unidentified woman in the schoolyard but as a young woman with a past, present, and, tragically lost, future. This intimate space was created through the tree-planting ceremony, and the deliberate and conscious effort to find space that could be pushed open and sustained, albeit for a short time. As with Meena, Rani, and the many mothers and widows before her, Duwatha had to find a way of moving forward while re-ordering and questioning the turbulent present.

Quietly carving the future

The determination of Duwatha to find her daughter and the way in which she had to deal with unanswered questions about her daughter's fate reflects the experiences of many parents and family members in Batticaloa and across the east who have had to carve paths forward while dealing with violence and loss. Moreover, it shows how those who were in relatively safer positions, like members of the *Valkai* group, can operate as conduits to connect with those facing immediate danger. Accordingly, we can argue that it is in the spaces of loss and grieving – spaces that few families in the east have escaped – that the power of violence and vulnerability has also highlighted the strength of connections working through and against structures of control and constraint. This has enabled people to endure the everyday. These strategies of endurance, I have suggested, are less visible than the other forms of everyday activism and conscious resistance for the very reason that they seek not to be separated from 'active living' that draws on the past and present of continuous pain and loss, but also on hope and investing in a different sense of the everyday and of the ordinary. Such strategies, I have argued, have been missing from any wider understanding of life in eastern Sri Lanka and, more generally, of how life goes on through everyday conflict. Moreover, these strategies provide a marker of how things could be.

It is also attempts to push for change that have directed my search for alternative meanings of the everyday, and an understanding of how the 'ordinary' might be perceived beyond what is banal and routine. My contention has been that while violent acts may embody complex aspects of meaning that relate to both order and disorder, continuity, and rupture in a given context, there is something more than just violence that causes us to question this understanding. As I have demonstrated, this should come from looking at what is done and feels possible within a certain context, as well as what is not done and what is not said. It is through the ways that people narrate or embody emotional spaces, and, in particular, how loss is translated and dealt with, that this can be understood.

At the beginning of this book, I explained that my work developed from the experiences and stories that unfolded and was also made possible by specific interactions with certain people, places, and space. However, these particularities and much of the detail of the work that was carried out could not be explicitly revealed. Specifically, the women with whom I lived and worked, and from whom in-depth and articulate explanations, stories and imaginations were spun out, have had to be largely faded into the background of my writing. Instead, I have focused on the stories and the lives that can be told. This has evidently made the task of writing this book much harder, and I have created what I refer to in the first chapter as an 'ethnography of process' (see page 23). It is the processes and the articulations, the embodiment, and imagination of the social context – incomplete and constantly reworked – that I have tried to capture in my work. Meanwhile, as I have written, I have found myself courting the dilemma of how to give credit to a group of people who, in essence, co-authored this work, and, yet, cannot – and, most often, do not want to – make claims to what is produced. They, therefore, appear as a 'present absence' in this book. This is also an apt description of much of the everyday spaces and encounters in Batticaloa – the 'present absence' of what had happened, is happening, and may happen in the future. While grappling with these issues, I have aimed to produce a collection of particular conversations and commentary about everyday life in Batticaloa where the engagement with and endurance of fear and violence both allow and disallow people to speak out. The 'present absence', however, does not negate the significance of the *Valkai* group or the women working with it, but rather reflects and emphasises the lived reality of everyday violence in Batticaloa, in which people must find strategies to endure, survive, and create hope for the future while working in quiet and less visible ways.

Returning to the ideas of the *Valkai* women in this final chapter, I attempt to tie together the threads of everyday understanding, meanings of the ordinary, and hope for the future which have run throughout the book. In doing so, I reveal the extent to which my understanding of everyday life in Batticaloa has been based upon the lives and visions of this group of people, and particularly the women who worked with them and what they had to say. Furthermore, I explain why I believe this understanding is vital to a wider sense of Sri Lanka, especially in relation to the present context of 'post-war' and a 'post-conflict' future.

Spaces of mourning and meaning

The currency of grief

The nature of life in Batticaloa and the task of dwelling upon the lives of individuals, with whom my own experiences and emotions are woven, means that in reality there is not any kind of conclusion in terms of 'ending' to be reached. Just as experiences, lives, and deaths go on in this context, so do attempts to make sense of their shape and meaning. Therefore, my intention in bringing the threads of this book together is not to provide a neat tying of ends with final answers and summaries, but rather to draw on some of the prominent themes that have emerged in this book, and consider the kinds of questions that are left. The main theme that I focus on here is grief. Grief, as a reaction to many kinds of loss, has seeped out from the stories of suffering and everyday endurance of the people of Batticaloa and the east. Grief, we learn, has its own currency – it can be used to isolate or to gather support, to justify action or revenge, or, as we have seen through the work of the *Valkai* group, to bring people together to question the past, present, and future. Drawing upon Butler's (2004) premise of the power of grief and mourning in revealing shared vulnerability, and the ties that can bind us as human beings, I suggest, in concert with my argument throughout this book, that there are different ways of experiencing and acting upon the past, present, and future when woven through with loss and grief. Recognising the many losses that have taken place, I suggest that these ways do not have to be solely about violence and suffering, but instead reveal a world of possibility and fragile hope. Thus, I also return to the themes of fear, risk, trust, and hope, which have been plaited through both existential and political meanings and experiences in everyday life, to argue that the role of the *Valkai* group, in particular, is central to striving for recognition and change of space. This also challenges a sense of the self and other, and their relationship within times of risk and loss. I also suggest that the significance placed upon achieving a balance, which locates suffering 'within' resistance rather than in opposition to it, could play an important part in understandings of healing, which have generally been structured around ideas of grief as debilitating and unproductive.

Ideas of space, trust, fear, grief, and hope are all themes that have come to characterise contexts of violence and suffering, and pepper the stories and narratives of everyday lives in the north and east of Sri Lanka. Yet, it is in the spaces where they take on meaning and are embodied that we need to look in order to develop a deeper understanding. In this conclusion, I suggest that through narrating the lives of people in Batticaloa, these themes can be brought alive through a deeper understanding and will, hopefully, contribute to recognition of the ways in which violence is understood and incorporated into the 'ordinary' of everyday life in Batticaloa. Moreover, they illustrate the need to remain aware of shifting contexts, changing boundaries, and alternative meanings even where forms of activism and conscious resistance are less visible and do not fit into specific categories. I relate these ideas to the broader concepts of grief, healing, and peace, and suggest this could lead to a contribution for a new perspective on war and peace – a perspective that does not divide the world into victims and perpetrators, nor concentrates on only the horror and suffering, nor presents the ethnographer as heroine, instead, it seeks to bring out the quiet negotiation and shaping of spaces which are encompassed in the endurance of the everyday.

Questions of everyday life have remained central to understanding lives in contexts of conflict and violence. I have shown from the beginning of this book that answers have mostly taken the form of accounts that highlight the extent of brute force and subsequent suffering or of the 'normalisation' of violence which has led to 'extraordinary' acts of survival and resistance. The window through which the lives of 'ordinary' people in such climates have been framed has often been the extent of totalised violence through tactics of 'dirty war' and the spaces of 'empowerment' that people, particularly women, have entered as a result of the changes wrought by conflict. This has added weight to questions of peace and development, which are intrinsically linked to understanding everyday violence, and gain value by arguing for transformation of 'civil society' and proposing humanitarian projects to enhance aspects of daily life for civilians (see Goodhand and Lewer 1999; Orjuela 2005; Walton 2010). While these answers are no doubt important for understanding the experiences and meaning of everyday lives, they remain incomplete. Treating violence as a continuum (Scheper-Hughes and Bourgois 2004: 1) and viewing everyday life through the dichotomy of struggle and survival creates too vague and all-encompassing conceptualisation of everyday violence, which fails to recognise aspects of life that do not fall into the accepted paradigm. It fails to look for what else goes on other than the immediate violence; what happens beyond the more obvious spaces of violence; how fear and risk are internalised and worked with; and, crucially, the aspects of everyday life that are not about violence. This is something to which I have drawn attention to throughout this book: the common binaries of suffering and resilience that frame the lives of those coping with violence as a daily reality; the ways in which violence is filtered through as an 'ordinary' experience pitted against the 'extraordinary' acts of resistance and survival to overcome the everyday (see Nordstrom 1997; Green 1999; Scheper-Hughes 2008). This framework, I have suggested, separates out the experiences of those who manage and those who do not, ignoring the reality that people's lives straddle both; people suffer and they survive, they give up and they resist, they dwell on the past and the move forward. It is in the texture of this straddling process that I have argued we can find the *endurance* of the everyday in which people also find spaces to push for different experiences and challenge the meaning of what is ordinary and everyday.

The stories and memories that emerge vividly from the tangle of violence and the everyday involve the interconnections of lives, deaths, bodies, pasts, presents, and futures. This is within a context of continued violence, protracted suffering, and the devastation of physical, social, and imagined landscapes. The war and the tsunami have done their part to carve up the spaces of eastern Sri Lanka to the extent that no one is free from the effects of everyday violence, while choices about the future have been narrowed by the heightened risk of loss. The struggle then resides in the ways that people devise everyday strategies to negotiate and work around the constraints and minimise the risks. It is in the tension between what is accepted and what is not, between knowing and not knowing, and in the entanglements of the everyday and fear that we can begin to understand what the everyday means and how it works. In Meena's account of growing up in the east, it is the overlapping flows of family, community, and militancy which constitute her endurance through the years of loss, and her ability to find spaces to push forward and forge connections. The experiences of Rani and mothers connected by the *Valkai* group also reveal the everyday reality of the suffocating intimacy of violence, fear, and silence. Where words are not spoken, familiarity and knowledge shape understanding and pain; and where bodies are dumped and buried in unmarked graves, it is the very real raw awareness of what is happening and being held back that shapes life. Furthermore, Rani's engagement with the tree planted in remembrance of her son tightens the ties that bind, while marking out small and fragile steps forward that can take on new meanings and new futures. The fishermen, also operated collectively as a group, tied by their environment and emotions; what was not always articulated in words was revealed by actions and routine. This was routine that appeared empty on the surface, and yet was crowded with meaning and courage – *endurance*. Moreover, my own experiences, as a researcher and as a young independent woman attempting to live out a new kind of life in a visibly frightening, emotionally engaging, and challenging environment were defined and shaped by the connections that worked and those that did not.

It is, therefore, the spaces and systems of interaction unfolding across people's lives that suggest that although violence shapes lives, it does not have to be 'a determining fact in shaping reality as people will know it, in the future' (Nordstrom 2004: 15). These spaces and systems are tested, challenged, and pushed to the limit by the effects of violence and, yet, reveal that the production of fear and violence, like other mechanisms of control, while powerful, is never absolute.

The value of (lost) lives and grieving

In *Precarious Lives*, Judith Butler (2004) proposes that processes of grieving and mourning are capable of making apparent more interdependency and vulnerability. In mourning, we become fractured and dislocated, she argues; that is, we lose something, which is a part of ourselves, and is also part of another. This, in turn, makes us mysterious or enigmatic to ourselves and causes us to question our very existence, past, present, and future, as rendered different by such loss (McRobbie 2006: 78). Engaging with matters of life and death, with burial, grief, and mourning, Butler argues that our proclamation of loss comprises a mode of address to others wherein we reveal our vulnerability. Through a critical analysis of the post 9/11 appropriation of grief by the US to justify and legitimise policies to wage war against the 'other', Butler suggests that through enduring such loss, we initiate a new circuit of communication with others as well as marking loss and opportunity. Therefore, rather than understanding mourning and grief through the common notions of isolation, withdrawal and suffering, it can instead provide a basis for new forms of political community through our exposed vulnerability and dependency on one another. This idea of using our dependency on others, and mobilising bodily vulnerability as a means of transcending fear and forging connections with others, resonates with what we have witnessed through the ties between the *Valkai* group and many of the mothers (and fathers) across the east including Rani, Meena, and the fishermen. While Butler takes the example of grieving families of soldiers in the USA and Britain, we could also look to the mothers and families in Batticaloa for evidence of how grief can be mobilised, though perhaps in more subtle and fragile ways. Analysing Butler's contribution to an understanding of state and social systems, McRobbie reframes Butler's ideas on mourning by asking, 'How might that moment of recognition of vulnerability become an opportunity to consider those others for whom such palpable and routine vulnerability is a normative condition of existence?' (2006: 79). According to Butler, it is the very ties and connections that render us dependent and a part of others that can be understood as a 'condition of our constant humanity' and that can become productive in creating new forms of connectability and sociability.

If we place this understanding within the shape and frame of Batticaloa's everyday experiences as explored in this book, we can see this in terms of the re-opening of spaces of vulnerability and interdependency against the destructive powers of control and manipulation which seek to isolate and shut such spaces down. As many stories have revealed, loss, suffering, death, and destruction have become an inevitable part of Batticaloa's physical and social landscapes, which shape everyday experiences and the meanings attributed to them. However, I have also demonstrated that dwelling in those everyday spaces – and questioning what it is to live in and around violence – illustrates that any understanding of life in Batticaloa must encompass not only violence but also the 'everything else' of everyday life, including the ability to carry on and to invest in the future. Factors such as silence, trust, fear, and risk reveal themselves as strategies by which people negotiate the everyday while searching for cracks and crevices in everyday spaces to instigate and encourage change. Central to this are the connections and ties through which people relate to one another and build up networks to transcend the context of violence and isolation. Butler's contention is that to look beyond the possibility of war and consider a 'meaningful peace' is to renew our understanding of injury and what it means to grieve. This is an issue central to the future of Sri Lanka as it enters a 'post conflict' stage following decades of war. As I argue later in this chapter (Dealing with fragments, page 160), by ignoring the injury of war and, thus, the need to grieve, the state in Sri Lanka has shut down space for 'focusing upon the connections between people and questioning the most basic human obligations to one another in order to illustrate human interdependence' (Butler 2004: 43). At the heart of this interdependence, argues Butler, is human vulnerability, and our general state of fragility (ibid.). Increased attunement to this provides the opportunity to make us 'more humane' and to recognise our moral responsibilities to one another.

Silence that heals

The importance of focusing on grief, according to Butler (2004), is that it unsettles the common understanding of mourning as a debilitating and unproductive process. Human reactions to the pain of loss are often to seek the closure of grief, refuse it, and even to anaesthetise it in order to carry on. This, Butler contends, becomes a part of the cycle of violence as revenge, for in denying grief and pain, relations of vulnerability are transformed into relations of power through which the violence continues. However, 'doing nothing' as Butler (2004) proposes, although seemingly counter-productive, can break the cycle of revenge and provide what Butler suggests is 'a fertile kind of action' (53). The emphasis is on the word 'action' here because 'doing nothing' is not a case of literally sitting back and remaining detached, but instead refers more to avoiding reactions that can aggravate further violence and prevent processes of healing from taking place. We can relate this to the work of the *Valkai* group and the processes of creating connections through loss – planting trees in remembrance and to symbolise new meanings. Therefore, in comparison to the LTTE and their celebrations of martyrdom which have pushed the rawness of loss and pain to justify further violence, the *Valkai* group aims to keep spaces open to envisage alternative everyday lives. These strategies of the *Valkai* group, to dwell in spaces of vulnerability and loss, in turn allow the process of grieving to take place in new unsettled spaces which challenge everyday violence by 'doing nothing'. Moreover, the mothers, in refusing to accept their situations of despair and forced hopelessness, do not seek to close grief and move on, but instead draw upon their shared vulnerability to challenge those who take their children and try to close spaces.[2]

The question of silence and the absence of words to talk about difficult experiences are important to acknowledge when discussing grief and shared vulnerability. While trauma's 'unspeakable' and 'amorphous' dimensions (Ross 2003) can be identified in silence, silence should not necessarily be viewed only as a legacy of terror, but instead as an intimate and embodied strategy of keeping up routine while simultaneously questioning meaning. The experiences of Rani, in particular, illustrate this through her engagement with her daily chores and the watering of her son's tree, '*kuti annar maram*'. As such, a space of the banal and the ordinary could be imagined as a place for optimism and resistance within the everyday experiences and the moral economy of war. Rani's experiences could no doubt be cast as traumatic, and causing existential crisis and suffering for her as an individual and in relation to her family. However, the individualistic and positivistic approach of trauma models for 'healing', such as those associated with Post Traumatic Stress Disorders (PTSD), do not always account for the intimate knitting of social and structural violence with issues of context, morality, and subjective and social meanings (see Hamber 2006; Lykes and Mersky 2006). Nor do the underpinnings of such models always recognise silence as a valuable resource, which is not always a characteristic of terror and loss, but also manifest in forms of 'engagement' with everyday life. As has been demonstrated through the work of the *Valkai* group as well as many others, silence can illustrate the way in which people in the most vulnerable spaces work out what can and cannot be done and find gaps for pushing change. Tree planting, for example, represents silence as a positive resource and marks presence amidst overwhelming absence. This is a presence that does not need to be recognised through words; the knowing, the feeling and the sharing is enough in that fragile and unfamiliar space. Therefore, if we combine Butler's notion of the power of grief with what we have seen in the role played by people in eastern Sri Lanka, particularly the mothers and the *Valkai* group, then we can argue that the space created by shared loss and grief illustrates a different sense of 'getting on' in uncertain times.

Grief as resilience

While I argue here that the mapping of subjective experience of loss is appropriate to revealing local and individual meanings attached to distress and grief, this is not to suggest that people experiencing violence in their everyday lives would not benefit from some kind of intervention and support. I emphasise this point because stating the nuances and local meaning of grief as in opposition to models of therapy and 'healing' also runs the risk of discounting actual distress and need for support. As I have already illustrated, the binary opposite to focusing on suffering is focusing on resilience. Nancy Scheper-Hughes (2008: 25) describes it as 'the sources of strength, toughness, hardiness, and relative immunity from personal and psychological collapse that we have come to associate with exposure to a variety of human calamities'. Scheper-Hughes uses this idea of resilience to highlight the limitations of the dominant psychological trauma model, and to argue for a rethinking of the notions of trauma, violence, and expectation. Referring to examples in her book, *Death Without Weeping* (1993), which offer an account of everyday life in the Brazilian slum of Alto do Cruzeiro, she suggests that mothers are forced to develop a 'high expectancy' of the death of their infants and thus pre-select babies to die after birth. Thus, she argues, '[t]he experience of too much loss, too much death where new life should be led to a kind of patient resignation ... that obliterated outrage as well as sorrow' (2008: 29). My contention is that the suggestion that sorrow is 'obliterated' seems to be as much of a generalised claim as that which suggests all mothers are traumatised. However, the experiences of mothers in Batticaloa that have been explored in this book, and the lives of those who have lost numerous times and face a future of more uncertainty and vulnerability, suggest that sorrow and grief is complicit in their resilience and resistance. As such, resilience would not imply 'immunity' but conversely sensitivity to loss and awareness of vulnerability. Where Butler argues we need to recognise the humanity of the 'other' in terms of their vulnerability and loss, this should also be recognised in terms of their courage and strength to move forward and find strategies for working with what is at hand.

In another example, Scheper-Hughes (2008) draws upon the experiences of young African National Congress (ANC) and Pan African Congress (PAC) militants to argue that rather than seeing themselves as 'victims' of violence, they claim to be 'victors'. Scheper-Hughes, thus, proposes that strength of character and 'relative invulnerability' are purchased at the price of relationships, of intimacy, and 'all those emotions and dispositions that render humans vulnerable to pain, to loss, to grief, to despair and to hopelessness' (2008: 43). This suggests that, although Scheper-Hughes claims to recognise human nature as 'both resilient *and* frail' (2008: 42 emphasis in original), her proposition of 'resilience in the face of adversity' prevents a consideration of grief, pain, and trauma as an *integral part* of everyday resistance.

Furthermore, such a perspective precludes a consideration of how stories of suffering and loss can be built upon to strengthen the strategies of support and trust already in place. Key to this, I suggest, is changing the ways in which we understand experiences of violence and moving away from concepts of resilience which deny suffering and grief, and instead focusing on everyday endurance.[3]

Questioning peace

Gendered bodies and (un)gendered meanings

As we become aware of a general state of fragility and physical vulnerability that bodies are connected across, we cannot discount gender as a factor, which highlights both how we are made by meaning which precedes us and also how we give meaning to individual lives and communities. The stories and ideas in this book highlight the elective gender practices upon which a major part of the struggle against violence and militarisation is contingent. At the beginning of this book, I argued that, although most of my informants were women and their perspectives shaped the vast majority of my experiences in Sri Lanka, at the same time I found it less useful to focus on women exclusively. I highlighted the fact that although men's voices are less salient in the stories and narratives that I tell, men remained intricately connected to every life, space, and place described. However, as the book developed, and as I examined power relations and the contradictions and injustices inherent in everyday life in Batticaloa, gender and gender relations clearly emerged as prominent themes. Moreover, as I have challenged the view of focusing on victims and heroes in warscapes, the role of women has emerged as central in that they are most often depicted by this binary, and, thus, their initiatives to endure the everyday become simplified and fixed. This has invariably led me to consider the role of particular women in eastern Sri Lanka, especially, those connected with the *Valkai* group, as they have challenged the culture of violence in Batticaloa. As I have shown, many observers have stressed that there is an essential link between women, motherhood, and non-violence, arguing that those engaged in mothering work have distinct motives for rejecting war that are contingent upon their ability to resolve conflict non-violently (as discussed in Chapter 1, page 29). While it is true that in comparison with men far fewer women take up arms, and that internal movements for peace are frequently led by women, it is also true that we need to look at the reasons why women are more visible in this case and the dynamics of any particular situation.

Throughout, I have remained wary of fixing women within a particular role and have suggested, for example, that the mothers and widows in the *Valkai* group were less concerned with consciously using their status as vulnerable women than simply working with what they could at a particular time. In Batticaloa, this equalled their role as mothers, who were more able to move about and avoid risk than men. In this sense, men were more the victims as they were often forced to stay in the shadows and avoid active participation in seeking their children, for example, even when they wanted to. In practice, men were and are always a part of this struggle, and many are themselves involved in efforts to challenge violence and push for change, but in different ways. This resonates with Butler's (2004: 48) argument that distinctive categories can actually deny the actual complexity of lives in question by seeking to provide single models of reason and notions of the subject. The mothers and *Valkai* women reflect what Butler refers to as the 'array of sometimes incommensurable epistemological and political beliefs and modes and means of agency' (ibid.) that shape the paths of activism or, as I have called it, of 'active living'. This framework is important precisely for the reason that it does not fix categories or spaces, and departs from notions of revenge and repetition of violence. In this sense, gender has revealed the possibilities of subjectivity and agency – of being gendered differently and of differently viewing gender. As Butler (2004) suggests, we are constrained by certain kinds of cultural forces but not determined by them, and, therefore, open to improvisation and malleability. Therefore, while there is a gendered story at

In light of new beginnings

play (as much as there is a violent story at play), I do not reduce it simply to being one of men or women, violence or peace, since all are dependent upon one another in order to see a way forward. Bourke (2007: 33) argues, 'there is always a very particular story to tell about violence, specific to its own time and place, including the ambiguities of its gendered dynamics' and it is this focus that allows me to bring the argument back to the importance of human bodies – men and women – as fundamentally dependent and vulnerable.

Drawing on the feminist legacy of ideas about intimacy, domesticity, and maternity, Butler reflects on the immediacy with which some deaths are articulated, made visible, and mourned (since we appear to seek comfort in what is familiar which creates a bond with others), and those that we do not/cannot mourn, and are, therefore, rendered invisible and dispensable. Her reflection is a critical comment upon the various modalities of power and the tragic repercussions for those unequivocally outside the frames of contemporary global modalities, whose lives ironically define the terms within which political culture is currently conducted. Therefore, Butler forces the critical questioning as to 'whose death is mournable and whose is not' (McRobbie 2006: 79). This kind of question has also emerged in relation to the many lives (and deaths) described in this book that have testified to the ability of the state to control the experiences and expendability of people in eastern Sri Lanka. Furthermore, the inability of the families of those killed or disappeared to find space to properly grieve, and often even bury the body of those they love, grates against the visibility of public ceremonies of mourning held by the LTTE and by the state. For Butler (2004), it is the thousands of Iraqi and Palestinian lives lost which remain unknown and unmarked that reveals the manifestation of the management of populations and bodies – disciplinary and discursive – in the strategies of US state power. She draws upon Foucault to identify the diverse technologies and normalising practices as conducted through language and in the convergence and repetition of statements, pronouncements, and iteration through which behaviour becomes known, thinkable, recognisable, and legitimated. Similarly, in applying this argument to the handling of the final offensive in Sri Lanka, in which thousands upon thousands of lives have been lost (see Chapter 1, page 21), the debate over numbers and the exact circumstances in which those deaths occurred has diluted the poignancy of each human life that has ended. The individuality of the many bodies maimed, fragmented, and crumbled has been overlaid with arguments over responsibility and legitimate use of violence. Thus, state power circumscribes the capacity of the subject to contest the terms upon which his/her existence is based and limits the space for resistance.

The significance of the contagious mobilisation of a vocabulary of fear (or risk) as a political instrument, and the effect of foreclosure that this can so easily achieve, reveals how state power is dispersed beyond a central command, instead taking on bodily and spatial characteristics. It is, thus, embodied, corporeal, and bio-political. However, as much as this kind of framework is needed to induce questioning of state powers and the loss of 'other' lives, there is also need for a more nuanced understanding of how this can productively play out in places where fear, secrecy, threat, and violence continue; where mourning is circumscribed and can only take place in private hidden spaces. Rather than argue for the visibility of deaths and space for mourning, which in the context of Batticaloa would put those involved at greater risk, we need a different way to draw on mourning as a personal experience in establishing balance and endurance. There is a need to recognise uncertainty and unpredictability as common factors in finding a sensitive and careful political instrument for pushing wider spaces of connection and support. Furthermore, if we are to seek value in this argument for Batticaloa, and Sri Lanka more generally, we need to close the gap of the 'other' and consider how we locate notions of political responsibility in ties of relations that are almost too close for comfort. In Batticaloa, the problem with distance is not physical, but lies in the rendering of what is familiar and trustworthy, or frightening, suspicious, and unknown. Distance lies between those who contest spaces and seek to control and manipulate lives. It also lies between those who are rendered vulnerable as they negotiate and attempt to repair the fragmentation of everyday life. Moreover, the overall context of fear and risk means that ties of relations are constantly stretched and tested, worn and broken. Therefore, it is the question of how these ties can be strengthened that I have addressed by drawing attention to the work of Meena, Rani, the *Valkai* group, and others who have demonstrated a commitment to living with a certain kind of vulnerability and susceptibility, which simultaneously enhances risk while investing in trust and hope.

Dealing with fragments

One of the most important questions that has arisen from discussions about violence and vulnerability throughout this book is where it leaves those who are exposed to risk daily and unable to escape climates of everyday conflict; what it means for their sense of the future; and how we can accommodate different meanings and bring into political discussion a different vocabulary and vision for everyday lives in violence. Such visions are invariably linked to concepts of development and 'peace-building' in contexts of conflict and civil war, and the possibility of ending war and of finding a meaningful peace. These are clearly pertinent questions given the situation in Sri Lanka as I finish writing this book. Today, the LTTE has been defeated and it is three years since the government declared victory. Many have observed that had this 'victory' been considered sensitively and carefully by the state, this could have been a unique opportunity to start a new chapter in Sri Lanka. However, all evidence since the war was officially declared over on 19 May 2009 tragically points to further betrayal of the people, particularly those in the north and east who are desperate for change based on openness and peace. There has been little recognition of the dignity and rights for those who have been shut up in IDP camps in the north, and little done to support those who have been displaced, over and over again with their families fragmented. In a recent conversation with one of the *Valkai* members (Rajan) who had just been to visit family in the north as well as visiting many areas across the east, I was told that the number of families trying to resettle with very little security, no assurances about the future, and no answers about the fate of their loved ones had led to an increased rate of suicide. Rajan described to me three cases whereby young women, who had lost family members during the last months of fighting, had hung themselves.[4]

There has also been an intensifying of the use of state machinery for a narrow political agenda and to further undermine democratic institutions, and in Batticaloa families talk about the deeper penetration of the military into everyday affairs (see UTHR 2009a and c).[5] As Anuloja and Rajan told me, 'it is like being in a prison and backed further and further against the walls'. Although a number of significant changes have taken place, such as the removal of checkpoints and the opening up of areas previously under LTTE-control, daily life is still laced with risk and fear.

The greater tragedy in Sri Lanka seems to be that the victory against the LTTE could have been a victory against repression and violence had the state sought a political transformation that recognised the need for transparency, honesty, and recognition of the suffering of the past. In turn, the state would have also needed to acknowledge their own role, alongside that of the LTTE and all other militant factions in the enormous loss of life. Sri Lankans, particularly those in the north and east, have been worn down by decades of war. Meeting the need for political space to draw on the threads of hope and trust that remain is essential to ensure a future that is different from the cycles of violence that haunts the past and present. Clearly, the legacy of state violence and violence from the LTTE and other Tamil militant groups cannot be forgotten. It is perhaps also too early to turn to ideas of forgiveness and reconciliation, given that wounds remain open and sore, and so many families and communities await the opportunity to begin stitching back together their everyday lives. There are some very powerful and important reports written about the current state of life and politics in Sri Lanka (see for example UTHR 2009c; Weiss 2011; ICG 2011a and b; 2012a and b). Therefore, I do not go into many of the details of life in Sri Lanka now other than to emphasise the continued (and in many cases heightened) state of impunity, controlled space, levels of fear, and use of violence to silence those who dare to speak out. As such, the propensity of the past to exacerbate hatred and fear is critical, and carries with it the weight of unfinished histories and voices that are yet to be heard. However, as I have tried to illustrate throughout this book, there is another way, which could open up spaces for grieving and vulnerability without exacerbating fear and hostility to generate more violence.

Shared helplessness

Butler (2004) contends that it is precisely our 'shared helplessness' which is as evident in the susceptibility of our desires and attachments to rejection and loss as in our enduring physical fragility that ties us together as human beings. She argues that a core part of any explanatory framework for global suffering must be an understanding of shared vulnerability, 'a vulnerability to the other that is part of bodily life, a vulnerability to a sudden address from elsewhere that we cannot pre-empt' (ibid.: 29). Mindfulness of this vulnerability, Butler argues, can become the 'basis of claims for non-military political solutions' and if stayed with, can generate new and create ways of addressing politics (ibid.). In other words, the importance of attending to vulnerability in this context is that it not only highlights the role of moral responsibilities, but also considers where this can take us and what this means for political futures. As Butler notes, 'to ask for recognition or to offer it is not to ask for recognition of what already is. It is to solicit a becoming, to instigate a transformation, to petition the future always in relation to the other' (ibid.: 46). Invoking the power of language to reflect 'with humility' on the suffering of others, therefore, can allow the consideration of an ethical vocabulary, which might provide terms for opposing everyday cultures. This is in contrast to stances of refusal which can lead to notions of resistance and heroism – as revealed by the position offered by Scheper-Hughes (2008) equating resilience with 'hardiness' and valour.

This focus can be also be related to the wider context of war and peace in Sri Lanka in which the experiences and meanings of everyday life could inform and shape ideas of sustainable peace following violence. Thinking back to the many stories and experiences in this book, which capture the small spaces that have been widened to create support and envisage change, it is clear that there is desire and hope for peace. We can link this with the focus in this chapter on human vulnerability in everyday living, and the need for a different vision and vocabulary that speaks not of more violence but of alternative solutions and spaces. As well as questioning what the actual meaning of peace can therefore be when it is coupled with notions of violence and violations, we also need to consider how the meaning of peace can be transformed and the spaces in which this can be done.

In determining the need for a new vision and vocabulary, the issue of where we locate the site of interaction and initiation is critical. It is easy to assert that the responsibility of instigating change lies with civil society and that a focus on its role and ideas of peace can take ideas of peace away from a state-centric framework (Uyangoda 2002: 214). However, in reality, the practicalities of such an approach are complex and extremely difficult. Throughout this book, it has become clear that any *simple* notion of a democratic civil society does not exist in the north and east of Sri Lanka, where the competing claims to power seriously compromise any right to express opinions, to move freely and to live without violence. Goodhand and Lewer (1999: 69–88) address this problem by stating that although it must be recognised, in the Sri Lankan context, that civil society in whatever form can contain the potential for greater interaction, this cannot bear the totality of responsibility for effecting deeper participation. Thus, the ambiguities of 'local' and of 'community' demand a sensitive and carefully mapped out approach to peace. However, this perspective misses the everyday strategies that have formed the central premise of this book, and which reveal that 'social energy' and the ability to face violence and threat do exist, but in more subtle and sensitive forms. Moreover, the very reason such strategies manage to exist in the first place is that they remain firmly embedded within the crevices and fluid spaces of everyday living, not seeking recognition and appreciation, but rather working at living on and through violence to effect change from within. As I have demonstrated, this is an approach that is sensitive to political shaping of action, but hostile to the effects of normal politics. Therefore, the point is that this work *is* being done – by those whose work is overlooked but to some extent *has* to be overlooked; for these people who set things in motion, it is about hope and change which is tightly tied to the everyday pockets of space to create more spaces of relative calm or peace. This peace is about making lives more bearable and making small investments in a more humane future. The question that needs to be addressed, therefore, is if and how this kind of work can be more broadly effective and mapped onto wider processes of peace-building.

A new beginning?

A search for balance

A frequent topic of conversation that arose in the Batticaloa household where I lived with members of the *Valkai* group, was about balance. That is, how to feel balanced or to sustain balance while confusion and chaos cut through everyday experiences and meaning. In other words, how to live in the midst of a landscape of suffering, and how to keep your feet down no matter what forces try to pull you off centre. One particular evening, towards the end of my time in Batticaloa, as we began discussing this topic, Anuloja, shared with me something she had written a number of years earlier when she had found herself reflecting on a similar question. Her words are written out below:

> Once balance is reached with-in and with-out it does not stay that way. There is nothing static in the growth process. The more open to self and environment I am the more I enter into the cycle of awareness; imbalance – search – balance. It's the spiral of life. A journey. It's a sense of movement so the me of yesterday is not the me of today. It's like travelling closer and closer to a beloved home. The home is not out there but here in our hearts. (Anuloja, member of the *Valkai* group 1998)

I have quoted Anuloja's words here not only because they so eloquently capture her search for meaning at that time, but because they also seem to grasp the essence of the lives and stories that have been told in this book in terms of the struggle faced by people across eastern Sri Lanka. By tracing the lives of individuals, the chapters here have shown the importance of trying to grapple with such issues of meaning and balance, and have emphasised how relations to violence and peace are far more intimate, personal, indissoluble than they might initially seem. Crucially, they address the links between violence, imagination, and anticipation, which are hinged upon a notion of balance, integral to everyday endurance. This is a balance of the experiences of grief and loss, of moving from the familiar to the unfamiliar, of letting go of the security of what you have and what you have lost. To be able to imagine a different space for the future, thus, entails a balancing of the past, present, and the future, of shadows of memories, and glimpses of dreams for the future. Where imaginings take place within the boundaries of what is known, of what is ordinary, they also escape beyond these confines to envisage an ordinary life that can hold alternative meanings and a different life. Therefore, while there will always be fragmented shards of memory – some reflecting light, others opening deeper wounds – a balance can still be found.

It is also this search for balance that I believe falls upon the shoulders of anthropologists and ethnographers to elucidate in order to bear witness to the complex dynamics of an everyday space. As I have noted within this book, this responsibility is not always because people cannot speak for themselves or because we, as ethnographers, are in a privileged moral position. Often, it is more the case that a climate of danger, or risk, and of an urgent need to attend to the practicalities of everyday life means that those who do not step away from a situation are unable to write. This is where I have located my responsibility to describe the unique present moment in Batticaloa that I entered into, while incorporating a sense of what took place before, what others have said, and what people spoke of for the future. In bringing together such threads, an attempt can take place to create something that does not focus exclusively on violence but equally does not embed it so deep in the crevices of everyday life that it becomes 'normal'. However, as the trope of witnessing suggests, anthropologists in conflict areas are able to pose both methodological and political questions, and especially expose the muddied nature of participation and observation, which are 'inherently political activities' (Hoffman 2003). Hoffman states, 'presence requires participation', for in reality there is no such thing as 'neutral, uninvolved observation' (2003: 3). Throughout this book, I have addressed concerns over issues of power and agency, and suggested that there are no pre-ordained answers as to how one conducts oneself in volatile contexts where questions of ethics, morality, and responsibility will continuously be raised. Therefore, the chapters illuminate the complexity of this reality, while also highlighting the relevance of building relationships within and across contexts, and questioning the substance of those relationships and what can be understood from inside and out. Mahmood (2002: 1) has argued that ethnography (particularly in emotionally and physically challenging spaces) tends to produce unusually close bonds with research subjects. The intimacy of these bonds, and the experience of bearing witness, is every aspect of one's scholarship, making the fallacy of the divide between field methodology, theory, and political engagement even more conspicuous (Mahmood 2002; Hoffman 2003). At the same time, it also makes the lines between empathy and identification particularly ambiguous, which for researchers in contexts of violent regions, raise far more questions about representation than they do of rapport.

My experiences of living in Batticaloa, leaving Batticaloa, and finding a way to write about Batticaloa have also been about finding a balance. When I first started writing after leaving the field, I experienced a painful period of confusion;

I found it impossible to translate what felt like a catastrophe of memories onto paper. There was so much that I wanted to say and I could not find a way. There was also much that I did not want to remember. However, these undesirable memories still forced their way into my consciousness, and, for a while, distorted reality, and my sense of 'being' in the present. In addition, the pressure I felt to do justice to the lives I had admired, learnt from, and grown to love became a paralysis to my writing, as did my lost hope for the future of Batticaloa. However, it has been in the process of thawing out these frozen thoughts, of re-locating and engaging with my memories and reality in relation to a firmer sense of the past, present, and future that I have found my balance again. In finding a space where both the sadness of loss and recognition of hope can exist, I have had to also engage with vulnerability and with the responsibility to ties of relationships. Therefore, my academic journey to describe the importance of endurance and balance in the everyday lives of people in Batticaloa is also well reflected in my personal journey to find a balance in my writing as well as to understand how my life has been shaped and changed by those in Batticaloa.

In conclusion

In 1989, Rajani Thiranagama wrote the following as a post script to *The Broken Palmyra*:

> Within this tragic history there is still an attempt by concerned people to think coherently of the future. There are debates going on as to the correct path for survival, organization and possible breakthroughs. There is, especially in the North, a limited attempt at organizing at the grass-roots level, so as to handle the repressive situation and violence from all sides. These are very small beginnings indeed ... For the people, any solution to the brutal and intense violence has to come from within the communities and cannot be imposed from outside. The development of these internal structures is a long and arduous task, a process which is only just beginning to be comprehended.

Reflecting on the state of life in the northern Sri Lanka at that time, Rajani recognised the enormity of the task facing Tamil-speaking communities while locating the fragile shoots of hope as 'small beginnings' embedded within the strategies of everyday endurance. Then, as now, the small beginnings of hope remain critical for the future of the north and east and for any sense of peace that can be built from the loss that war has brought. Hope also relies on space – political space to work out a sense of what lies in the future, practical space to manage the affairs of reconstruction and development, emotional space to face up to losses and grieve for those who will not return, and personal and collective spaces to overcome the legacies of violence and work together without fear.

There are many voices, which, sadly, despite underpinning the foundations of and echoing throughout this book, cannot be identified and named. Forced into silence in this written form however, they have not been silenced in Batticaloa, and in their own ways, through their own means, they continue to call out for justice while they push through boundaries and borders claiming witness to the

Plate 7.1 Children playing in the sea, Batticaloa (2005)

continued struggle that everyday endurance faces. It is these voices that have created this work of stories, memories, and hopes for the future, which dwell in the spaces of Batticaloa and testify to the everyday endurance of the people.

In drawing to the end of this book, I find that much remains unfinished; there are many spaces that are yet to be discovered and understood, and lives that are yet to be given meaning. And as daily life in eastern Sri Lanka moves on in a context of 'post conflict' that continues to be highly militarised and stained with fear, these spaces demand further questioning of the meaning of the everyday and the ordinary. Widening my focus from what has been made possible and of what has been able to work, my hope is that sensitive and careful research can further strengthen the connections and ties of those who actively but quietly continue to push for change. If balance can be attended to, if unfamiliar and frightening spaces can be further opened and made safer, and if the value of grief can reflect on the value of life, then it can be hoped that individuals and families across eastern Sri Lanka will no longer, like Rani and her children, need to plant trees to remember lives. Instead, they can focus on and enrich the spaces that *Kuti annar maram* and other trees have opened up, to invest in a different future and new beginnings.

Notes

1 A 'martyrs family' is a family where one of the family members has died fighting for the LTTE.
2 The apparent urgency and need to foreclose grief and move into action can be located in medical models shaped by Western discourse such as PTSD, which have sought to brand experiences of violence and loss as 'trauma', and often draw attention to an apparent failure of local mental health support groups to alleviate emotional incapacity to face loss. While I do not enter into an in-depth discussion in this chapter about the role of PTSD, I refer the reader to Becker (1995), Somasundaram (2007), and Young (1995).
3 Such a perspective could also lead to a reassessment how the PTSD model is framed and utilised, for although in theory it makes universal assumptions, this does not mean that in practice it is not malleable to more culturally specific ideas (see Somasundaram 2007).
4 This was conveyed to me in an informal conversation, and while I cannot provide evidence to back up the claims about the rising suicide rate I have heard from a number of sources in Sri Lanka that this is becoming a much greater issue.
5 The UTHR reports (2009a and 2009c) provide detailed accounts of what took place during the last stages of war as well as the current moves of the Sri Lankan state *vis-a-vis* the people locked up in internment camps. They also debate the need to find alternative spaces for peace, amidst an increasingly militarised and authoritarian government.

Bibliography

Abu-Lughod, L. (1993). *Writing Women's Worlds: Bedouin Stories*, Berkeley, CA: University of California Press.
Agarwal, B. (1990). 'Gender and Land Rights in Sri Lanka', Working Paper No. 49, Rural Employment Policy Research Program Policy Series, World Employment Program Research, ILO, Geneva.
—— (1996 [1994]). *A Field of One's Own: Gender and Land Rights in South Asia*, New Delhi: Cambridge University Press.
Agence France-Presse (AFP) (2004). 'Army Deployed as Tamils Flee East Sri Lanka Amid Arson Attacks, War Fears', 31 March 2004, www.reliefweb.int/rwarchive /rwb.nsf/db900sid/. Last accessed 1 December 2009.
Agreement on a ceasefire Between the Government of the Democratic Socialist Republic of Sri Lanka and the Liberation Tigers of Tamil Eelam (2003), www.slmm.info/CEASEFIRE_AGREEMENT/Ceasefire_Agreement/. Last accessed 12 September 2009.
Alison, M. (2003). 'Cogs in the Wheel? Women in the Liberation Tigers of Tamil Eelam', *Civil Wars*, 6(4): 55–82.
Amnesty International (AI) (1990a). 'Sri Lanka: The Indian Peace Keeping Force and "Disappearances"', 31 August 1990, www.amnesty.org/en/library/info/ASA37 /030/1990/en. Last accessed 16 October 2009.
—— (1990b). 'Sri Lanka: An Update on Human Rights', 31 August 1990, www.amnesty.org/en/library/info/ASA37/002/1991/en. Last accessed 12 October 2009.
—— (2005). 'Sri Lanka: Waiting to Go Home – the Plight of the Internally Displaced', AI_LKA_UPR_S2_2008anx_asa370042006.pdf. Last accessed 12 September 2009.
—— (2007). 'Sri Lanka Armed Groups Infiltrating Refugee Camps', 14 March 2007, www.amnesty.org/en/library/info/ASA37/007/2007. Last accessed 12 October 2009.
Arasaratnam, S. (1994). 'Sri Lanka's Tamils under Colonial Rule', in B. Pfaffenberger and C. Manogaran (eds.), *The Sri Lankan Tamils: Ethnicity and Identity*, Oxford: Westview Press, pp. 28–53.
Arendt, H. (1958). *The Human Condition*, Chicago: Chicago University Press.
Asian Development Bank (ADB) (1999). 'Country Briefing Paper: Women in Sri Lanka', www.adb.org/Documents/Books/Country_Briefing_Papers/Women_in_SriLanka/def ault.asp. Last accessed 6 December 2009.
Asian Development Bank (ADB), JBIC, and WB (2005). 'Preliminary Damage and Needs Assessment', www.adb.org/Tsunami/sri-lanka-assessment. Last accessed 17 April 2012.
Athukorala, P. and B. P. Resosudarmo (2005). 'The Indian Ocean Tsunami: Economic

Bibliography

Impact Disaster Management and Lessons', Division of Economics, Research School of Pacific and Asian Studies, Australian National University, Canberra.

Bähre, E. (2007). 'Reluctant Solidarity: Death, Urban Poverty and Neighbourly Assistance in South Africa', *Ethnography*, 8(1): 33–59.

Bajoria, J. (2009). 'The Sri Lankan Conflict', Council on Foreign Relations (CFR), New York, www.cfr.org/publication/11407/. Last accessed 12 December 2011.

Bakhtin, M. M. (1993). *Toward a Philosophy of the Act*, Austin: Texas University Press.

Balasingham, A. (1983). *Women and Revolution: The Role of Women in Tamil Eelam National Liberation*, London: Fairmax Publishing.

—— (1993). *Women Fighters of Liberation Tigers*, London: LTTE Publication Section.

—— (1998). *Will to Freedom: An Inside View of Tamil Resistance*, London: Fairmax Publishing.

Barry, J. (2005). *Rising up in Response – Women's Rights Activism in Conflict*, London: Urgent Action Fund for Women's Human Rights.

Bastian, S. (2009). 'The Politics of Foreign Aid in Sri Lanka: Promoting Markets and Supporting Peace', *South Asia Economic Journal*, 10: 229–37.

Becker, D. (1995). 'The Deficiency of the Concept of Post-Traumatic Stress Disorder when Dealing with Victims of Human Rights Violations', in R. Kelber, C. Figley, and B. Gersons (eds.), *Beyond Trauma: Cultural and Societal Dynamics*, New York: Plenum Press, pp. 99–144.

Bohle, H. G. (2007). 'Living with Vulnerability: Livelihoods and Human Security in Risky Environments', *InterSecTions* (Interdisciplinary Security ConnecTions), 6: 1–32.

Bohle, H. and Fünfgeld, H. (2007). 'The Political Ecology of Violence in Eastern Sri Lanka', *Development and Change*, 38(4): 665–87.

Bose, S. (1994). *States, Nations and Sovereignty*, London: Sage Publications.

Bourdieu, P. (1977). *Outline of a Theory of Practice*, Cambridge: Cambridge University Press.

Bourke, J. (2007). *Rape: A Cultural History*, London: Virago.

British Refugee Council (BRC) (2002). 'Sri Lanka: Return to Uncertainty', August 2002, www.internaldisplacement.org/8025708F004CE90B/httpCountry_Documents?ReadForm&country=Sri%20Lanka&count=10000. Last accessed 12 October 2009.

Burke, A. and Mulakala, A. (2011). 'An Insider's View of Donor Support for the Sri Lankan Peace Process, 2000–2005', in J. Goodhand, B. Korf, and J. Spencer (eds.), *Conflict and Peacebuilding in Sri Lanka: Caught in the Peace Trap?* London: Routledge, pp. 150–67.

Butalia, U. (2000 [1998]). *The Other Side of Silence: Voices from the Partition of India*, New Delhi: Penguin.

Butler, J. (2004). *Precarious Life: The Powers of Mourning and Violence*, London: Verso.

Calhoun, C. (2008). 'The Imperative to Reduce Suffering: Charity, Progress, and Emergencies in the Field of Humanitarian Action', in M. Barnett and T. C. Weiss (eds.), *Humanitarianism in Question: Politics, Power and Ethics*, Ithaca, New York: Cornell University Press, pp. 73–97.

Campbell, R. (2002). *Emotionally Involved: The Impact of Researching Rape*, London: Routledge.

Canagaratnam, S. O. (1921). Monograph of the Batticaloa District of the Eastern Province, Ceylon, Colombo, Sri Lanka: H. R. Cottle.

Centre for Information Resources Management (CIRM) (2005). 'Administrative Map of Batticaloa District: District, DS Division, GN Division boundaries', www.ifsp-srilanka.org/html/administrative_map_batticaloa.html. Last accessed 28 November 2011.

Centre for Policy Alternatives (CPA) (2007). 'Fact-Finding Visit to Batticaloa', 10 and 11 April 2007, www.cpalanka.org/page.php?id=0&pubid=341&key=9bdd5f06c37bdab66735ca41a9457925. Last accessed 12 September 2009.

Chandraprema, C. A. (1991). *Sri Lanka The Years of Terror*, Colombo, Sri Lanka: Lake House Bookshop.

Channel 4. (2011). *Sri Lanka's Killing Fields* and (2012) *Sri Lanka's Killing Fields: War Crimes Unpunished*, www.channel4.com/info/press/programme-information/sri-lankas-killing-fields-war-crimes-unpunished. Last accessed 18 May 2012.

Clark, N. (2005). 'Disaster and Generosity', *Geographical Journal*, 171: 384–6.

Clarke, A. (2005). 'The Day after Tsunami: New Waves of Human Spirit and Perseverance in Sri Lanka', *Daily Mirror*, Colombo, Sri Lanka.

Cock, J. (1994). 'Women and the Military: Implications for Demilitarization in the 1990s in South Africa', *Gender and Society*, 8(2): 152–69.

Cockburn, C. (1998). *The Space Between Us: Negotiating Gender and National Identities in Conflict*, London: Zed Press.

—— (2007). *From Where We Stand: War, Women's Activism and Feminist Analysis*, London: Zed Press.

Connell, R. W. (2002). 'Masculinities, the Reduction of Violence and the Pursuit of Peace', in C. Cockburn and D. Zarkov (eds.), *The Postwar Moment: Militaries, Masculinities and International Peacekeeping – Bosnia and the Netherlands*, London: Lawrence & Wishart, pp. 33–40.

Coomaraswarmy, R. (1996). 'Tiger Women and the Question of Women's Emancipation', *Pravada*, 4(9): 8–10.

—— (2002). 'Violence, Armed Conflict and the Community', in S. Jayaweera (ed.), *Women in Post-Independence Sri Lanka*, New Delhi: Sage, pp. 79–98.

Coomaraswarmy, R. and Fonseka, D. (eds.) (2004). *Peace Work: Women, Armed Conflict and Negotiation*, New Delhi: Women Unlimited.

Crook, S. (1998). 'Minotaurs and Other Monsters: "Everyday Life" in Recent Social Theory', *Sociology*, 32(3): 523–40.

Daniel, V. (1984). *Fluid Signs: Being a Person the Tamil Way*, Berkeley, CA: University of California Press.

—— (1994). 'The Individual in Terror', in T. Csordas (ed.), *Embodiment and Experience: The Existential Ground of Culture and Self*, Cambridge: Cambridge University Press, pp. 229–47.

—— (1996). *Charred Lullabies: Chapters in an Anthropography of Violence*, Princeton, NJ: Princeton University Press.

Daniel, V. and Thangarajah, Y. (1995). 'Forms, Formations and Transformations of the Tamil Refugee', in V. Daniel and E. Knudsen (eds.), *Mistrusting Refugees*, Berkeley, CA: University of California Press, pp. 225–56.

Das, V. (1994). 'Moral Orientations to Suffering: Legitimation, Power and Healing', in L. C. Chen, A. Kleinman, and N. C. Ware (eds.), *Health and Social Change in International Perspective*, Boston: Harvard School of Public Health, pp. 139–67.

—— (1995). *Critical Events: An Anthropological Perspective on Contemporary India*, Delhi: Oxford University Press.

—— (1997). 'Language and Body: Transactions in the Construction of Pain', in A. Kleinman, V. Das, and M. Lock (eds.), *Social Suffering*, Berkeley and Los Angeles, CA: University of California Press, pp. 67–91.

—— (2003). 'Trauma, Testimony and the Making of Political Community', Paper presented to the Department of Anthropology, 10 February 2003, Duke University, Durham.

—— (2007). *Life and Words: Violence and the Descent into the Ordinary*, Berkeley, CA: University of California Press.
—— (2008). 'Violence, Gender, and Subjectivity', *Annual Review of Anthropology*, 37: 283–99.
Das. V. and Poole, D. (eds.) (2004). *Anthropology in the Margins of the State*, Sante Fe, NM: School of American Research Press.
De Alwis, M. (1997). 'Motherhood as a Space for Protest: Women's Political Participation in Contemporary Sri Lanka', in B. Amrita and P. Jeffrey (eds.), *Appropriating Gender: Women's Activism and the Politicization of Religion in South Asia*, London and New York: Routledge, pp. 185–201.
—— (2002). 'The Changing Role of Women in Sri Lankan Society', *Social Research: An International Quarterly of Social Sciences*, 69(3): 675–91.
—— (2004a). 'The "Purity" of Displacement and the Reterritorialization of Longing: Muslim IDPs in North Western Sri Lanka', in W. Giles and J. Hyndman (eds.), *Sites of Violence: Gender and Conflict Zones*, Berkeley, CA and London: University of California Press, pp. 213–20.
—— (2004b). 'A Rising in the East', *Polity*, 2(1): 12–14.
—— (2009a). 'Interrogating the "Political": Feminist Peace Activism in Sri Lanka', *Feminist Review*, 91: 81–93.
—— (2009b). 'A Double Wounding: Aid and Activism in Post-Tsunami Sri Lanka', in M. de Alwis and E. L. Hedman (eds.), *Tsunami in a Time of War: Aid, Activism and Reconstruction in Sri Lanka and Aceh*, New York, US and Colombo, Sri Lanka: International Centre for Ethnic Studies, pp. 121–38.
De Alwis, M. and Hedman, E. L. (2009). 'Introduction', in M. de Alwis and E.-L. Hedman (eds.), *Tsunami in a Time of War: Aid, Activism and Reconstruction in Sri Lanka and Aceh*, New York, USA and Colombo, Sri Lanka: International Centre for Ethnic Studies, pp. 9–28.
De Certeau, M. (1984). *The Practice of Everyday Life*, S. Rendall (trans.), Berkeley, CA: University of California Press.
De Mel, N. (1998). 'Agent or Victim? The Sri Lankan Woman Militant in the Interregnum', in M. Roberts (ed.), *Sri Lanka: Collective Identities Revisited*, Vol. II, Colombo, Sri Lanka: Marga Institute, pp. 199–220.
—— (2001). *Women and the Nation's Narrative: Gender and Nationalism in Twentieth Century Sri Lanka*, Lanham, MD: Rowman & Littlefield.
—— (2002). 'Fractured Narratives: Notes on Women in Conflict in Sri Lanka and Pakistan', *Development*, 45(1): 99–104.
—— (2007). *Militarizing Sri Lanka: Popular Culture, Memory and Narrative in the Armed Conflict*, London: Sage.
De Silva, K. M. (1986). *Managing Ethnic Tensions in Multi-Ethnic Societies: Sri Lanka 1880–1985*, Lanham: University Press of America.
De Silva, M. (1994). 'Women in the LTTE: Liberation or Subjugation?', *Pravada*, 3(7): 27–31.
Deleuze, G. (1993). *The Fold: Leibniz and the Baroque*, London: Athlone Press.
Deleuze. G. and Guattari, F. *(1994). What is Philosophy?*, H. Tomlinson and G. Burchell (trans.), New York: Columbia University Press.
Department of Census and Statistics (1981). *Estimated Mid Year Population by Ethnic Group, 1980–1989*, www.statistics.gov.lk/. Last accessed 13 November 2011.
—— (2008). *Population by Ethnic Group, Census Years, Statistical Abstract 2008*, www.statistics.gov.lk/Abstract_2008_PDF/abstract2008/pagesPdf/chapter2.htm. Last accessed 13 November 2011.

Department of Census and Statistics Special Enumeration (2007). 'Basic Population Information on Batticaloa District – 2007: Preliminary Report Based on Special Enumeration', Department of Census and Statistics Special Enumeration, Sri Lanka.

Dirks, N. B. (2008). *Castes of Mind: Colonialism and the Making of Modern India*, Delhi: Permanent Black.

Dorfman, A. (1983). *Widows*, S. Kessler (trans.), New York: Seven Stories Press.

Dumont, L. (1953). 'The Dravidian Kinship Terminology as an Expression of Marriage', *Man*, 53: 34–9.

—— (1957). *Hierarchy and Marriage Alliance in South Indian Kinship*, RAI Occasional Paper 12, London: Royal Anthropological Institute.

—— (1966). 'Descent or Intermarriage? A Relational View of Australian Section Systems', *Southwestern Journal of Anthropology*, 22: 231–50.

—— (1970). *Homo Hierarchicus*, Chicago: University of Chicago Press.

—— (1983). *Affinity as a Value: Marriage Alliance in South India, with Comparative Essays on Australia*, Chicago: University of Chicago Press.

Eastmond, M. (2007). 'Stories as Lived Experience: Narratives in Forced Migration Research', *Journal of Refugee Studies*, 20(2): 248–64.

Eddleston, M., Ariaratnam, C. A., Mayer, W. P., Perera, G., Kularatne, A. M., Attapattu, S., Sheriff, M. H., and Warrell, D. A. (1999). 'Epidemic of Self-poisoning with Seeds of the Yellow Oleander Tree (Thevetia peruviana) in Northern Sri Lanka', *Tropical Medicine and International Health*, 4(4): 266–73.

Emmanuel, S. (2005). 'Sri Lankan Women's Small but Significant Gains in the Post Tsunami Reconstruction Process', *Forum News*, 18(2): 8–9.

—— (2008). *Strategic Mapping of Women's Peace Activism in Sri Lanka*, Colombo, Sri Lanka: Women and Media Collective.

European Union Report (2009). *Map of Sri Lanka*, http://commons.wikimedia.org/wiki/File:Extent_of_territorial_control_in_sri_lanka.png#filehistory. Last accessed 21 May 2012.

Feldman, A. (1991). *Formations of Violence: The Narrative of the Body and Political Terror in Northern Ireland*, Chicago: The University of Chicago Press.

—— (2000). 'Violence and Vision: The Prosthetics and Aesthetics of Terror', in V. Das, A. Kleinman, R. Mamphela, and P. Reynolds (eds.), *Violence and Subjectivity*, Berkeley, CA: University of California Press, pp. 46–78.

Fernando, U. and Hilhorst, D. (2006). 'Everyday Practices of Humanitarian Aid: Tsunami Response in Sri Lanka', *Development in Practice*, 16(3/4): 292–302.

Finnström, S. (2008). *Living with Bad Surroundings: War, History, and Everyday Moments in Northern Uganda*, London: Duke University Press.

Foucault, M. (1977). *Discipline and Punish: The Birth of the Prison*, New York: Pantheon.

Fraser, I. (2005). 'Small Fish Trampled in Post-Tsunami Stampede', *Forced Migration Review*, Special Issue (July): 39.

Freks, G. and Klem, B. J. (2005). 'Tsunami Response in Sri Lanka', Report on a Field Visit from 6–20 February, Clingendael Institute, Wageningen University.

—— (2011) 'Muddling the Peace Process: The Political Dynamics of the Tsunami Aid and Conflict', in J. Goodhand, B. Korf, and J. Spencer (eds.), *Conflict and Peacebuilding in Sri Lanka: Caught in the Peace Trap?*, London: Routledge, pp. 168–82.

Fuglerud, O. (1998). 'Space and Movement in the Sri Lankan Conflict', Working Paper, Centre for Development and the Environment, University of Oslo.

—— (2004). 'Local Communities and State Ambitions in Eastern Sri Lanka', in M. Mayer, D. Rajasingham-Senanayake, and Y. Thangarajah (eds.), *Building Local Capacities for*

Peace: Rethinking Conflict and Development in Sri Lanka, New Delhi: Macmillan, pp. 65–79.
Gaasbeek, T. J. (2010). 'Actors in a Masala Movie: Fieldnotes on the NGO Tsunami Response in Eastern Sri Lanka', in D. B. McGilvray and M. R. Gamburd (eds.), *Tsunami Recovery in Sri Lanka*, London and New York: Routledge, pp. 125–42.
Galtung, J. (1996). *Peace by Peaceful Means: Peace and Conflict, Development and Civilisation*, London: Sage Publications.
Garfinkel, H. (1952). 'The Perception of the Other: A Study of Social Order', unpublished Ph.D. dissertation, Department of Sociology, Harvard University, California.
—— (1967). *Studies in Ethnomethodology*, Englewood Cliffs, NJ: Prentice-Hall.
Gilsenan, M. (1996). *Lords of the Lebanese Marches: Violence and Narrative in an Arab Society*, London: I. B. Tauris.
Good, A. (1980). 'Elder Sister's Daughter Marriage in South Asia', *Journal of Anthropological Research*, 36: 474–500.
—— (1981). 'Prescription, Preference, and Practice: Marriage Patterns among the Kondaiyankottai Maravar of South India', *Man* (N.S.), 16: 109–29.
—— (1991). *The Female Bridegroom*, Oxford: Clarendon Press.
—— (2007). *Anthropology and Expertise in the Asylum Courts*, Oxford and New York: Routledge-Cavendish.
Goodhand, J. and Hulme, D. (1999). 'From Wars to Complex Political Emergencies: Understanding Conflict and Peace-Building in the New World Disorder', *Third World Quarterly*, 20(1): 13–26.
Goodhand J. and Klem, B. (with D. Fonseka, S. I. Keethaponcalan, and S. Sardesai) (2005). *Aid, Conflict, and Peace Building in Sri Lanka 2000–2005*, Colombo, Sri Lanka: Asia Foundation.
Goodhand, J. and Lewer, N. (1999). 'Sri Lanka: NGOs and Peace-Building in Complex Political Emergencies', *Third World Quarterly*, 20(1): 69–88.
Government Survey Department of Sri Lanka (2005a). *Map of Sri Lanka Districts and Provinces*, Sri Lanka: UN Humanitarian Information Center for Sri Lanka.
—— (2005b). *Batticaloa District: Administrative Map*, Sri Lanka: UN Humanitarian Information Center for Sri Lanka.
Green, L. (1994). 'Fear as a Way of Life', *Cultural Anthropology*, 9(2): 147–72.
—— (1995). 'The Paradoxes of War and Its Aftermath: Mayan Widows in Rural Guatemala', *Cultural Survival Quarterly*, 19(1): 73–5.
—— (1999). *Fear as a Way of Life: Mayan Widows in Rural Guatemala*, New York: Columbia University Press.
Groundviews (2011). 'A Robust Debate on No Fire Zones (NFZs) and International Humanitarian Law: Artful Dodging of War Crimes in Sri Lanka?', Groundviews, 26 May 2011, www.groundviews.org/2011/05/26/a-robust-debate-on-no-fire-zones-nfzs-and-international-humanitarian-law-artful-dodging-of-war-crimes-in-sri-lanka/. Last accessed 12 May 2012.
Gunaratna, R. (2001 [1994]). *Sri Lanka: A Lost Revolution? – The Inside Story of the JVP*, Kandy: Institute of Fundamental Studies.
Hallisey, C. (2010). *Between Intuition and Judgement: Moral Creativity in Theravada Buddhist Ethics*, Harvard, MA: Harvard Divinity School.
Hamber, B. (2006). 'Nunca Mas and the Politics of the Person: Can Truth Telling Prevent the Reoccurrence of Violence?', in T. A. Borer (ed.), *Telling Truths: Truth Telling and Peace Building in Post-Conflict Societies*, Notre Dame and Indiana: University of Notre Dame Press, pp. 207–30.

Hariharan, R. (2004). 'Karuna in a No-Win Situation', *South Asian Analysis Group* No. 1147 and 8, www.southasiaanalysis.org/papers12/paper1165.html. Last accessed 1 November 2009.

Harris, S. (2006). 'Disaster Response, Peace and Conflict in Post-Tsunami Sri Lanka Part 1: The Congestion of Humanitarian Space', Centre for Conflict Resolution Working Paper 16, Department of Peace Studies, University of Bradford.

Harrison, P. (2000). 'Making Sense: Embodiment and the Sensibilities of the Everyday: Environment and Planning D', *Society and Space*, 18: 497–517.

Hasbullah, S. H. and Korf, B. (2009). 'Muslim Geographies and the Politics of Purification in Sri Lanka after the 2004 Tsunami', *Singapore Journal of Tropical Geography*, 30: 248–64.

Hearn, J. (1998). *The Violences of Men: How Men Talk About and How Agencies Respond to Men's Violence to Women*, London: Sage.

Herring, R. J. (1972). 'The Forgotten Paddy Lands Act in Ceylon: Ideology, Capacity and Response', *Modern Ceylon Studies*, 3(2): 99–124.

Hoffman, D. (2003). 'Frontline Anthropology: Research in a Time of War', *Anthropology Today*, 19(3): 9–12.

Hollup, O. (1994). *Bonded Labour: Caste and Cultural Identity among Tamil Plantation Workers in Sri Lanka*, Sri Lanka: Charles Subasinghe & Sons.

Hoole, R. (1995). *A Murder and the Problem of Truth: The Suffocation of Truth and Its Political Implications*, UTHR publications, www.uthr.org/Rajan/truth.htm. Last accessed 1 May 2012.

___ (2001). *Sri Lanka – The Arrogance of Power: Myths Decadence and Murder*, Colombo, Sri Lanka: University Teachers for Human Rights (Jaffna).

Hoole, R., Somasundaram, D. K., Sritharan, K., and Thiranagama, R. (1988). *The Broken Palmyra: The Tamil Crisis in Sri Lanka – An Inside Account*, Claremont, CA: Sri Lanka Studies Institute.

Hughes, D. (forthcoming). *Violence, Torture and Memory in Sri Lanka: Life after Terror*, Abingdon and New York: Routledge.

Human Rights Watch Report (1992). *Sri Lanka. Stop Killings of Civilians*, May 1992, www.hrw.org/legacy/reports/1995/Srilanka.htm. Last accessed 15 November 2009.

—— (2004). *Living in Fear: Child Soldiers and the Tamil Tigers in Sri Lanka*, November 2004, www.hrw.org/en/reports/2004/11/10/living-fear. Last accessed September 2009.

—— (2005). *Sri Lanka – Child Tsunami Victims Recruited by Tamil Tigers: LTTE May Seek Children to Replace Lost Forces*, 13 January 2005, www.hrw.org/en/news/2005/01/13/sri-lanka-child-tsunami-victims-recruited-tamil-tigers. Last accessed 15 November 2009.

—— (2007a). *Complicit in Crime: State Collusion in Abductions and Child Recruitment by the Karuna Group*, January 2007, www.hrw.org/en/reports/2007/01/23/complicit-crime. Last accessed 13 November 2009.

—— (2007b). *Sri Lanka – Return to War: Human Rights under Siege*, August 2007, www.hrw.org/reports/2007/srilanka0807/1.htm. Last accessed 15 November 2009.

—— (2007c). *Sri Lanka: Karuna Group and LTTE Continue Abducting and Recruiting Children*, 29 March 2007, hrw.org/reports/2007/srilanka0107/. Last accessed 5 October 2009.

—— (2007d). *Sri Lanka: Civilians Who Fled Fighting Are Forced to Return*, 16 March 2007, www.hrw.org/reports/2007/srilanka0807/1.htm. Last accessed 8 October 2009.

—— (2008a). *Recurring Nightmare: State Responsibility for 'Disappearances' and Abductions in Sri Lanka*, 5 March 2008, www.hrw.org/en/node/62398/section/6#_ftn114. Last accessed 18 May October 2012.

—— (2008b). *Sri Lanka: Human Rights Situation Deteriorating in the East: Armed Faction is Killing, Kidnapping Civilians*, Human Rights Watch press release, 24 November 2008, www.hrw.org/en/news/2008/11/24/sri-lanka-human-rights-situation-deteriorating-east. Last accessed 5 October 2009.

—— (2009a). *Don't Abuse the Displaced*, 9 March 2009, www.hrw.org/en/news/2009/03/09/sri-lanka-don-t-abuse-displaced. Last accessed 9 December 2009.

—— (2009b). *Sri Lanka: Adopt International Inquiry for Aid Worker Killings, Third Anniversary of ACF Murders Marked by Government Inaction, Intimidation*, 3 August 2009, www.hrw.org/news/2009/08/03/sri-lanka-adopt-international-inquiry-aid-worker-killings. Last accessed 11 January 2013.

Hume, M. (2007). 'Unpicking the Threads: Emotion as Central to the Theory and Practice of Researching Violence', *Women's Studies International Forum*, 30(2): 147–57.

Inter-Agency Standing Committee Country Team (IASC) (2006a). 'Situation Report #35 on 25–27 September 2006', Colombo, Sri Lanka, www.reliefweb.int/rw/RWFiles2006.nsf/ … iasc-lka … /iasc-lka-27sep.pdf. Last accessed 9 September 2009.

—— (2006b). 'Sri Lanka: Escalation of Conflict Leaves Tens of Thousands of IDPs without Protection and Assistance: A Profile of the Internal Displacement Situation', 16 November 2006, www.internal-displacement.org/idmc/website/assets.nsf/7cf378e8013c9a4880257090004b29cd/8c66e519775d0508c12572270041ee05/$FILE/SriLanka_overview_nov2006.pdf. Last accessed 9 September 2009.

Internal Displacement Monitoring Centre (IDMC) (2006). 'Sri Lanka: Escalation of Conflict Leaves Tens of Thousands of IDPs without Protection and Assistance: A Profile of the Internal Displacement Situation', 16 November 2006.

International Crisis Group (ICG) (2006). 'The Failure of the Peace Process', Asia Report No. 124, 28 November 2006, www.crisisgroup.org/en/regions/asia/south-asia/sri-lanka/124-sri-lanka-the-failure-of-the-peace-process.aspx. Last accessed 14 January 2011.

—— (2008). 'Sri Lanka's Eastern Province: Land, Development, Conflict', Asia Report No. 159, 15 October 2008, www.crisisgroup.org/en/regions/asia/south-asia/sri-lanka/159-sri-lankas-eastern-province-land-development-conflict.aspx. Last accessed 16 May 2012.

—— (2011a). 'Reconciliation in Sri Lanka: Harder then Ever', Asia Report No. 209, 18 July 2011, www.crisisgroup.org/en/regions/asia/south-asia/sri-lanka/209-reconciliation-in-sri-lanka-harder-than-ever.aspx. Last accessed 11 May 2012.

—— (2011b). 'Sri Lanka: Women's Insecurity in the North and East', Asia Report No. 217, 20 December 2011, www.crisisgroup.org/en/regions/asia/south-asia/sri-lanka/217-sri-lanka-womens-insecurity-in-the-north-and-east.aspx. Last accessed 1 May 2012.

—— (2012a). 'Sri Lanka's North I: The Denial of Minority Rights', Asia Report No. 219, 16 March 2012, www.crisisgroup.org/en/regions/asia/south-asia/sri-lanka/219-sri-lankas-north-i-the-denial-of-minority-rights.aspx. Last accessed 18 May 2012.

—— (2012b). 'Sri Lanka's North II: Rebuilding under the Military', Asia Report No. 220, 16 March 2012, www.crisisgroup.org/en/regions/asia/south-asia/sri-lanka/220-sri-lankas-north-ii-rebuilding-under-the-military.aspx. Last accessed 22 July 2012.

IRIN. 'Sri Lanka: IDPs in Transit Centre Face Uncertain Future', 18 April 2007, www.irinnews.org/Report.aspx–ReportId=71682. Last accessed 5 September 2009.

Jackson, M. (1996). 'Introduction: Phenomenology, Radical Empiricism, and Anthropological Critique', in M. Jackson (ed.), *Things as They Are: New Directions in Phenomenological Anthropology*, Bloomington, IN: Indiana University Press, pp. 1–50.

—— (2002). *The Politics of Storytelling: Violence, Transgression and Intersubjectivity*, Copenhagen: Museum Tusculanum Press.

Jeganathan, P. (1998). '"Violence" as an Analytical Problem: Sri Lankanist Anthropology after July 1983', *Nethra (Journal of the International Centre for Ethnic Studies)*, 2(4): 7–47.

—— (2004). 'Checkpoint: Anthropology, Identity, and the State', in V. Das and D. Poole (eds.), *Anthropology in the Margins of the State*, Sante Fe, New Mexica: School of American Research Press, pp. 67–80.

Kalyvas, S. N. (2006). *The Logic of Violence in Civil War*, Cambridge: Cambridge University Press.

Kapadia, K. (1995). *Siva and Her Sisters: Gender, Caste, and Class in Rural South India*, Boulder, CO, San Francisco, CA, and Oxford: Westview Press.

Kapferer, B. (1998 [1988]). *Legends of People, Myths of State: Violence, Intolerance and Political Culture in Sri Lanka and Australia*, Second edn, Belair: Australia: Crawford Press.

Kaplan, R. (1996). *The Ends of the Earth: A Journey to the Frontiers of Anarchy*, New York: Vintage Books.

Kearney, R. N. (1975). 'Educational Expansion and Political Volatility in Sri Lanka: The 1971 Insurrection', *Asian Survey*, 15: 727–44.

—— (1985). 'Ethnic Conflict and the Tamil Separatist Movement in Sri Lanka', *Asian Survey*, 25(9): 898–917.

—— (1987) 'Territorial Elements of Tamil Separatism in Sri Lanka', *Pacific Affairs*, 60(4): 561–77.

Kearney, R. N. and Miller, B. D. (1985). 'The Spiral of Suicide and Social Change in Sri Lanka', *Journal of Asian Studies*, 45(1): 81–101.

—— (1987). *Internal Migration in Sri Lanka and Its Social Consequences*, Boulder, CO: Westview Press.

Keenan, A. (2003). *Democracy in Question: Democratic Openness in a Time of Political Closure*, California: Stanford University Press.

Kelly, L. (1988). *Surviving Sexual Violence*, Cambridge: Polity Press.

Kelly, T. (2008). 'The Attractions of Accountancy: Living an Ordinary Life During the Second Palestinian Intifada', *Ethnography*, 9(3): 351–76.

Klein, N. (2007). *The Shock Doctrine: The Rise of Disaster Capitalism*, London: Penguin Books.

Korf, B. (2007). 'Antimonies of Generosity: Moral Geographies and Post-Tsunami Aid in Southeast Asia', *Geoforum*, 38(2): 366–78.

Korf, B. and Silva, K. T. (2003). 'Poverty, Ethnicity and Conflict in Sri Lanka', Paper presented at University of Bonn, Department of Sociology, Centre for Development Research and University of Peradenyia.

Korf, B., Hasbullah, S., Hollenbach, P., and Klem, B. (2009). 'The Gift of Disaster: The Commodification of Good Intentions in Post-Tsunami Sri Lanka', *Disasters*, 34(1): 560–77.

Korf, B., Engeler, M., and Hagmann, T. (2010). 'The Geography of Warscape', *Third World Quarterly*, 31(3): 385–99.

Kurukulasuriya, U. (2012). 'Rajapaksa – Tiger Deal on WikiLeaks and Political Analysis', *Colombo Telegraph*, www.colombotelegraph.com/index.php/rajapaksa-tiger-deal-on-wikileaks-and-political-analysis. Last accessed 14 May 2012.

Lankanewspaper (2006). 'NGO Porn Scandal Shocks Batti, Ampara', 23 April 2006, www.lankanewspapers.com/news/2006/4/6567.html. Last accessed September 2009.

(2007). 'Sri Lankan Rupee Spiraling Down to the Bottom', 20 November 2007, www.lankanewspapers.com/news/2007/11/21660_space. Last accessed 21 July 2012.

Bibliography

Lawrence, P. (1997). 'Work of Oracles, Silence of Terror: Notes on the Injury of War in Eastern Sri Lanka', unpublished Ph.D. thesis submitted to the Faculty of the Graduate School of the University of Colorado.
—— (1999). 'The Changing Amman: Notes on the Injury of War in Eastern Sri Lanka', in S. Gamage and I. B. Watson (eds.), *Conflict and Community in Contemporary Sri Lanka*, London: Sage Publications, pp. 218–28.
—— (2000). 'Violence, Suffering, Amman: The Work of Oracles in Sri Lanka's Eastern War Zone', in V. Das, A. Kleinman, R. Mamphela, and P. Reynolds (eds.), *Violence and Subjectivity*, Berkeley, CA: University of California Press, pp. 171–204.
—— (2003). *The Ocean Stories: Children, Imagination, Creativity, and Reconciliation in Eastern Sri Lanka*, Colombo, Sri Lanka: International Centre for Ethnic Studies.
Leach, E. R. (1961). *Pul Eliya, A Village in Ceylon: A Study of Land Tenure and Kinship*, Cambridge: Cambridge University Press.
Le Billon, P. (2000). 'The Political Economy of War: What Relief Agencies Need to Know', HPN-Network Paper 33, Overseas Development Institute, London.
Le Billon, P. and Waizenegger, A. (2007). 'Peace in the Wake of Disaster? Secessionist Conflicts and the 2004 Indian Ocean Tsunami', *Transactions of the Institute of British Geographers*, 32(3): 411–27.
Lee, R. M. (1995). *Dangerous Fieldwork*, Thousand Oakes, CA: Sage.
Lefèbvre, H. (1991). *The Production of Space*, D. Nicholson-Smith (trans), Oxford: Blackwell.
Levi, P. (1988). *The Drowned and the Saved*, New York: Summit Books.
Lykes, M. B. and Mersky, M. (2006). 'Reparations and Mental Health: Psychosocial Interventions towards Healing, Human Agency and Rethreading Social Realities', in P. De Greiff (ed.), *The Handbook of Reparations*, Oxford: Oxford University Press, pp. 589–622.
Mahmood, C. K. (1996). *Fighting for Faith and Nation: Dialogues with Sikh Militants*, Philadelphia: University of Pennsylvania Press.
—— (2002). 'Anthropological Compulsions in a World in Crisis', *Anthropology Today*, 18(3): 1–2.
Manchanda, R. (2001). 'Where are the Women in South Asian Conflicts?', in R. Manchanda (ed.), *Women, War, and Peace in South Asia: Beyond Victimhood to Agency*, Delhi/Thousand Oaks, CA: Sage Publications, pp. 9–41.
Manikkalingham, R. (2002). 'Political Power over Ethnic Identity', *Frontline*, 19(13), www.frontlineonnet.com/fl1913/19130580.htm. Last accessed 12 July 2012.
Marcus, G. E. and Cushman, D. (1982). 'Ethnographies as Texts', *Annual Review of Anthropology*, 11: 25–69.
Marcus, G. E. and Fischer, M. M. J. (1986). *Anthropology as Cultural Critique: An Experimental Moment in the Human Sciences*, Chicago: University of Chicago Press.
Martin, E. (2007). 'Violence, Language, and the Everyday Life', *American Ethnologist*, 34(4): 741–5.
Massey, D. (1994). *Space, Place, and Gender*, Minneapolis: University of Minnesota Press.
—— (1995). *Spatial Divisions of Labor: Social Structures and the Geography of Production Capitals*, Second edn, New York: Routledge.
Maunaguru, S. (1995). 'Gendering Tamil Nationalism: The Construction of "Women" in Projects of Protest and Control', in P. Jeganathan and Q. Ismail (eds.), *Unmaking the Nation: The Politics of Identity and History in Modern Sri Lanka*, Colombo, Sri Lanka: Social Scientists Association, pp. 158–76.
Mbembe, A. (1995). 'Figures of the Subject in Times of Crisis', *Public Culture*, 7(2): 323–52.

McDowell, C. (1996). *A Tamil Asylum Diaspora Sri Lankan Migration, Settlement, and Politics in Switzerland*, New York: Berghahn.

McEntire, D. A. (2001). 'Triggering Agents, Vulnerabilities and Disaster Reduction: Towards a Holistic Paradigm', *Disaster Prevention and Management*, 10(3): 189–96.

McGilvray, D. B. (1973). 'Caste and Matriclan Structure in Sri Lanka: A Preliminary Report on Fieldwork in Akkaraipattu', *Modern Ceylon Studies*, 4: 5–20.

—— (1982a). 'Dutch Burghers and Portuguese Mechanics: Eurasian Ethnicity in Sri Lanka', *Comparative Studies in Society and History*, 24(2): 235–63.

—— (1982b). 'Mukkuvar Vannimai: Tamil Caste and Matriclan Ideology in Batticaloa, Sri Lanka', in D. McGilvray (ed.), *Caste Ideology and Interaction*, Cambridge: Cambridge University Press, pp. 34–98.

—— (1982c). 'Introduction', in D. McGilvray (ed.), *Caste Ideology and Interaction*, Cambridge: Cambridge University Press, pp. 1–8.

—— (1997). 'Tamils and Muslims in the Shadow of War: Schism or Continuity?', *South Asia*, 20: 239–53.

—— (1998a). *Symbolic Heat: Gender, Health and Worship among the Tamils of South India and Sri Lanka*, Ahmedabad: Mapin Publishing.

—— (1998b). 'Arabs, Moors and Muslims: Sri Lankan Muslim Ethnicity in Regional Perspective', *Contributions to Indian Sociology*, 32: 433–83.

—— (2008). *Crucible of Conflict: Tamil and Muslim Society on the East Coast of Sri Lanka*, Durham and London: Duke University Press.

McGilvray, D. and Raheem, M. (2007). 'Muslim Perspectives on the Sri Lankan Conflict', *Policy Studies*, 41, Washington, DC: East–West Center.

McRobbie, A. (2006). 'Vulnerability, Violence and (Cosmopolitan) Ethics: Butler's Precarious Life', *The British Journal of Sociology*, 57(1): 70–85.

Menon, N. (2004) *Recovering Subversion: Feminist Politics Beyond the Law*, Delhi: Permanent Black/Ubana and Chicago: University of Illinois Press.

Miller, B. H. (2011). 'We Remember: After 21 Years', *Groundviews*, http://groundviews.org/2011/11/02/we-remember-after-21-years%E2%80%A6. Last accessed 15 July 2012.

Mines, M. (1994). *Public Faces, Private Voices: Community and Individuality in South India*, Berkeley, CA and London: University of California Press.

Montani, A. (1999). 'On the Move: A Cultural Study of Contested Space on the East Coast of Sri Lanka', unpublished Ph.D. dissertation, University of Edinburgh.

Moore, M. (1990). 'Economic Liberalisation versus Political Pluralism in Sri Lanka?', *Modern Asian Studies*, 24(2): 341–83.

Nagar, R. (2000). 'Mujhe Jawab Do! (Answer Me!): Women's Grass-Roots Activism and Social Spaces in Chitrakoot (India)', *Gender, Place and Culture*, 7(4): 341–62.

Narayan, K. (1992). *Storytellers, Saints, and Scoundrels: Folk Narrative in Hindu Religious Teaching*, Philadelphia: University of Pennsylvania Press.

Nissan, E. (1996). *Sri Lanka: A Bitter Harvest*, London: Minority Rights Group.

—— (1998). 'Historical Content', in *Demanding Sacrifice: War and Negotiation in Sri Lanka*, Accord, 4, London: Conciliation Resources.

Norad (2011) 'Pawns of Peace: Evaluation of Norwegian Peace Efforts in Sri Lanka, 1997–2009', *Report 5/2011 – Evaluation*, Norway: Evaluation Department, Norad.

Nordstrom, C. (1992). 'The Dirty War: Civilian Experience of Conflict in Mozambique and Sri Lanka', in K. Rupesinghe (ed.), *Internal Wars and Governance*, New York: Macmillan, pp. 27–43.

—— (1994). *Warzones: Cultures of Violence, Militarization and Peace*, Canberra, Australia: Peace Research Centre.

—— (1997). *A Different Kind of War Story*, Philadelphia: University of Pennsylvania Press.
—— (1998). 'Terror Warfare and the Medicine of Peace', *Medical Anthropology Quarterly*, 12(1): 103–21.
—— (2004). *Shadows of Violence (Shadows of War: Violence, Power, and International Profiteering in the Twenty-First Century)*, Berkeley, CA: University of California Press.
Nordstrom, C. and Martin, J. (eds.) (1992). *The Paths to Domination, Resistance, and Terror*, Berkeley, CA: University of California Press.
Nordstrom, C. and Robben, A. C. G. M. (eds.) (1996). *Fieldwork under Fire: Contemporary Studies of Violence and Survival*, Berkeley, CA: University of California Press.
Obeyesekere, G. N. (1964). 'The Natural History of a Land Tenure System', Ph.D. dissertation, University of Washington, Seattle, University Microfilms, Ann Arbour, Michigan.
—— (1974). 'Some Comments on the Social Background of April 1971 Insurgency in Sri Lanka', *Journal of Asian Studies*, 33(3): 367–84.
—— (1978). 'The Fire-Walkers of Kataragama: The Rise of Bhakti Religiosity in Buddhist Sri Lanka', *Journal of Asian Studies*, 37: 457–76.
Orjuela, C. (2003). 'Building Peace in Sri Lanka: A Role for Civil Society?', *Journal of Peace Research*, 40(2): 195–212.
—— (2004). 'Civil Society in Civil War: Peace Work and Identity Politics in Sri Lanka', Ph.D. dissertation, Department of Peace and Development Research (Padrigu), Goteborg University, Sweden.
—— (2005). 'Dilemmas of Civil Society Aid: Donors, NGOs and the Quest for Peace in Sri Lanka', *Peace and Democracy in South Asia*, 1(1): 1–12.
Ortner, S. B. (1984). 'Theory in Anthropology since the Sixties', *Comparative Studies in Society and History*, 26: 126–66.
Peace Brigade International (PBI) (1998). 'International Human rights NGO Forced to Leave by Sri Lankan Government', www.peacebrigades.org/archive/lanka/slp98-5a.html). Last accessed 22 May 2012.
Peebles, P. (1990). 'Colonization and Ethnic Conflict in the Dry Zone of Sri Lanka', *The Journal of Asian Studies*, 49(1): 30–55.
Peluso, N. and Watts, M. (2001). 'Violent Environments', in N. Peluso and M. Watts (eds.), *Violent Environments*, Ithaca, New York: Cornell University Press, pp. 3–38.
Perera, M. (1991). 'Female Headed Households: A Special Poverty Group', in *Women, Poverty and Family Survival*, Colombo, Sri Lanka: CENWOR, pp. 27–64.
Perera, S. (1995). 'Societies of Terror: The Absence of a Body and the Problems of Mourning and Coping', in S. Perera, *Living with Torturers and Other Essays of Intervention: Sri Lankan Society, Culture and Politics in Perspective*, Colombo, Sri Lanka: International Centre for Ethnic Studies, pp. 1–8.
—— (1998). 'Beyond the Margins of a Failed Insurrection: The Experiences of Women in Post-Terror Sri Lanka', *Edinburgh Papers In South Asian Studies*, 11: 1–21.
Peteet, J. (2011). 'Icons and Militants: Mothering in the Danger Zone', *Signs*, 23(1): 103–29.
Pickering, S. (2001). 'Undermining the Sanitized Account Violence and Emotionality in the Field in Northern Ireland', *British Journal of Criminology*, 41: 485–501.
Pirani, C. and Kadirgamar, A. (2006). 'Internationalization of Sri Lanka's Peace Process and Governance: A Review of Strategic Conflict Assessments', *Economic and Political Weekly*, 6: 1789–95.
Punyasena, W. (2003). 'The Façade of Accountability: Disappearances in Sri Lanka', *Third World Law Review*, 23(1): 115–58.

Rajasingham-Senanayake, D. (1998). 'After Victimhood: Cultural Transformation and Women's Empowerment in War and Displacement', Paper presented at the Conference on Women in Conflict Zones, International Centre for Ethnic Studies (ICES), Colombo, Sri Lanka.

—— (1999). 'Post Victimisation: Cultural Transformation and Women's Empowerment in War and Displacement', in S. Thiruchandran (ed.), *Women, Nation and Narration: Collective Images and Multiple Identities*, New Delhi: Vikas Publishers, pp. 136–51.

—— (2004a). 'Between Victim and Agent: Women's Agency in Displacement', in P. Essed, G. Frerks, and J. Schrijvers (eds.), *Refugees and the Transformation of Societies: Agency, Ethics and Politics*, Oxford: Berghan Publishers, pp. 151–64.

—— (2004b). 'Between Reality and Representation Women's Agency in War and Post-Conflict Sri Lanka', *Cultural Dynamics*, 16 (2–3): 141–68.

Reynolds, H. (1980). 'The Auspicious Married Woman', in S. B Wadley (ed.), *The Powers of Tamil Women*, New York: Maxwell School of Citizenship and Public Affairs, Syracuse University, pp. 35–60.

Ries, N. (2002). 'Anthropology and the Everyday: From Comfort to Terror', *New Literary History*, 33: 725–42.

Ring, L. A. (2006). *Zenana: Everyday Peace in a Karachi Apartment Building*, Bloomington: Indiana University Press.

Robben, A. C. G. M. and Suarez-Orozco, M. M. (eds.) (2000). *Cultures under Siege: Collective Violence and Trauma*, Cambridge: Cambridge University Press.

Ross, F. C. (2003). *Bearing Witness: Women and the South African TRC*, London and New York: Pluto Press.

Rupasinghe, K. (ed.) (1998). *Negotiating Peace in Sri Lanka: Efforts, Failures and Lessons Learnt*, Vol. I, Second edn., Colombo, Sri Lanka: Foundation for Co-Existence (FCE).

—— (ed.) (2006). *Negotiating Peace in Sri Lanka: Efforts, Failures and Lessons Learnt*, Vol. II, Colombo, Sri Lanka: Foundation for Co-Existence (FCE).

Ruwanpura, K. N. (2006). *Matrilineal Communities, Patriarchal Realities: A Feminist Nirvana Uncovered*, New Delhi: Zubaan.

—— (2009). 'Putting Houses in Place: Re-Building Communities in Post-Tsunami Sri Lanka', *Disasters: The Journal of Disaster Studies, Policy and Management*, 33(3): 436–56.

Ruwanpura, K. N. and Humphries, J. (2004). 'Mundane Heroines: Conflict, Ethnicity, Gender, and Female Headship in Eastern Sri Lanka', *Feminist Economics*, 10(2): 173–205.

Sachs, H. (1992). *Lectures on Conversation*, Oxford: Blackwell.

Samarasinghe, S. W. R. de A. (1990). *The Vanishing Aborigines: Sri Lanka's Veddas in Transition*, New Dehli, India: International Centre for Ethnic Studies in Association with NORAD and Vikas Publishing House.

Samarasinghe, G. and Galapatti, A. (1998). 'Living in Conflict Zones, Past and Present: Women and Psychosocial Suffering', Paper presented at the Conference on Women in Conflict Zones, Colombo, Sri Lanka, 11–13 December.

Samaraweera, V. (1997). 'An "Act of Truth" in a Sinhala Court of Law: On Truth, Lies, and Judicial Proof among the Sinhala Buddhists', *Cardozo Journal of International and Comparative Law*, 5: 133–63.

Samuel, K. (2003). 'Activism, Motherhood, and the State in Sri Lanka's Ethnic Conflict', in W. Giles, M. de Alwis, E. Klein, and N. Silva (eds.), *Feminists Under Fire: Exchanges Across War Zones*, Toronto: Between the Lines Press, pp. 167–80.

—— (2006). *A Hidden History: Women's Activism for Peace in Sri Lanka 1982–2002*,

Colombo, Sri Lanka: Social Scientists Association.
Sandywell, B. (2004). 'The Myth of Everyday Life: Toward a Heterology of the Ordinary', in M. Gardiner and G. E. Seigworth (eds.), *Rethinking Everyday Life: And Then Nothing Turns Itself Inside Out*, London: Routledge, pp. 160–80.
Scarry, E. (1985). *The Body in Pain*, Oxford: Oxford University Press.
Scheper-Hughes, N. (1993 [1992]). *Death without Weeping: The Violence of Everyday Life in Brazil*, Berkeley, CA: University of California Press.
—— (1995). 'The Primacy of the Ethical: Propositions for a Militant Anthropology', *Current Anthropology*, 36(3): 409–40.
—— (1996). 'On the Call for a Militant Anthropology – Reply (White Writing)', *Current Anthropology*, 37(2): 344–6.
—— (2008). 'A Talent for Life: Reflection on Human Vulnerability and Resilience', *Ethnos*, 73(1): 25–56.
Scheper-Hughes, N. and Bourgois, P. (eds.) (2004). *Violence in War and Peace: An Anthology*, Oxford: Blackwell Publishing.
Scheper-Hughes, N. and Sargent, C. (eds.) (1998). *Small Wars: The Cultural Politics of Childhood*, Berkeley, CA: University of California Press.
Schilling, D. (2003). 'Everyday Life and the Challenge in Post War France: Braudel, Lefebvre, Certeau', *Diacritics*, 33(1): 23–40.
Schonthal, B. (2011). 'Translating Remembering', in C. J. Holt, R. Kirk, and S. Orin (eds.), *The Sri Lanka Reader: History, Culture, Politics*, Durham, NC: Duke University Press, pp. 542–56.
Schrijvers, J. (1998). 'We Are Like Coconut and Flour in the Pittu: Tamil-Muslim Violence, Gender and Ethnic Relations in Eastern Sri Lanka', *Nêthrà*, 2(3): 10–39.
—— (1999). Fighters, Victims and Survivors: Constructions of Ethnicity, Gender and Refugeeness among Tamils in Sri Lanka', *Journal of Refugee Studies*, 12 (3): 307–33.
Schutz, A. (1972). *The Phenomenology of the Social World*, London: Heinemann.
Segal, L. (1999). *Why Feminism? Gender, Psychology, Politics*, Cambridge: Polity Press.
Seligmann, C. G. and Seligmann, B. Z. (2003) [1911]. *The Veddas*, New Delhi: Navrang.
Senanayake, D. S. (1985 [1935]). *Agriculture and Patriotism*, Colombo, Sri Lanka: Ministry of Lands and Land Development.
Skultans, V. (1998). *The Testimony of Lives: Narrative and Memory in Post-Soviet Latvia*, London and New York: Routledge.
Sluka, J. A. (1995). 'Peace Process Images, Symbols and Murals in Northern Ireland', *Critique of Anthropology*, 16: 381–7.
—— (2000). *Death Squad: The Anthropology of State Terror*, Philadelphia: University of Pennsylvania Press.
Smirl, L. (2008). 'Building the Other, Constructing Ourselves: Spatial Dimensions of International Humanitarian Response', *International Political Sociology*, 2(3): 236–53.
Somasundaram, D. (1998). *Scarred Minds: The Psychological Impact of War on Sri Lankan Tamils*, London: Sage Publications.
—— (2007). 'Collective Trauma in Northern Sri Lanka: A Qualitative Psychosocial-Ecological Study', *International Journal of Mental Health Systems*, 1(1): 5.
Spencer, J. (1989) 'Anthropology as a Kind of Writing', Man New Series, 24(1): 145–64.
—— (1990a). *A Sinhala Village in a Time of Trouble: Politics and Change in Rural Sri Lanka*, Delhi: Oxford University Press.
—— (1990b). 'Introduction: The Power of the Past', in J. Spencer (ed.), *Sri Lanka: History and the Roots of Conflict*, London: Routledge, pp. 1–16.
—— (1990c). 'Writing Within: Anthropology, Nationalism, and Culture in Sri Lanka',

Current Anthropology, 31(3): 283–94.
—— (2007). *Anthropology, Politics and the State: Democracy and Violence in South Asia*, Cambridge: Cambridge University Press.
—— (2011). 'Reflections on an Illiberal Peace', in J. Goodhand, B. Korf, and J. Spencer (eds.), *Conflict and Peacebuilding in Sri Lanka: Caught in the Peace Trap?*, London: Routledge, pp. 201–12.
Sri Lanka Monitoring Mission (SLMM). Statement 3 January 2008, www.slmm-history.info/SLMM_Archive/Operational_statements/2008/16%2F01%2F08+SLMM+Press+Statement.9UFRrM3W.ips. Last accessed 9 January 2013.
Stirrat, J. (2006). 'Competitive Humanitarianism Relief and the Tsunami in Sri Lanka', *Anthropology Today*, 22(5): 11–16.
Suarez-Orozco, M. M. (1990). 'Speaking of the Unspeakable: Toward a Psychosocial Understanding towards Terror', *Ethos*, 18(3): 353–83.
Sunday Leader (2007). 'President's Tiger deal Exposed', 8 July 2007, *Sunday Leader*, www.thesundayleader.lk/20071118/archives.htm. Last accessed 9 August 2008.
Swamy, N. (1994). *Tigers of Lanka: From Boys to Guerillas*, Colombo, Sri Lanka: Vijitha Yapa.
Tambiah, S. J. (1973). 'Dowry and Bridewealth and the Property Rights of Women in South Asia', in J. Goody and S. J. Tambiah (eds.), *Bridewealth and Dowry*, Cambridge: Cambridge University Press, pp. 59–169.
—— (1986). *Sri Lanka: Ethnic Fratricide and the Dismantling of Democracy*, Chicago: University of Chicago Press.
—— (1992). *Buddhism Betrayed? Religion, Politics and Violence in Sri Lanka*, Chicago: University of Chicago Press.
—— (1997). *Levelling Crowds: Ethnonationalist Conflicts and Collective Violence in South Asia*, Chicago: University of Chicago Press.
Tambiah, Y. (2005). 'Turncoat Bodies: Sexuality and Sex Work under Militarization in Sri Lanka', *Gender and Society*, 19(2): 243–61.
Taraki (1990 [1991]). *The Eluding Peace (An Insider's Political Analysis of the Ethnic Conflict in Sri Lanka)*, Paris: ASSEAY.
Taussig, M. (1987). *Shamanism, Colonialism, and the Wild Man: A Study in Terror and Healing*, Chicago: University of Chicago Press.
—— (1992). *The Nervous System*, New York: Routledge.
Telford, J., Cosgrave, J., and Houghton, R. (2006). *Joint Evaluation of the International Response to the Indian Ocean Tsunami: Synthesis Report*, London: Tsunami Evaluation Coalition.
Terry, F. (2002). *Condemned to Repeat?: The Paradox of Humanitarian Action*, Ithaca, NY: Cornell University Press.
Thangarajah, Y. (1995). 'Narratives of Victimhood as Ethnic Identity among the Veddhas', in P. Jeganathan and Q. Ismail (eds.), *Unmaking the Nation: The Politics of Identity and History in Modern Sri Lanka*, Colombo, Sri Lanka: Social Scientists Association, pp. 158–76.
The Times (2009). 'Slaughter in Sri Lanka', *The Times Online*, 29 May 2009, www.timesonline.co.uk/tol/comment/leading_article/article6382706.ece. Last accessed 13 November 2009.
Thiranagama, R. (1988). 'No More Tears Sister: The Experiences of Women', in R. Hoole, D. K. Somasundaram, K. Sritharan, and R. Thiranagama (eds.), *The Broken Palmyra: The Tamil Crisis in Sri Lanka–An Inside Account*, Claremont, California: Sri Lanka Studies Institute, pp. 305–30.

Thiranagama. S. (2005). 'Stories of Home: Generation, Memory, and Displacement among Jaffna Tamils and Jaffna Muslims', unpublished Ph.D., The University of Edinburgh.

—— (2009). 'A New Morning? Reoccupying Home in the Aftermath of Violence in Sri Lanka', in S. Jansen and S. Lofving (eds.), *Struggles for Home: Violence, Hope and the Movement of People*, London: Berghahn Books, pp. 129–48.

—— (2011). *In My Mother's House: Civil War in Sri Lanka*, Philadelphia: University of Pennsylvania Press.

Thiruchandran, S. (1999). *Women, Narration, and Nation: Collective Images and Multiple Identities*, New Delhi: Vikas Publications.

Trautmann, T. R. (1981). *Dravidian Kinship*, Cambridge: Cambridge University Press.

—— (1987). *Lewis Henry Morgan and the Invention of Kinship*, Berkeley, CA: University of California Press.

Trawick, M. (1997). 'Reasons for Violence: A Preliminary Ethnographic Account of the LTTE', *South Asia*, 20: 153–80.

—— (2002). 'Interviews with High School Students in Eastern Sri Lanka', in D. P. Mines and S. Lamb (eds.), *Everyday Life in South Asia*, Bloomington: Indiana University Press, pp. 366–80.

—— (2007). *Enemy Lines: Warfare, Childhood, and Play in Batticaloa*, Berkeley, CA: University of California Press.

United Nations (2012). 'Executive Summary of the Report of the Panel of Experts', www.un.org/en/rights/srilanka.shtml. Last accessed 15 May 2012.

United Nations High Commissioner for Refugees (UNHCR) (2005). 'Sri Lanka: IDP Movements by District between January 2002–May 2005, internal displacement May 2005, UNHCR', www.internal-displacement.org. Last accessed 6 November 2009.

University Teachers for Human Rights (Jaffna) (UTHR) (1989). 'Bombing in Jaffna', Report No. 1, January 1989, www.uthr.org/SpecialReports/spreport1.htm. Last accessed 12 September 2009.

—— (1990a). 'The War and Its Consequences in the Ampara District, Thirunelvely, Jaffna, Sri Lanka', Report No. 3, www.uthr.org/Reports/Report2/Report2.htm. Last accessed 9 October 2009.

—— (1990b). 'The War of June 1990', Report No. 4, www.uthr.org/Reports/Report4/Report4.htm. Last accessed 20 May 2012.

—— (1991). 'The Debasement of Law and Humanity and the Drift towards Total War (August 1991)', Report No. 8, www.uthr.org/Reports/Report8/Report8.htm. Last accessed 16 September 2009.

—— (1992a). 'Human Rights and the Issues of War and Peace', Briefing No. 1, August 1992, www.uthr.org/Briefings/Briefing1.htm. Last accessed 18 May 2012.

—— (1993a). 'Land, Human Rights and the Eastern Predicament', Report No. 11. 15 April 1993, www.uthr.org/Reports/Report11/Report11.htm. Last accessed 22 May 2012.

—— (1993b). 'From Manal Aaru to Weli Oya and the Spirit of July 1983', Special Report No. 5, 15 September 1993, www.uthr.org/SpecialReports/spreport5.htm. Last accessed 1 May 2012.

—— (1995). 'The Exodus', Special Report No. 6, 6 December 1995, www.uthr.org/SpecialReports/spreport6.htm. Last accessed 12 September 2009.

—— (2002). 'Towards a Totalitarian Peace: The Human Rights Dilemma', Special Report No. 13, 10 May 2002, www.uthr.org/SpecialReports/spreport13.htm. Last accessed 12 September 2009.

—— (2005). 'Impunity in the Name of Peace: Norway's Appeasement Strategy Claims Another Victim', UTHR Statement, 17 August 2005, www.uthr.org/Statements/

Impunity%20in%20the%20name%20of%20Peace.htm. Last accessed 15 August 2009.

—— (2006). 'The Choice between Anarchy and International Law with Monitoring', Special Report No. 23, 7 November 2006, www.uthr.org/SpecialReports/spreport23.htm. Last accessed 18 May 2012.

—— (2007). 'Can the East be Won through Human Culling?', Special Report No. 26, 3 August 2007, www.uthr.org/SpecialReports/spreport26.htm#_Toc173926115. Last accessed 23 May 2012.

—— (2009a). 'A Marred Victory and a Defeat Pregnant with Foreboding', Special Report No. 32, 10 June 2009, www.uthr.org/SpecialReports/spreport32.htm. Last accessed 1 May 2012.

—— (2009b). 'Third Anniversary of the ACF Massacre', Special Report No. 33, 4 August 2009, www.uthr.org/SpecialReports/spreport33.htm. Last accessed 15 September 2009.

—— (2009c). 'Let Them Speak: Truth about Sri Lanka's Victims of War', Special Report No. 34, 13 December 2009, www.uthr.org/SpecialReports/Special%20rep34/Uthr-sp.rp34.htm. Last accessed 1 May 2012.

Uyangoda, J. (2002). 'Spoiler Dynamics', *Peace Monitor*, 4(3): 17–18, www.cpalanka.org. Last accessed 13 November 2009, www.flonnet.com/fl2218/stories/20050909006100400.htm. Last accessed 19 April 2006.

—— (2005). 'Post-Tsunami Recovery in Sri Lanka', *Polity*, 2(1): 4–7.

Vigh, H. (2008). 'Crisis and Chronicity: Anthropological Perspectives on Continuous Conflict and Decline', *Ethnos*, 73(1): 5–24.

Vittachi, V. T. (1958). *Emergency '58 – The Story of the Ceylon Race Riots*, London: Andre Deutsch.

Walker, R. (2013). 'Taking a Back Seat: The Uses and Misuses of Space in a Context of War and Natural Disaster', *Humanitarianism and Responsibility: A Special Issue of The Journal of Human Rights*, 12(1): 69–86.

Walton, O. (with Sarravanmuttu, P.) (2010). 'In the Balance? Civil Society and the Peace Process 2002–2008', in J. Goodhand, J. Spencer, and B. Korf (eds.), *Conflict and Peacebuilding in Sri Lanka: Caught in the Peace Trap?*, London: Routledge, pp. 183–200.

Weerasinghe, R. (1987). *Female-Headed Households in Two Villages in Sri Lanka*, Colombo, Sri Lanka: Women's Education Centre.

Weiss, G. (2011). *The Cage: The Fight for Sri Lanka and the Last Days of the Tamil Tigers*, London: The Bodley Head Ltd.

Whitaker, M. P. (1990). 'A Compound of Many Histories: The Many Pasts of an East Coast Community', in J. Spencer (ed.), *Sri Lanka: History and the Roots of Conflict*, London: Routledge, pp. 145–63.

—— (1996). *Amicable Incoherence: Manipulating Histories and Modernities in a Batticaloa Tamil Hindu Temple*, Amsterdam: VU University Press.

—— (1999) 'Tigers and Temples: The Politics of Nationalist and Non-modern Violence in Sri Lanka', in S. Gamage and I. B. Watson (eds.), *Conflict and Community in Contemporary Sri Lanka: 'Pearl of the East' or the 'Island of Tears'?*, London: Sage Publications, pp. 183–95.

Williams, R. (1977). *Marxism and Literature*, London: Oxford University Press.

Wilson, A. J. (2000). *Sri Lankan Tamil Nationalism: Its Origins and Development in the Nineteenth and Twentieth Centuries*, Sydney: C. Hurst & Co.

Wittgenstein, L. (1953). *Philosophical Investigations*, G. E. M. Anscombe (trans.), Oxford: Basil Blackwell.

—— (1980). *Philosophical Remarks*, Chicago: University of Chicago Press.
Women and Media Collective (WMC) (2006). 'Sri Lanka: Statement – Defend Women's Right to Work', 5 October 2006, www.wluml.org/node/2953. Last accessed 12 September 2009.
Wood, E. (2007). 'Field Research During War: Ethical Dilemmas', in L. Joseph, M. Mahler, and J. Auyero (eds.), *New Perspectives in Political Ethnography*, New York: Springer, pp. 205–23.
—— (2009). 'Armed Groups and Sexual Violence: When Is Wartime Rape Rare?', *Politics Society*, 37: 131.
World Bank (2005a). 'Rebuilding Sri Lanka: Opportunity in Chaos', *Tsunami Aftermath Special Report*, Vol.1 1, Issue 7, Asian Development Bank.
—— (2005b). 'Sri Lanka Development Forum: The Economy, the Tsunami and Poverty Reduction', Poverty Reduction and Economic Management Sector Unit, South Asia Region, Colombo, Sri Lanka.
World Health Organization (WHO) (2005). 'Tsunami Situation Report No. 38', 22 February 2005, www.searo.who.int/LinkFiles/Situation_Reports_NEWWHO22 Feb2005.pdf. Last accessed 12 September 2009.
Yalman, N. (1967). 'The Raw: the Cooked: Nature: Culture: Observations on Le Cru et le Cuit', in E. Leach (ed.), *The Structural Study of Myth and Totemism*, London: Tavistock Publications, pp. 71–89.
—— (1971 [1967]). *Under the Bo Tree: Studies in Caste, Kinship, and Marriage in the Interior of Ceylon*, Berkeley, CA: University of California Press.
Young, A. (1995). *The Harmony of Illusions: Inventing Post-Traumatic Stress Disorder*, Princeton, NJ: Princeton University Press.

Index

abducted children *see* child abduction
active living
  as activism 50–2
  spaces in 29–31
  Valkai group 14–15, 30–1
    vision 55–6
  vulnerability 158–9
activism
  spaces for 45–50
  of women 17–19
aerial bombardment, of civilians 113, 114–15
agents, in everyday violence 88–9
aid organisations, post-tsunami 9–10, 138–9
Amman temples, oracle of 21
anti-Tamil violence 113–14
  riots 6, 105, 106–7
Anuloja
  family life 66
  helping returned children 44
  Valkai group foundation 49–50
  on *Valkai* group vision 55–6
Anuradapura, massacre 35–6
anxiety, of researchers 63
armed combatants, women as 16, 17
army camps 38
  husbands detained in 107–8
Ashraf, M.H.M. 33
atrocities, everyday lives 88–9

Bähre, E. 55
Bakhtin, M.M. 92
balance, search for 163–5
Bandaranaike, S.W.R.D. 5
Batticaloa, researcher's life in 62–7
Batticaloa district

administrative boundaries xxi
  continuity and change 37–41
  devastation xi–xii
  DS divisions 31
  ethnic mix 4, 32
  K-Party in 8
  tsunami 9–10
Batticaloa Peace Committee 40, 109
bereavement, Meena's story 100–3
Black July pogrom 6, 7
Black Tigers 5
boat ownership 139
Bohle, H. 138–9, 140
border villages, lines of control 93
Buddhist constitution 5
Buddhist people 4
Buddhist site, massacre at 35–6
Burgher people 4, 25n.3, 32
  discrimination against 34
Butler, Judith 154–6, 158–9, 162

case studies, overview 24
caste system 32, 34
  Meena's story 106
ceasefire
  international peacekeepers 7–8
  peace talks 10–11
Ceasefire Agreement (CFA) 8, 41
census data, ethnicity in Batticaloa 4, 32
checkpoints 38
  civilian powerlessness 75–6
  gendered behaviour 73
  picture of domination 93
  Red Cross ID card 120
  risk of searches 67
child abduction xiii
  during ceasefire 11

escape from camps 43–4
  by LTTE 6, 41
    Meena's story 122–3
  in LTTE split 8
  mothers' meetings 52–5
child conscription, international law 5–6
childhood, Meena's story 100–3
children
  in LTTE make-up 5–6
  suffering
    conflict and violence 75–6, 118
    fatherless 117–20
    tsunami effects 123–4
civilian displacement *see* displaced people
civilian life, the situation *(suyal nilamai)* 83–6
civilians
  armed 36
  as human shields 13
civil society, hopes for future 162–3
civil society groups 40–1
civil war 1–8
coastal belt
  communities 31–2
  military activity 38
  post-tsunami 9, 137–46
Colombo
  feelings in 78
  riots in 6
  women's journey to 49
colonisation schemes 32, 35
commando police unit *see* Special Task Force (STF)
communication, silence in 80–1
conflict
  continuous state 95–6
  roots of 3–11
  the situation *(suyal nilamai)* 83–6
  women's active living 15–20
consent, research subjects 71–2
control
  contests over shoreline 138–40
  lines of in everyday life 93
  narrowing spaces 46–8
  and power 29–30
  tactics 1–3
conversations in the darkness xi–xiii
cruelty, step-parenting 100, 101, 102
culture, ethics and 69

daily life, balance in 144–6
daily reality, shelling 83–4
daily strategies 90–2
danger, unknown spaces 46–8
Das, V. 94, 95
de Certeau, M. 47, 64, 90–1, 136
detentions
  from Eastern University camp 114
  factional politics 122–3
  Meena's story 107–8, 116, 124–5
    by TMVP 124–5
dirty war 1
disappeared persons xiii
  documenting by researchers 60–1
  by government forces 7
  protests about 17
  statistics 37–8
  tree-planting ceremonies for 50–2
  women's journeys for information 49
discrimination, against Tamils 120–1
displaced people 3
  Black July 6
  encampment 83–4
  forced eviction 36
  fragmented lives 160–1
  by LTTE 8
  in LTTE clearance 44–5, 113–16
  statistics 37–8
  Tamil plantation workers 34
  by tsunami 9
Divisional Secretariat (DS) 31
documenting
  ethical and moral issues 67–9
  in fear and secrecy 78–81
dowry system 104
DS (Divisional Secretariat) 31
Duwatha's story 148–9

earning money, Meena's story 110–11, 118
Eastern Province
  administrative districts 31
  ethnic communities 31–7
  ethnic mix 4, 32
  landscape 38
  military 'clearance' of LTTE 44–5
  occupation, Meena's story 109–17
  people of 31–7
Eastern University 113, 114
economic hardship
  in Eastern Region 38
  see also poverty
economic migrants 102–3
Eelam People's Revolutionary Liberation Front (EPRLF) 37, 58n.13

Index

emotional support, by *Valkai* group 14–15
emotions, documenting 67–8
endurance
　balancing the everyday 145–6
　carving the future 150–1
　evening conversations xii
　everyday life 2–3, 88–9, 96
　'for another first time' 92–4
　household chores in 131–4
　in loss and displacement 130–1
　and resilience 153–4
environmental disturbance, post-tsunami 142–4
environmental entitlement, violence and 140
EPRLF (Eelam People's Revolutionary Liberation Front) 37
Eravur DS division 31
　violence in 106, 113
ethical dilemmas, in research 60–2, 71–2
ethical issues, in safety 67–9
ethnic conflict 1–8
　LTTE incitement 30, 35–7
ethnicity
　Eastern Province 30, 31–7
　mixed, Meena's story 100–1
ethnographic research
　everydayness 87
　morals and ethics 60–2
　relationships in 62–9
　search for balance 163–5
　theoretical framework 89–90
ethnography of process 23, 150
everyday
　balance in 144–6
　concept 83–6
　　violence in 86–90
　fragility of 136
　tactical resistance in 90–1
everyday life
　encountering 130–4
　endurance 96, 131–4
　fear in 69–70
　return to fishing 142–6
　search for balance 163–5
　spaces of empowerment 152–3
　study overview 23–5
　violence in xi–xiii
　　cultural phenomenon 64–5
everyday violence 1–3
　personal histories 47–8
experiences, connections through 76–8

extra-judicial killings 6–7
extraordinary, concept 86–7

factional politics, detained people 122–3
family life
　in Batticaloa xi–xiii, 60, 66–7
　relationships in 75
fear
　everyday life 69–70
　in finding abducted child 52–4
　of researchers 63
feelings, tree-planting ceremonies 50–2
female kin, networking 100–25
female oracles, roles of 39
feminist groups 17–19
Fieldwork under Fire 64, 65
First Eelam war 6
fish, environmental disturbance 142–4
fishermen, post-tsunami 24, 137–46
fishing communities, migration 35
food stamps 118
'for another first time' 92–4
foreigners, identities 70–3
Foucault, M. 29
fragmented lives 160–1
future lives
　carving paths forward 150–1
　sense of 160–1

Garfinkel, H. 92
gender
　peace bodies 157–63
　in researcher's relations 72–3
　roles in war 15–19
　vulnerability 73–5
gendered framework, in everyday violence 88–9
gendered vulnerabilities 119–22
giving, toxic discourse of 42–3
government, peace talks with LTTE 40–1
government forces
　gender and power 73–4
　support for TMVP 43–4
　violence in break of ceasefire 7
　see also Special Task Force (STF); Sri Lankan Army (SLA)
government policy, post-tsunami 9–10
grief
　currency of 151–4
　and interdependancy 154–6
　as resilience 156–7
　spaces of 151–6

Gumesh 132, 134–6

Hallisey, C. 69
harthals (shut-downs) 11
healing, in silence 155–6
helplessness, shared 161–3
Hindu people 4
Hindu Saivites 34
Home Guards, formation 36
hope, for the future 150–1, 165–6
hospital, embodied silence 80–1
household chores, in endurance 131–4
household heads, women as 16
humanitarianism, competitive 9–10, 42–3
human rights activists, shortcomings 17–18
human rights groups, informal 2
human rights violations, 'clearing' the east 12–13, 44–5
Human Rights Watch (HRW)
　child recruitment in conflict 5
　disappeared persons xiiin.3

identity, researchers and subjects 69–76
income generation, by women 16
Independence, preparation for 4–5
Indian Ocean tsunami *see* tsunami
Indian Peace-Keeping Force (IPKF) 7
　offensive 36
　reign of terror 111–13
Indian Tamils 33–4
　discrimination against 101
Indo-Sri Lankan Accord (ISLA) 7
infant mortality 104–5
informants, risk to 65
information spread 29
informed consent, ethical dilemma 71–2
inheritance systems 32
Internally Displaced People (IDP)
　camps shelled 84
　see also displaced people
international agencies
　failure to help returned children 44
　ineffective 41
　tsunami aid 42–3
international aid, post-tsunami 9–10
International Non-Governmental Agencies (INGOs), peace aid 40–1
international peace-keepers 7, 8
intimacy, evening conversations xii
IPKF *see* Indian Peace-Keeping Force (IPKF)

irrigation system 35, 44
ISLA (Indo-Sri Lankan Accord) 7

Jaffna, battle over 7
Janatha Vimukthi Peramuna (JVP) 5
　aid disputes 9
　insurgencies and terrorism by 6–7
Jathika Hela Urumaya (JHU), aid disputes 9

Kaavya 77
Kalyva, S.N. 47
Kamla
　family life 66
　helping returned children 44
　Valkai group foundation 49–50
Karuna, Colonel (Vinayagamoorthi Muralitheran) 8
　TMVP and 43–5
Kattankudy DS division 31
　violence in 36
Kilinochchi
　army advance on 12
　battle over 7
　LTTE capital xi
　women's journey to 49
killings, extra-judicial 6–7
kinship practices, in marriage 103–4
Kokkadichcholai
　massacre 39–40
　Meena's childhood 100–3
K-Party 8
　see also Karuna, Colonel (Vinayagamoorthi Muralitheran); *Tamil Makhal Viduthalai Pulikal* (TMVP)
Krishna
　family life 66
　helping returned children 44
　Valkai group foundation 48–50
kuti annar maram (older brother's tree) 134–6

language, in social relationships 94–5
Lawrence, Patricia 39
Liberation Tigers of Tamil Eelam (LTTE)
　areas of control xx, 11
　ceasefire 7–8
　child abduction 6–7
　contest over coastal areas 138
　emergence of 5–6
　factional politics 8, 43–5, 122–3

final battle xi, 1, 11–14
gender and power 73–4
harthals called by 11
and IPKF 7
massacres of civilians 35–6
Meena's story 105–6
motivational tree-planting 51, 159
peace talks with PA 40–1
presidential elections 11–12
strategies to incite ethnic violence 30, 35–7
struggle for power 35–7, 37–8
support gained 106–7
lifeworld, concept 91–2
loss, searching for closure 148–51
LTTE *see* Liberation Tigers of Tamil Eelam (LTTE)

Malay people 4
marriage
 kinship practices 103–4
 Meena's story 103–4
 patterns 32
massacres
 by government forces 39–40
 by LTTE 35–6
 records by Batticaloa Peace Committee 109
Mattakkalappu (muddy lagoon) *see* Batticaloa
Meena
 childhood 100–7
 IPKF and 111–17
 making ends meet in widowhood 117–26
 STF arrival 107–11
 weaving stories 98–100
memories, search for balance 163–5
men, and war 15–16
migration, by Tamils 102–3
military encampments 38
moral issues
 in research 60–2
 in safety 67–9
mosques, massacres at 36
Mothers' Front 17–18
mothers' meetings 30–1
 safe spaces 52–5
 by *Valkai* group 15
mourning 24–5
 during conflict 159–60
 and hope for change 136

searching for closure 148–51
spaces of 151–6
see also tree-planting ceremonies
Mukkuvar people 32
Mullaitivu 13
Muralitheran, Vinayagamoorthi 8
Muslim communities, in Eastern Province 31–3, 36–7
Muslim political parties, aid disputes 9
Muslims, diverse population 4

narrative analysis, of violence and silence 19–20
networking
 female kin 100–25
 post-tsunami 46
 for support 29–30
 by *Valkai* group 14–15, 49–50
non-governmental organisations (NGOs), post-tsunami 139
non-violent action, by *Valkai* group 14–15
Non-Violent Peace Force (NP) 49
Nordstrom, C. and Robben, A.C.G.M. 64, 65
Norwegian government, peacekeepers 8

objectification, sexual gaze 73–4
older brother's tree *(kuti annar maram)* 134–6
oracles 21, 39
oral histories, power of 19–20
ordinary, concept of 83–6
ordinary life
 descent into 94–7
 return to fishing 142–6
 routine and 131–4, 137–46
outsiders
 in conflict areas 89–90
 researchers 60–1

peace
 gendered bodies 157–63
 hopes for future 162–3
peace aid
 INGOs 40–1
 middle-class orientation 122
Peace Brigade International (PBI) 49
peace-related studies, failures 61
peace talks 40–1
 fragile ceasefire 10–11
People's Alliance (PA), peace talks 40–1
People's Liberation Front *see* Janatha

Vimukthi Peramuna (JVP)
People's Liberation Organisation of Tamil
    Eelam (PLOTE) 7
  Meena's story 105
  struggle for power 37
perpetrators *see* agents
personal histories
  everyday violence 47–8
  weaving the story 98–100
Pirabakaran *see* Prabhakaran, Velupillai
places, or spaces 46–7
plantation workers, Indian Tamils 33–4
PLOTE *see* People's Liberation
    Organisation of Tamil Eelam
    (PLOTE)
podiyars 32
police stations, strategic silence in 79–80
political culture, hope for the future 159–66
political violence 33–40
Post-Tsunami Operational Management
    Structure (P-TOMS) 9
poverty
  marriage practices 103–4
  Meena's story 102–3, 109–11
  survival strategies 109–11, 118–19
power
  gender relations 158–63
  inequality 73–5
power and control, lack of space 29–30
power-cuts, evening conversations xi–xiii
P-Party, northern LTTE 8
Prabhakaran, Velupillai 5
practical support, by *Valkai* group 14–15
prawn farm massacre 101, 111
present absence 151
P-TOMS (Post-Tsunami Operational
    Management Structure) 9

Rajan
  family life 66
  Valkai group foundation 49–50
Rajapakse, Mahinda 11–12
Rani
  silence of 21–2
  story of 130–4
  tree-planting meaning 51, 134–6
Ranjini
  family life 66
  Valkai group foundation 49–50
recruited children *see* child abduction
refugee camps, Tamil women's identities
    16–17

refugees, from Sri Lanka 103
relationships
  in ethnographic research 62–9
  family life, in Batticaloa 66–7
  researchers and subjects 69–76
researchers
  ethical questions 81
  family life, in Batticaloa 66–7
  local views on 60–1
  relationships with subjects 69–76
  vulnerability 69–70
resilience
  and endurance 153–4
  in everyday violence 87
  grief as 156–7
restrictions, lack of space 29–30
restrictive spaces, LTTE camp 52–4
Ries, N. 88–9
riots, anti-Tamil 6, 105, 106–7
risks
  ethical positions in 67–9
  in finding abducted child 52–4
  to informants 65
  unknown spaces 46–8
roots of conflict 3–11
round-ups, Meena's story 107–8
routine, in endurance 131–4, 141–6

safety, ethical and moral issues 67–9
Saktirani, oracle 21
Sarvodaya (NGO) 105
  Meena's placement 110
  volunteer work 117
Sathurukandon massacre 39, 109
Scheper-Hughes, Nancy 68–9, 87, 153,
    156–7, 162
searching, for abducted daughter 148–50
security forces
  control over coastal areas 138–40
  detention of Sivam 141–2
Selvam
  family life 66
  relationships 75
sexual gaze, objectification 73–4
sexual violence
  everyday lives 88
  by father-in-law 104
  by IPKF soldiers 7, 111–13
  against widows 121–2
shelling, near displaced people 83–4
silence
  healing 155–6

Index

narrative analysis 19–20
  types of 79–81
  in unspeakable trauma 20–2
Sinhala communities
  displacement from east 106
  in Eastern Province 31–2, 35–6
Sinhala language 4, 5
Sinhala political parties
  aid disputes 9
  presidential elections 11–12
Sinhalese constitution 5
Sinhalese people, majority population 4–5
Siththi, cruelty of 100, 101, 102
  drinking 103
situation, the *(suyal nilamai)*
  civilian life in conflict 83–6
  people's responses to 85
Sivam's story 137–46
SLA *see* Sri Lankan Army (SLA)
Sluka, J.A. 68–9
social event, temple rituals 39
social relationships
  language in 94–5
  researchers and subjects 69–76
  in *Valkai* group work 52–5
social theory, in everyday 89–94
South Asian tsunami *see* tsunami
spaces 29–31
  borders within borders 93
  evening conversations xii
  mothers' meetings 52–5
  of mourning and meaning 151–6
  or places 46–7
  tree-planting ceremonies 51–2
  understanding 45–50
Special Task Force (STF) 30, 107–9
  arrests of Meena's husband 109–10
  atrocities by 36
  terror tactics 39
Sri Lanka, maps xx–xxii
Sri Lankan Army (SLA)
  aerial bombardment 113, 114–15
  final battle against LTTE 11–14, 159
  riot suppression 6–7
  shelling by
    near displaced people 83–4
    night-time xi–xii
  struggle for power 37–8
Sri Lankan government, areas of control xx, 11
Sri Lankan Monitoring Mission (SLMM) 8, 41

Sri Lankan Muslim Congress (SLMC) 33
starvation, Meena's story 109–11, 118
state violence *see* Sri Lankan Army
subjectivity, through violence 95
suffering, unspeakable 20–2
suicide commando unit, Black Tigers 5
suicides
  after loss 161
  after sexual abuse 112
  connections through 77–8
  post-tsunami 137
support, by *Valkai* group 14–15, 55–6
survival strategies
  Meena's story 109–15
  silence in 79–80

tactical resistance 90–1
tactics, in research 63–4
Tamil communities
  diaspora 6
  in Eastern Province 31–7
  hope for the future 165–6
Tamil culture, women in 16–17
Tamil Eelam xi
  advocated by TULF 6
  end of the dream 14
  Muslims' views 33
Tamil Eelam Liberation Organisation (TELO) 7, 37
  Meena's story 105
Tamil Liberation Front (TULF) 6
Tamil Makhal Viduthalai Pulikal (TMVP) xiii, 8
  Colonel Karuna and 43–5
  harthals called by 11
  people detained by 124–5
  support for government forces 44–5
Tamil militant groups 5–6, 7
  struggle for power 36–8
  violence by, Meena's story 107–9
Tamil people, largest minority 4–5
Tamil People's Liberation Tigers *see Tamil Makhal Viduthalai Pulikal* (TMVP)
Tamil-speaking communities 1, 4–6
Tamil Tigers *see* Liberation Tigers of Tamil Eelam (LTTE)
TELO (Tamil Eelam Liberation Organisation) 7
temple rituals, social event 39
Terror, the *(Bheeshanaya)* 6–7
terror tactics 1–3
  of STF 39

theoretical framework
  in everyday 89–90
  overview 23–4
Thiranagama, Rajani 165
TMVP *see* Tamil Makhal Viduthalai Pulikal (TMVP)
torture, Meena's husband 116–17
training, with NGOs 120–1
transport infrastructure 38, 41
trauma, unspeakable 20–2
tree-planting ceremonies 30–1, 134–5
  intimate space in grief 149
  motivational by LTTE 51, 159
  symbolic relevance 50–2
  Valkai group in xiii, 15
trust
  knowing whom to 65
  Valkai group vision 55–6
  Valkai group work 52–5
tsunami 8–10
  aftermath 30–1, 45
  effects on children 75
  enormity of xi–xii
  impact of 42
  loss in 123–4, 130–1
  reconstruction 138–40
  shared experiences 76
  violence in 95–6, 123–4
tsunami volunteers, foreigners 71
TULF (Tamil Liberation Front) 6

United National Party (UNP), insurgencies and terrorism by 6–7
universal suffrage 4–5
University Teachers for Human Rights (Jaffna) 67
UNP (United National Party) 6–7

Valachchenai DS division 31
  violence in 51
Valkai group
  activism 18–19
  emergence of xiii
  evolvement 14–15
  founder members 48–50
  hidden identities 22–3
  researcher's identity 71
  tsunami aftermath 30–1, 45–6
  vision 55–6
  work of 2

Vanni Party, northern or mainstream LTTE 8
Vavuniya, early fieldwork 77
Veddas (indigenous people) 4
  discrimination against 34
victims, in everyday violence 88–9
violence
  continuous state 95–6
  coping mechanisms 39–40
  disputed and undisputed factors 55–6
  environmental entitlement and 140
  ethical positions in 67–9
  everyday experience 1–3
  in everyday lives xi–xiii, 86–90
    study overview 23–5
  Meena's story 107–9
  narrative analysis 19–20
  narrowing spaces 46–8
  post-tsunami 10–11
  research roles 62
  unfinished history 160–1
  writing about 20–2
vulnerability
  active living 158–9
  gendered 73–5, 103–4, 119–22
    search for detainees 107–9
  and interdependancy 154–6
  poverty and 103–4
  of researcher 69–70

Wickremasinghe, Ranil 8, 11
widowhood
  stigma 16
  see also Meena; Rani
widows' society, formation 118–19
women
  activism of 17–19
  empowerment 152–3
  family networking 100–25
  female Tigers 112
  IPKF reign of terror 111–13
  in peace movements 157–63
  post-tsunami 14–15
  and war 15–20
women's rights, emergence of *Valkai* group xiii
writing, ethical and moral issues 67–9

EU authorised representative for GPSR:
Easy Access System Europe, Mustamäe tee 50,
10621 Tallinn, Estonia
gpsr.requests@easproject.com

www.ingramcontent.com/pod-product-compliance
Ingram Content Group UK Ltd.
Pitfield, Milton Keynes, MK11 3LW, UK
UKHW021835140426
5217IPUK00021B/1457